archive of tongues

....

archive
of tongues

*an intimate history
of brownness*

MOON CHARANIA

duke university press · durham and london · 2023

© 2023 Duke University Press. All rights reserved
Printed in the United States of America on acid-free paper ∞
Designed by Aimee C. Harrison · Project Editor: Bird Williams
Typeset in Minion Pro, IBM Plex Mono, and IBM Plex Sans
by Copperline Book Services.

Library of Congress Cataloging-in-Publication Data
Names: Charania, Moon, [date]- author.
Title: Archive of tongues : an intimate history of brownness /
Moon Charania.
Description: Durham : Duke University Press, 2023. | Includes
bibliographical references and index.
Identifiers: LCCN 2022060454 (print)
LCCN 2022060455 (ebook)
ISBN 9781478019473 (paperback)
ISBN 9781478016830 (hardcover)
ISBN 9781478024101 (ebook)
Subjects: LCSH: Charania, Moon, [date]—Family. | South Asian
diaspora. | Women immigrants—Social conditions. | Minority
women—Social conditions. | Immigrant families—Social conditions. |
Motherhood—Political aspects. | Sex discrimination against women. |
Feminist theory. | BISAC: SOCIAL SCIENCE / Feminism & Feminist
Theory | SOCIAL SCIENCE / Ethnic Studies / Asian Studies
Classification: LCC HQ 1735.3 .C46 2023 (print)
LCC HQ1735.3 (ebook)
DDC 909/.04914--dc23/eng/20230411
LC record available at https://lccn.loc.gov/2022060454
LC ebook record available at https://lccn.loc.gov/2022060455

Cover art: Imran Qureshi, *Love me love me not*, 2015. 198 × 137 cm.
Courtesy of the artist and Nature Morte.

For my mother, whose words cut . . . through everything.

And for Zoya, who inherited these lexical intimacies
but who might just find a way to shake loose
the spell of this inheritance.

CONTENTS

PREFACE

....

This book is a brown maternal archive. It is an archive of the stories, memories, songs, shapes, ghosts, attachments, and vernaculars that live on my mother's tongue. Textured, whispered, melancholic, womanly, lesbian, failed, and analytic, this is the tongue I share. The stories, memories, chronologies, experiences, and speech acts that I detail are real, in that they were all directly shared with me by my mother. Others are my memories of her and my memories of her recounting her memories (with me and with others). Both her memories and my memories of her memories are presented here, with some details obscured and remixed to shield (certain) identities. But if I am to be (even more) truthful, many of the "events" in this book are records of things that never happened or happened but had little consequence. There is no collective memory here, only idiosyncratic, minor, minimal, miniscule historiographic traces, even as many of these nonevents left no trace at all. They are, instead, matters of feminine memory, maternal memory, brown memory. These are my mother's stories, and this is my intimate, anxious, tender, erotic, raging, and careful curation of my mother's life. But like all witnessing and retelling, this archive is shaped by materiality and speculation, by lived conditions and by fabulation, by cognitive observation and by affective longing, by fact and by fiction. This book is the skin, heart, blood, and bones of one brown mother, just as it is my memories, reflections, indictments, and witnessing of her life and mine.

As such, I am in this project—as narrator, as interpreter, as daughter, as beloved, as shadow, and so many other ways I cannot articulate. My mother is me. I am her. This strangely Lacanian experience of negotiating my mother's stories, stories that are inside me on many levels, compels a reading of critical theory as an intimate encounter with one's own ideas and with the subject who is also the self. This double genitive positions my mother as both inside and outside—inside as philosopheme, outside as part of my life, inside as analysand and outside as analyst, inside as self and outside as *other*. Such a hybrid multivocal witnessing is a collaboration that enlists and mediates the contradictions of reading the mother through the daughter (inevitably and simultaneously Lacanian and Fanonion and Kristevan—a project that perhaps reflects its own iteration of glorified psychoanalytic tragedies). I offer a sensual and structural reading of the brown maternal that underscores the texture of this project as one of a mother-daughter dyad, in which memory, trauma, and subjectivity are passed from one to the other, like the vagaries of a diasporic utterance that sounds like an old childhood lullaby. Indeed, I have a perverse relation to this archive, to my mother, to the maternal. Julietta Singh's words resound: "The archive is a stimulus between myself and myself."[1]

Archive of Tongues is a narrative and theoretical experiment in which I confront and reflect upon how we read and write feminized, racialized maternal pasts and the debris they leave behind; how we might *listen to* the vernaculars, grammars and speech acts that emerge from (my) brown mother's tongues across time and space; how the brown mother's tongue/s expose a whole world where aspirations of *the good life* are cast aside for the everyday necropolitical; and how we might understand the affections, erotics, solidarities, socialities that are born out of impossible situations. This is not to suggest that the mother tongue evokes/requires/acquires a transhistorical quality. Rather, I want to think about how the brown mothers' tongue reconfigures itself across diaspora-time, rejects the linearity of historicity, challenges the notion of futurity, conflates yesterdays and tomorrows, queers epistemology and temporality, and opens the way for other modes of consciousness to be considered seriously—those of ghosts, for example, and the maid, the wife, the lesbian, and the whore.

By engaging in a multinarration of what has been historically an Orientalizing narrative, I hope that my reader will do the work of *not* falling into the trap of appropriation and instead will think with me about what political and ethical questions weigh most heavily in this deeply gendered, sexualized, racialized, and felt archive. I hope that my reader will *read* with greater "thickness," as Anjali Arondekar and Geeta Patel propose in their work on the impossibility of area studies, by which they refer to historicized, material, multilayered, and interdisciplinary readings.[2] I hope that my reader will understand that such an archive lends itself also to an anxious reading, disrupting how a reader conventionally reads, demanding from the reader (just as it demands/demanded from me) a different practice, one that is in relation to uncomfortable affect, one that is willing to sit with a level of opacity that may be unfamiliar. I share this archive as one that deliberately subalternizes the brown mother and her feminine and feminized knowledges. My use of the term *subaltern* gestures to a Spivakian argument that class privilege is defined by access to knowledge production and that access to knowledge production is a politics of power that travels across geopolitical differences; I am thinking here of Spivak's point that White critique and postcolonial theory are contiguous class formations. I have stakes in this framing of subalternity.

In subalternizing the brown maternal, I think about how brown maternal memory, intimacy, sociality, and speech underscore not only the failures of White, Western, Northern scholarship but also certain strands of postcolonial studies, feminist studies, and queer studies. The very condition of archivization of my mother's tongues—a mode of knowledge production not seen as such—implicates many of the tensions and aporias that shape these fields. By offering (her) archival tongues, I limn these fields' epistemological questions about what constitutes an archive or evidence, what makes an utterance a truth or a lie, what is instituted as knowledge and what is dismissed as gossip. I reject the imperative to produce my mother as an abstract subject within the scholia of Foucauldian terminology (whose interest in the subject never included figures like the brown mother or, for that matter, the racial *other*). Subsequently, I also understand that just as I interpellate my mother as a subject in relation to the world, I simultaneously hollow her out in the very act of naming her as subject and her subjectivity as theoretically relevant. This dialectic between constitution of subject and emptying of subjectivity is perhaps inevitably part of the fiber of scholarly and disciplinary research. I do my best to fail at this mandate.

My mother's stories compelled a gathering around bad objects—abjection, oppression, femininity, brownness, melancholia, negativity, shame, embarrassment, disability, illness, and violence. Stories of self-induced abortions, dead babies, rapes, beatings, madness, magic, fabulation, dystopia, mysticism, instinct, gut, and gore sat somewhere deep inside of her, maybe in her brownness, maybe in her heart. I could not exactly tell. For her, both the category brown woman and the category brown maternal were sites of negation, abjured and overdetermined. I sit in a feminist contemplation of these bad objects and "bad feelings" ("ugly feeling," to invoke Sianne Ngai's 2005 phrase) and read them sensuously, promiscuously, nakedly, replacing the systematic forms of interpretation, reason, logics, methods, renouncing Anglo-Bourgeois values of legibility and privatization of pain.[3]

Walter Benjamin noted that to "articulate the past historically does not mean to recognize it 'the way it really was.' It means to seize hold of a memory as it flashes up at the moment of danger."[4] Following Benjamin, I write to make my mother's private experiences public knowledge, to unravel the unrelenting demand to privatize our past, to shake our comportment of the present, to lay bare the impossibility of separating the psychological need to protect those we love and the intellectual effort to uncover harm and hurt. There is no simple excavation or symbolic revival. Language is ideological. Subjectivity is partial. Theory can be empty and unfulfilling. All I have is what Toni Morrison called insistent memory, mutated from fact into fiction, then into folklore, and then into nothing.[5]

Regardless, this rendering of the private self public and, conversely, the public self as opaque is a destabilizing epistemological practice (although, ironically, a common methodological one). It is also important to say that I do not find privacy to be a feminist notion: its very contours are shaped by patriarchal and colonial logics. The assumption that privacy is a sanctuary, a site of dignity, a space to be who you are is mediated and modulated by access to resources, as well as gender, class, and sexual norms and expectations. It's worth more explicitly pointing out that for queer people and women the private domestic space is one of policing, abuse, confinement, silence, and shame more than a sanctuary. What, then, is privacy but a concept worthy of critique, perhaps even abandonment? Through this public telling of private stories, I seek to critique privacy by speaking what some may consider a private language. I try to think about all the ways we fail at privacy, or where privacy breaks down, the vagaries and compulsions of privacy, the disappointments and violences of privacy. If privacy is sanctuary, intimacy, and opacity, then it is also secrecy, shame, humiliation, and risk. The internal sociality of this text and the social relations of this book's production erode the very possibility of bourgeois notions of privacy. I take this erosion seriously.

It became clear to me, in writing this book, that my mother's itinerant encounters, memories, modalities, affects—all the sights, sounds, smells, secrets, socialities—that eventually became her mother tongue, came also to be mine. I bring this fleshy merger—her tongue in my mouth—this subject-object, mother-daughter coagulation, to bear in this book. I move inadequately from one tongue to another, or perhaps I am insufficient to work the many tongues in my mouth. Arundhati Roy, when asked whether the English language is always colonial, responded that even one's mother tongue is "actually an alien, with fewer arms than Kali perhaps, but many more tongues."[6] Even in my best effort to write back to or against this coloniality, the language I use already contains my ruin. What can I offer, then, with this tongue in my mouth? Seduction, coercion, hauntings, irreverence, intimacy, perversion, theory? I do not know where this tongue will commence, nor do I know what this tongue will command (from me, from you), but I cannot stop reaching for it.

....

GRATITUDES

....

I am made of tongues. Mine, my mother's, her mother's, her mother's mother and other mothers, aunties, sisters, daughters, friends, teachers, mentors, and lovers. These tongues taught me, trained me, tamed me, tormented me, tainted me, tempered me, and took care of me. These tongues shape my feminist grammars, impulses, intimacies, practices, and solidarities. So intimately entangled am I with these tongues that at times it is hard to tell where theirs end and mine begins. Without these tongues, this book would not exist.

This kind of solidarity is difficult to express. We know when it's there, we feel it, we connect with it, are grateful for it. It's a visceral, bodily charge as much as love, as much as the erotic. This kind of solidarity is rare and wild; it gives oneself over to another regardless of self-interest. It is a deeply resonant affinity that requires constant affective labor, constant epistemological undoing. This is the kind of solidarity that has made this book possible.

I am grateful for my core community of thoughtful interlocuters with whom I think and write and learn: Tiffany King, Jane Ward, Ghassan Massouwi, Elizabeth Beck, Kristen Abatsis-McHenry, Stevie Larson, and Cory Albertson. At different moments in the process of writing this book, each of them read, edited, advised, and counseled me in ways that profoundly shaped not only this book but also my relation with and to the academy. I am deeply dependent on the presence of these committed readers, thinkers, and writers in my life and in this project. I am fortunate to have each of them, as Toni Morrison phrased in *Beloved*, as "friends of my mind."

I am not sure where I would be as a writer and thinker without Wendy Simonds. She is easily the most important and most intimate working friendship of my life. She has read every article, every chapter, every version of this manuscript, redlining sections with her incisive editing until the final click. I am immensely thankful to C. Riley Snorton, who in a tremendous act of friendship and solidarity, read entire parts of my early manuscript one afternoon in New Orleans—an afternoon of exchanging ideas and thoughts that charted this project toward new critical grammars and that suffused me with new, unexpected possibilities and solidarities. The very first time I met Jasbir Puar I immediately sensed that we would become fast friends—a lovely, unexpected night in London spent connecting over feminist ideas and struggles at a conference that was more than a little lackluster. Over the years, our friendship has grown into fierce femme sisterhood. I could not be more grateful to Jasbir for her meticulous reading of my work, who, even from afar, managed to get at the heart of this text, pushing me to write *for* and not against, untangling my ideas without ever abjuring them. Amber Jamila Musser's voice and support hovers over this project. It was an unexpected encounter when Amber joined a cooking group Jasbir and I had put together at the start of the COVID-19 pandemic. Pandemic fear, isolation, and lockdown forced us to create a world of connection, solidarity, levity, and laughter in a way that none of us had ever anticipated and with people not part of our physical worlds. Connecting with Amber as we Zoom-cooked spicy Pakistani dishes week after week was a precious gift from the feminist goddesses, as our friendship strengthened and took new turns. Amber's generous reading of this manuscript was a gesture of that feminist friendship and her ethics to lift junior faculty. For me her reading affirmed the extraordinary brown maternal world of words and how it resonates with other worlds and world making. Jyoti Puri has been, without a doubt, one my most passionate and genuine allies in the academy, always reading my work with nuance, capaciousness, porosity, generativeness, and love, always reaching out to include me in dynamic thought collectives. I owe a special thanks to Beverly Guy-Sheftal and Cynthia Spence, both of whom opened up intellectual space and financial resources for my work and invited me into the warm embrace of Black feminist world making at Spelman College. I am especially grateful to Beverly's intuitive advice throughout my time at Spelman, simultaneously humorous, irreverent, and priceless. I feel lucky to work in the shadow of her dynamic Black feminist presence.

My warmest thanks to my Duke University Press reviewers, who pushed and challenged this project at many stages. I owe a debt of gratitude to my editor Miriam Angress, who took an interest in this project when it was merely a seedling and no matter the challenges steadfastly advocated for this book. I am thankful to the James Weldon Johnson Institute and the UNCF Mellon Foundation, who provided me an invaluable opportunity of a semester free of teaching and for being such an important resource for early-career scholars. Previous and smaller iterations of this book have been published in *Meridians: feminism, race, transnationalism* (a journal published twice a year by Duke University Press) and *Queer Theories: A Transnational Reader*, edited by L. A. Saraswati, Barbara Shaw, and Heather Rellihan (Oxford, UK: Oxford University Press, 2020). I want to thank Ayu L. Saraswati and Ginetta Condelario for giving my early experimental thoughts on the brown maternal a feminist home.

I am thankful to my family for their support of me, even as my life and work have presented challenges and complexities in their own lives. I am especially thankful to my father, who sat with me for hours at a time, recounting his difficult journey of migration, family politics, and racialized experiences, even when it meant going to places that he had tried so hard to leave behind.

Sara Shroff, my lesbian, feminist, brown girl-cousin-sister-love, I cannot thank enough for working with me in this book and in life. She is always there, laughing at a shared memory, reaching up to clarify a word, shaking up a queasy-making loyalty I hadn't quite worked through, offering up a translation and a folklore, leaning in to whisper an important fact, deepening my analysis with a simple word or memory in my ear. Sharabi-style, Karachi-style, she will always be a comrade in my life.

I still remember in vivid detail how, from the very first moment I met her, Erin's handsome tenderness, feminist masculinity, and Southern astuteness struck me. To my life partner, I owe enduring love and debt for never failing to orient me toward pleasure as I pursued a project marked by pain. Her belief in this project has been unyielding, even as it meant becoming vulnerable in the ink of this book.

No two people have shaped me more profoundly than my mother, Maher, and my daughter, Zoya. The lifeworld in which I came to be my mother's youngest daughter and the world making involved in being Zoya's mother have unflinchingly made me who I am. The very act of writing this book strengthened both these bonds—that of being a daughter and that of being mother. Zoya grew up watching me write this book, moving through her teenage years, jettisoning old identities to fashion new ones, learning in wanted and unwanted ways the sticky inheritance of her mother and her mother's mother. The dialectic of loss and desire that shaped the years of writing this book and watching Zoya grow into the dynamic brown feminist presence she is today is the greatest gift I have been granted. Everything she is already exceeds my wildest dreams.

I lack the words to thank my mother, who shared with me so many stories, advice, memories, observations, and in doing so, relived sadness and suffering. I still have not figured out if, through this extraordinary commitment to telling, retelling, overtelling, still telling, she metabolized pain or anesthetized it. What I do know is that writing my mother's stories was to intercourse with her hauntings and mine, even when writing, like the English language, like translation, like my academic training, always betrays. But if I do nothing more than affirm the psychic presence of my mother or turn the face of history toward her history (to paraphrase June Jordan), then I have already done something more extraordinary than I thought possible.

Mother, loosen my tongue, or
adorn me with a lighter burden.

—AUDRE LORDE, *ZAMI: A NEW SPELLING OF MY NAME*

PROLOGUE

....

I look for her shape. . . .
—PATRICIA WILLIAMS, *ALCHEMY OF RACE AND RIGHTS:*
DIARY OF A MAD LAW PROFESSOR

I see my mother's face in my eyelid's inner flesh. . . .

I see my mother's face—elusive and material, fantastic and contingent. Avalanche of emotions. Site of my exile. The lights, shadows, colors, vibrancy, tactility, sounds, scents, spirits. All familiar. Familial. I search for my mother's face. My mother searches for her mother's face. Her mother, now dead, searched in vain for *her* mother. There is a history here that does not belong solely to the order of genetics. I remind myself that I am searching for something for which there is no coherent articulation. I think I am possessed by my mother's dispossession, and her mother's, and her mother's. . . .

I see my mother's face in an old photo from 1979. We are in Alaska, she reminds me. Her younger brother, a successful immigrant with many white employees, lives there, and she and I have come for a visit. The photo, I think, is lovely. Her brown eyes. Her soft mouth. Her full cheeks. Her forehead broad. Her face clear and smooth in a picture that looks blurry and faded. Her eyes refuse the simplicity of the gaze. She is wearing a blue-and-white-striped western dress, fitted around her rounded body, an unusual departure from her usual going-out sari. Her hair is wrapped in a bun that sits low at the nape of her neck. She never wore her hair down. She has a half smile on her face, giving the impression that the camera clicked too early, but I know it's because she's shy and self-conscious that her photo is being taken. But she is also proud of making it here, that her brother made it here. She understands the importance of arrival (in America), the significance of success, of mobility, of the photograph, of the memory. I know this because I know her. Knowing her gives me this knowledge, because her face is as silent as the photograph. My two-year-old self sits on a wicker chair, legs crossed, looking up at her, as she stands shyly in front of a burning fireplace. . . .

I see my mother's face, resting on a cheap, plastic, ribbed pillow, her creamy, brown body soaking in a small tub filled with warm water. She is naked, round, beautiful. I am reminded again of her touch. Her labor floods my body. I want to get in the water with her. She doesn't want me to. This is her time. But she will let me sit in the bathroom, as she alternatively closes her eyes or opens them slowly to fill my ears with stories. I like her stories when she speaks. I stare at her body when she is silent. I am in awe of her body. I am struck by her speech. I feel her presence in me. I commit her stories to memory. I learn nothing. I learn everything. She is my love. My ghost. My salvation. My inquiry. My subject. My story. My mother. . . .

I see my mother's face, her eyes searching for a memory, combing for a correction, a revised detail, possibly a tender moment. This is where she pauses the most. She wasn't one to repress the unpleasant, the disgusting, the violent, the carnal. The fleshy tongue in her mouth produced fleshy stories about fleshy femininity. And she did not need to search for those. Those memories sat at the tip of her tongue, the distance between memory as flesh (tongue) and memory as utterance (story) short and extemporaneous. They simply rolled off, uninvited, unpleasant, uncensored, uncultivated, untender. She was quick with these stories; like spit, she spat them out with an urgency; often even before one had sat down, she had taken them to the bowels of the earth. Yes, she knew too many things firsthand, secondhand, third removed. Yes, she had learned along the way not to fight. Yes, she was easy to defeat. Yes, she joined them in her own demise. But who fails to recognize such a figure? Who doesn't know this story?

I see my mother's face, lined and wrinkled, her oiled hair pulled back in a thinning and graying bun, her nylon pants and cotton T-shirt hanging on her too-thin body. Her saris have been hibernating in the closet for eighteen years. It is noon and time for her prayer. She looks tired, even though the day has just begun. She has begun to take daily naps, after her noon prayer. She is surprised she is still alive, but death, she says, is the one thing *Allah* has kept in his hands. Then she tells me that our relation, the affective force between her and me, is from another life. Our relationality is the residue of something leftover, something that needed completion, actualization, materiality, touch. She calls this *lein-dein*, a complicated Urdu figure of speech that alludes to leftover debt from a previous life. She tells me it is why she never went through with the abortion when she realized she was pregnant with me, even when she was so close to getting it, even when she knew she needed it, even when she knew it would've made her life easier, even when she had her feet in stirrups, her knees apart, and a male doctor between her legs, asking her for the third time if she was sure. It was 1975. She had married a man who had five (White) children waiting for him in America. She had given him two more children. She didn't need or want a third one. She was sure. But still she closed her legs.

introduction

a story on tongues

What is my mother tongue, my mammy tongue,
my mummy tongue, my momsy tongue,
my modder tongue, my ma tongue?
— M. NOURBESE PHILIP, *SHE TRIES HER TONGUE,*
HER SILENCE SOFTLY BREAKS

When I was a little girl, my mother used to tell me a story. It was a story she repeated at various points throughout my childhood and well into my young adulthood. It was a strange, silly, and over-the-top story. Like many of my mother's stories, this story was abject and centered around flesh. And for a long time, I thought this story was yet another example of my mother's obsession with oppression. But my mother narrated this story with such mysterious seriousness, with such dailiness, continuity, factuality, steadiness that I eventually came to hold space for this story in my life, that I eventually realized that my growing was *marked* by this story.[1] This story was about the tongue.

Think about the human tongue, my mother would say. The tongue is soft and vulnerable, fleshy, and pink. We need it to eat, to speak. We need it to enjoy food and sex. The tongue is all muscle and no bone—supple; it has a huge range of motion and shape and agility. No matter how much you use it or don't, it never loses its volume. The tongue, she would say, is tirelessly flexible. But this tongue, for all its softness, lives between thirty-two teeth—hard, strong, dense, and sharp. Any given second, the teeth can damage, tear, wound the tongue. But the tongue has no choice. It must learn to live among the teeth, between and within the hardness that could individually or collectively destroy the tongue.

My mother does not remember the origins of this story, unsure if it came from her mother or her grandmother or a story she strung together from other stories she had heard throughout her life. But every time she offered this story, it was an invitation to think (with her) about difficulty and violence and un/livability, to think with her about the ways that women are often "imprisoned by the peculiarities of the body."[2] The very idea of the tongue living so intimately with that which can destroy it functions as a necro-metaphorization—a metaphor not just of death but of *death worlds*, a metaphor of a life that is perpetually threatened with or close to death.[3] But just as she inextricably enmeshed the tongue in a field of imminent violences, her story also pointed to the ways the tongue ruptures these possibilities and is instead perpetually surviving, resisting, maneuvering, negotiating, flitting, fleeing its oppressive conditions. The tongue, as my mother tells it, insists on and survives through its perspectival agility. This private metaphoric story of the tongue's place in the mouth, among teeth, was one moment when I realized that my mother speaks in tongues.

As the primer of my childhood, I now take this story into serious consideration. This strange little story—a play on words, a play on tongues—holds within it what Chela Sandoval might call a "methodology of the oppressed"—an alternative consciousness and oppositional expression.[4] For as long as I can remember, my mother constructed the tongue in this way, as experimental (always tentative), subversive (possibly insubordinate), and unsovereign (never belonging just to itself). For her, the tongue is a troubled condition borne in the body, both a closure of flesh (in the mouth) and a going beyond flesh (language). As a piece of flesh that functions in a structure of constraints, enclosures, governance, and training, the tongue has to survive its own conditions in order to then tell the story of its survival. This story offered a lesson on the nonsovereignty of our bodies—a lesson that violence was not just out in the world, exterior, anterior, posterior but that violence haunts the very way our bodies are built. The irony of the body to commit violence against itself and the ability of the body to survive and thrive (by which I mean to live intentionally) within its own inflicted or immanent violence was not lost on me. Even as a little girl, I realized this story on the tongue undid the common sense of the body taught to me in schools run by men, in books written by men.

Over time, this story became for me an object of theory, an episteme in formation, not in the sense of theoretical distillation but rather as implicitly theoretical in its inquisitive commitments and its descriptive style.[5] I came to see my mother's tongue as having inherited incommensurable ways of knowing the unknowable—incommensurable because they unraveled conventional modes of empiricism, logic, comfort, and fact. I came to see my mother's tongue as a relation to a condition, a maneuvered sociality, a denied pedagogy. It is a pedagogy that is not pedagogical because it is rife with bad education, feminine insurgency, and indices of failure. It is a pedagogy of how to exist once you accept that oppression is immovable, a social fact of social life. It is a pedagogy that refuses to do what language, in its more colonial guises, is often called on to do. It is a pedagogy that renders oppression (allegorized through the fleshy, pink tongue among hard teeth) carnal, sexual, arbitrary, ideological, quotidian, and spectacle.

For my mother, tongues are a thingness that is feminized. They are fleshy and vulnerable, even as they are agile and manipulative, just as they too perform a way of being that is within (the mouth) and without (language). The tongue is given meaning, even saturated with meaning, just as it too is dismissed as meaning nothing. It is the ideological and fleshy site from which one must be severed in order for one to become a subject (i.e., the mother [in the] tongue). That language gets collapsed into tongues and tongues into language is not entirely figurative. It literally invokes the (maternal) body. As a deeply erotic, intimate, and tenuous apparition, the tongue, like women's bodies, is often regarded as dirty and excessive, particularly in terms of sexuality. My mother's story assembles and fissures this dirty, irreverent, and fugitive femininity, and in so doing, gestures to queer sexuality, to dirty sex, to a too literal and an appropriately oblique relation to the libidinous. It captures and stays close to immodesty and eroticism, sensation and feeling, language and flesh. In feminizing the tongue—soft flesh surrounded by hardness—my mother signals to femininity as one way into other knowledges, memories, eccentricities, feelings, stories, and socialities.

Like so many of my mother's stories, this little story was messy, discursive, paratactic. On one hand, at least tautologically, it invoked an ideological desire to talk about power—in the story, both power (structural) and pleasure (libidinal) are bound up together. On the other hand, her expressions and enunciations on tongues only registered as scandalous, excessive, and unsavory. Certainly there was something promiscuous within her line of thought (*and that it was seen as promiscuous*) that always felt surprising, unknown, and accidental, something secret, hidden, worth searching for, the opacity of her words often arresting meaning. Trinh Min Ha wrote that the mark of a "mother's talk is a practice of indirection that is at times overt and other times secret."[6] I think of how this story about the tongue marks Minh Ha's point, a story that seems to state the obvious just as it too reveals a secret (way of thinking). In this way, then, I think of tongues as also alluding to the secrets, memories, inheritances, metaphors, and opacities in brown mothers' ways of explaining the world. Riddled with riddles and moving with metaphor, my mother's stories often confounded me, puzzled me, frustrated me. I searched and searched for what was important about her metaphors over and above candor, what was important about her opacities over and above transparencies.

Metaphors, for my mother, are serious things. So are archives. But the conventional archive—that which evidences the past or past events through texts, documents, materials—was not one with which my mother would have engaged or for that matter understood, in part because of the dialectic between access and knowledge (production), what in Urdu is called *Talim*, and in part and perhaps more frankly, because she would find it boring. While others built their knowledge by collecting information through rational and regularized processes, my mother, in contrast pursued means that were oral, irregular, inappropriate, improper, embarrassing, shameful. She did it sometimes surreptitiously, other times boldly, and other times ordinarily; like cooking, like telling stories, it looked like complacency and cliché and acceptance to the dominant order. I learned to listen closely to what she had to offer me, and I found myself deeply enmeshed in flesh thick with fissured, fragmented, polyvocal, polysemic, dirty, feminized, maternal vernaculars.

The tongue of which my mother speaks and the tongues through which I now write this book are an archive of a feminized world that has been made abject, and violated, evaded, or just not dealt with, misogynistically dismissed; reduced to myth, folklore, old wives' tales, illiteracy, catty speech, gossip, riddles, conspiracy theories, paranoias, and secrets. Her broken, distorted, unfinished, feminized, lyrical Urdu/Gujrati/Hindi/English vernacular, her ethnicized and gendered tongue pushes at the borderlands of formal knowledge and informal knowledge, of intellectual history and being (left) out of intellectual history, of useful knowledge and knowledge without use (or not knowledge at all, extraneous, gratuitous, solipsistic). I am now a collector and curator of my mother's tongues, perhaps retrospectively, perhaps nostalgically.

What new orientations, different ethics, necessary disruptions can I crystalize by politicizing my mother's tongue, tethering flesh to knowledge, to being, to the archive? I offer this archive of tongues as a brown maternal tactic, drawing out what Christina Sharpe calls in her genre-bending book, *In the Wake: On Blackness and Being*, "an unscientific method of gathering knowledge that comes from observing where one stands in relation to the empire of oppression."[7] Such a form of knowledge gathering, like the very life of a tongue, is a patent refusal of separation of mind and body, flesh and survival—"theory in the flesh" as Cherrie Moraga offered.[8] I offer this brown, maternal tactic as one means by which we might replace the reigning epistemology of logic, empiricism, cognition, and method with feeling, orality, opacity, and ethic. Just as my mother transfigured the tongue into feminized flesh searching for survival (a linguistic-ideological move that she equates with an embodied reality), I transfigure tongues into an intellectual practice that speaks to affect, memory, fragmentation, multiplicity, and opacity. I treat tongues as a working strategy that is responsive to the feminine, the maternal and the racial-ethno-class formations of language and sociality. By telling a different story of tongues—one that is admittedly brown, maternal, sensual, and feminine—I turn inward toward the interior, the domestic, and the unconscious. As flesh that survives every day its conditions of being, tongues shift our ontological understanding of relations we may not know we engage with and modes of violence and oppression and sociality we may not identify.

The life of the tongue is a life teeming with contradictory fidelities, spilling over with sex (wanted or not), brimming with modes of disobedience, seething with cautious practices of solidarity, safety, and survival. To be clear, it is not my project to relativize "tongues," such that culture and language and sociality become the site of admissible difference, nor is it to offer my mother's tongues as an antidote to inauthenticity. Rather, I chose tongues because they provide an analytic for messiness, polyvocality, and destabilization, because as Keguro Macharia writes, "imprecision is also method."[9] I choose the tongue because as a site, as a mode, as a part of the body, it emerged organically in my mother's narrative arc and I did not want to subsume her vernaculars, her approach, her methodologies by translating them under other critical frames that would intentionally or unintentionally marginalize my mother as a thinker/as an actor. I choose the tongue, too, because of its proximity, its touching, its tonguing, with so many other words—*body, sex, erotic, language, maternal, resistance, precarity,* and *flesh*. I choose the tongue because it was so resonant in my mother's daily life—as errant, as disobedient, as promiscuous.

For her, and now for me, tongues *are* the flesh of feminine excess. Tongues *are* speech acts of flesh.

By speech acts of flesh, I refer to the ways language is *of* our flesh, *of* our body, *of* our cells. To gather around the tongue means to gather around the somatic function of the body and the mind; it is to straddle the gap between the body as flesh—interior, naked and bare—and flesh as language—exterior, refined, elaborate. Speech acts of flesh, then, refer to both somatic function and epistemological function—knowledge and histories as stored in the cellular, fleshy structures of the body, deposited on and dispensed by the tongues and talk of brown mothers. By speech acts of flesh, I refer also to the way the tongue is an embodied and unstable and feminized archive. Reading about, writing about, listening to tongues intensify the body (and sex) in all its attenuations—an intensification that occurs through, and not despite, precarity. As an analytic grammar, tongues reveal that language itself is an intensification of bodily capacity, one manner in which the body can articulate itself, one kind of matter, tangible and abstract (as Mel Chen writes, language is not opposed to matter; rather language *is* matter).[10] Following then, as fleshy sites of capacitation, tongues too are also a key site of debilitation, one way in which the faculties, capacities, and mobilities of brown mothers are cut off. As such, these speech acts of flesh, simultaneously capacitating and debilitating, are tightly entangled with racialized, classed, gendered, and sexualized ways of being in the world.

By offering tongues, the imperative of this project is not just to excavate stories of untold violence (although this too is an overwhelming and worthy task in of its own) but also to create an intellectual practice (methods), an ethics of care (feminism), a way of noticing *other* and *othered* socialities and knowledges (queering) that emerge in the midst of brown, maternal trauma. However, I do not claim tongues as a liberatory hermeneutic, as I, like many others, are far too aware of such failed seductions. bell hooks once wrote, "Theory is not inherently healing, liberatory or revolutionary. It fulfills this function only when we ask that we do so and direct our theorizing to this end."[11] In hooks's spirit, then, I offer this archive of tongues to awaken a longing, to sensate that tongue-in-cheek, to stretch out the way language works to make us see something that perhaps before we could not see. I offer tongues because I believe theory must reckon with the secret expressions of the oppressed.

The Mother in the Tongue, Or
the Tongue in the Mother

....

Her tongue is all de weapon a woman got.
—ZORA NEALE HURSTON, *THEIR EYES WERE WATCHING GOD*

Let me begin by saying that I reject the psychoanalytic imperative that the daughter first "turn away" from her primary love object: the mother. Conversely and rebelliously, I turn toward my first love: my mother. But my investigation is not one of an atomized, brown mother—an insular, Oedipal narrative of desire that refuses the affective charge, the libidinal desires, the erotic infusion of mother-daughter relations. It is instead a serious investigation of brownness through the provocation of the maternal: the effacing of the brown maternal and the abject, brown, maternal body are driving vexations in this book.

But the fact remains that to raise the specter of the brown mother means turning slightly, if not fully, toward psychoanalysis, despite psychoanalysis's own dismissal, disavowal, detestation of mothers. I turn to psychoanalysis, because as Avery Gordon has written, "This is where the human sciences have been most willing to entertain ghosts."[12] Compelled also by the fact that psychoanalysis exposes the antagonisms that live inside the subject, I am reminded of Albert Memmi, who wrote that psychoanalysis can be a mechanism for understanding the obscure and the obsolete.[13] Drawing too from Ranjana Khanna, I see psychoanalysis as a reading practice that allows me to get at the psychic life of colonial and postcolonial predicaments and to take on the intimate, the domestic, the perverse, the experimental, the fantastical, the imagined, the maternal, and the mythic and to put them in dialogue with my mother's diasporic utterances.[14] But to posit the brown, immigrant, domesticated mother as a central figure through whom we might think of (and access) knowledge/production, to actually do this thing we name decolonizing knowledge requires first trekking, if briefly, through the deep historical disavowal of the mother in the Western theoretical canon, with psychoanalysis as *mea culpa*.

When Gilles Deleuze (1997) wrote, "It is not my language that is maternal, it is my mother who is a language,"[15] his words weren't necessarily about his mother or, for that matter, about mothers at all. Deleuze referred to the mother as a collection of words that have been put in his mouth and ears, an organization of things that have been put in his body. The Mother for Deleuze was this organizing entity, what Deleuze would refer to as Life (although this was Life as abstraction and not life as flesh). His Mother emerged as the metaphysical, metaphorical, therefore disembodied. The figure of the Father, conversely, is foreign, that which is accessed exteriorly, hence, Knowledge. So Deleuze, like many others, betrays the figure of the mother in order to get at what he names Philosophy/Knowledge (and Deleuze was one of the few theorists who actually liked his mother).

In psychoanalysis, language is the name of the Father, achieved through a (necessary and productive) rejection of the desire-producing *Mother*. Lacan tells us that the Mother has to be learned as the *other* (the *other* in the *Mother*) in order for the self to emerge.[16] For Lacan, the Name-of-the-Father is the fundamental signifier securing the entry of the subject into the symbolic order: Father's Law. In Lacanian thought, the symbolic order which constitutes the "I" must be paternal, even as he ironically describes how patriarchy *is* the structural and systemic name of the father. This separation is fundamentally subject formation for Lacan, in that this refusal of the mother creates the conditions for the Cartesian split (a split, we know, is an impossibility in the patriarchal, Orientalist and colonial context). Lacan, of course, also noted that we learn language, loss, and desire all at the same time. In order to enter language, we must be severed from the immediacies of bodily satisfaction. We might not be able to have the mother, but we get to have language instead. The brutal severance from the mother (for psychoanalysts, it is exhaustingly always about the mother's breasts) opens up a labyrinth of longing, which is then paved with language (i.e., the imagination is born). Lacan, along with the familiar cast of characters of Freud, Marx, Derrida, and others, want to forget the mother.[17] And they all do so in particularly dull, reductive habituations and self-congratulating misogynistic ways.

In *The Theorist's Mother*, Andrew Parker traces this loathing of the maternal in Western philosophy and perhaps aptly captures his own as well, as his cover image displays an oversized stone breast sculpture with innumerous nipples (read "the overfeeding mother").[18] Parker's book cover is reminiscent of the artwork of seventeenth-century Francois Perrier, for whom feminine sexuality takes refuge in motherhood to live out its perversions and madness.[19] Parker's treatise focuses namely on Marxism's and psychoanalysis's long-possessed ability to reproduce themselves and their ongoing schools of thought without a trace of the mother. Parker notes that revolution for Marx required forgetting the mother tongue.[20] In *Capital*, Marx argued that ideas have to be translated out of their mother tongue into a foreign language in order to circulate, be exchangeable. Freud, of course, totally pathologized the mother and saw her as a repressive force. Derrida, unsurprisingly, named philosophy itself as masculine so that the philosopher is always a paternal figure; thus the deconstruction of the phallogocentric is the deconstruction of philosophy itself, even as he, too, could not imagine a thinking, much less a philosophizing, mother. From Freud's self-analysis to Sartre's psychobiography to Alain Badiou's disdainful maternal narratives, Parker traces the Anglo-European abjection of the maternal. And lest we forget, this abject mother with her overfeeding breasts and overbearing tongue is a White mother. Even Donald Winnicott's "good enough mother" (developed some twenty years after Freud) is a White mother.[21] The (White) maternal rises and recedes within the archives of theory, repressed or loathed, foreclosed or displaced. Indeed, it would not be a stretch to say that the mother of color and her tongue are unthinkable within their epistemological frames. If these dead white men could speak, they would be hard pressed to allow a Black or brown mother to pass through their tongues (except, of course, when they might be feeding off her breasts).

But psychoanalytic feminists looking into the archive of the mother—the few that chose to do so—couldn't quite resuscitate her either. Nancy Chodorow, for example, showed that traditional psychoanalysis failed the mother by positing that motherhood was fact and that fatherhood was idea, extending this to motherhood as body and fatherhood as mind.[22] Chodorow argues that this is the dichotomy that inevitably and pathologically produces the longstanding difficulty to dismantle the sexual division of labor. However, Chodorow, even as she opened a space to understand the unending and embodied labor of the mother's work, essentialized maternity as white and the subsequent gender division of labor as universally and evenly experienced (as oppressive). Melanie Klein, notably, shifted the focus from the mother as fanatical figure from which the child must separate to the obsessive fantasies the infant has of the mother: the fanatical and even destructive child.[23] Klein reversed the pathological claim that it is the mother who obsesses over her attachment to the infant and, in so doing, initiated a mother-centered psychoanalysis. But Klein's construction of the good breast/bad breast object (Kleinian object-relations theory) and the sadistic infant who wants to consume, perhaps even, destroy the mother, meant that Kleinian psychoanalysis dwelled on the drives, where drives for Klein are relationships, thus eventually moving away from the mother altogether. Intervening in Klein's notion of introjection is the psychoanalytic duo, Nikolas Abraham and Maria Torok, who explain that introjecting's (= casting aside) initial moment occurs first when the infant discovers the emptiness of her mouth, a mouth absent of the breast (even if the mother is physically present).[24] The emptiness of the mouth, Abraham and Torok explain, is a void the infant fills with cries and sobs and the experience of her own tongue searching the empty mouth for sustenance. The "transition of a mouth filled with breast to a mouth filled with words" is the first model of introjection and one that requires the presence of the mother, as the figure that gives and sustains meanings of words: "the mother's constancy is the guarantor of the meaning of words."[25] The intervening experience of the empty mouth, the tongue hopelessly and repeatedly searching the mouth for its lost object is the key moment that language replaces breast as object.

But perhaps the most masterful feminist subversion in psychoanalysis is made by Julia Kristeva, even as she acknowledged that even speaking of the mother sets one up to be "accused of normativism, read: of regression."[26] Kristeva was highly critical of the "paternal tongue," which is influence and logic and social order as we know it. She argued prolifically against Freud and Lacan, taking the position that entry into language is not the result of lack or separation but is motivated by pleasure and excess, indeed the body's own longing, its own urge to speak.[27] Building a case for maternal passion, which she posits transforms the libido to love ("sexuality is deferred by tendency to tenderness") and maternal sublimation, Kristeva writes that the child develops language *with* the mother, not through or against her. She further argues that Winnicott's "good-enough mother" involves a "depassioning" that transforms the fear of mothering monstrosity (the overmothering mother) into that which is misread as serenity, thus just enough.[28] The overmothering mother that Kristeva pushes against (against whom Winnicott developed the "good enough" mother) often directly or indirectly involves the specific dynamic of the mother-daughter relationship. The mother-daughter dyad as always and already too close for comfort, thus most available to psychoanalytic critique, is the unfortunate clutch on which Kristeva leans. For all her feminist genius, Kristeva implies that maternal passion's flip side is narcissism and melancholy, the effect of which can be a psychically dangerous symbiotic fusion between the mother and the daughter.[29]

Part of that same moment of feminist psychoanalysis, Luce Irigiray, conversely and importantly, recognized the mother-daughter relation as one that is disrupted by patriarchy. She observed and argued (not incorrectly) that "Western culture is founded not on the much-feared patricide on which the Oedipal complex lies but rather on the more common murder of the mother."[30] Her radical thesis that the culture we live in and the myths we live by are predicated on the death of the mother-as-subject and on the subsequent erasure of what she refers to as maternal genealogy is important to how I think about the maternal body. Irigiray encouraged women to develop what she calls a female language with one another that doesn't subscribe to patriarchal impositions on female relations.[31] However, despite her important—sometimes radical, sometimes romantic—intervention, Irigiray saw the mother, perhaps inevitably under the conditions of patriarchy, as a suffocating figure, particularly toward the daughter.[32] In "One Doesn't Stir without the Other," one of the most salient sensations that emerge from reading Irigiray, is that of the glut of the mother, overfeeding, overstuffing her daughter (which is what demands a flight to the father or a third abstraction, Knowledge).

Even feminists not attached to (rewriting) the psychoanalytic script fell into this trope. Judith Butler, for example, recognized the mother as the original site of desire, but for Butler, desire for the mother and motherhood is laced with melancholy and taboo, shaped by the compulsory obligation to (only) reproduce.[33] Simone de Beauvoir's memoir on her mother, *A Very Easy Death*, expresses somewhat differently this dynamic, as she describes the ideological distance the feminist daughter has (to have) with her mother. De Beauvoir describes her mother's love: "Her love for us was deep as well as exclusive, and the pain it caused us as we submitted to it was a reflection of her own conflicts. . . . With regard to us, she often displayed a cruel unkindness that was more thoughtless than sadistic: her desire was not to cause us unhappiness but to prove her own power to herself."[34] Here again, we hear the echoes of Lacan, who called mother-daughter relationships a devastation!

While I recognize that feminists and feminist psychoanalysts took on the mother differently and that their analytics and analysis differ from one another in a great many ways, my goal is not to parse each tendency and the field of differences between them in detail. Rather, as I hope to make clear—even belabor—is that, regardless, Anglo-American and European feminists limned the figure of the mother in ways from which I urge departure. Produced and imagined as threatening, withholding, devouring, abandoning, the maternal (in a particular pathological dyad with the daughter) continues to circulate from psychoanalytic negation to the second wave feminist generations' "kill your mother" formation. Even contemporary postcolonial feminists and white queer scholars resuscitated this narrative of the failed mother from which we must depart or without whom we cannot (yet) contend (recalling here the otherwise lovely and powerful works of Sara Suleri (*Meatless Days*), Manju Kapur (*Difficult Daughters*), Cathy Hong (*Minor Feelings*), and Jordy Rosenberg ("Daddy Diacectic"). In all these epistemic frames and writings, we see the carte blanche impulse to forget the mother, where forgetting the mother is the *sine qua non* of individuation.

What is more, while these feminists disputed the psychoanalytic privileging of the male infant, rewrote the pathological overnursing mother as a by-product of patriarchy, and in some small ways, gave language back to the mother (Kristeva), they were all speaking if not literally, then ideologically, about white middle-class motherhood (or its ascendant). Even in *Of Woman Born*, where Adrienne Rich wrote: "We know more about the air we breathe, the seas we travel, than about the nature and meaning of motherhood," she, like her feminist comrades, was holding space for a white mother.[35] Indeed, I would say that in all of these feminist resuscitations, there is a way in which White (and White adjacent) mothers, despite whatever "wound" they may carry, are always positioned in the space of life—a space from which Black and brown mothers are evacuated. Therefore, while all these thinkers critiqued the Oedipus complex as patriarchal and sexist, they seemed to forget that the exaltation of the Oedipus complex as the primary condition for language acquisition also bolsters White supremacy, as it produces the very ethos through which Black and brown mothers are always and already seen as failed or failing (at language).

In writing about my mother, I want to disrupt this embedded homology of whiteness and motherhood and this homology of the maternal as failure, pathology, forgettable, or just *good enough*. I want to instead center the brown mother in myriad ways, as subject position, embodied experience, political location, symbol, and metaphor. Certainly, the collective history and theorizing of Black women put them in a different relationship to the canonical categories of the Freudian paradigm, that is, to the father, to the maternal, and to the female-sexed body. The history of chattel slavery produced a very polarized approach to the maternal: either the maternal as absence, dearth, negation, and neglect (read Black) or the plentitude of the maternal, the idealization of maternal love and care (read White). This colonial binary erased the complex experiences of ambivalence, survival, and politics that shape colonized mothering for Black and brown mothers. Black feminist scholars, then, consecrated a particular kind of feminist politics by highlighting the difficult structure of Black maternity and its attendant grammars of loss, abjection, and rejection.

For Hortense Spillers, merely thinking of the Black mother marks an epistemological limit in psychoanalysis, and thus Spillers bends psychoanalysis toward a consideration of the mother (of color).[36] For example, Spillers points out that the processes of violent enfleshment of Black bodies denied the possibility for the symbolic; thus protective gender identity (allocated only for White women/mothers) were also accompanied by the violent erasure of Black mothers and mothering. Spillers points out that, under colonial conditions, the paternal became synonymous with whiteness and the maternal with absence—"mother-dispossessed"—a condition produced and amplified by the materialities of race, empire, coloniality and capitalism. In Spiller's work, the Black mother is posted as the underbelly of modern life, and the violence of colonial modernity erased Black mothers and Black mothering—the Black maternal as the container of social hatred. Building on Spillers, Fred Moten argues that the Black maternal was turned into the raw material for commodification and that the Black mother cannot be thought of outside of this commodification.[37] Rizvana Bradley, in thinking about maternal function in contemporary Black cinema, observes that "the warped absence of the black maternal" signals a number of epistemological difficulties, ranging from issues of representation and visuality to practices of world making and notions of dignity.[38] These thinkers grapple with the ways this condition of absence and disappearance reveals the specter of the lost (even if present) mother in blackness.

Amber Jamila Musser's work offers an important intervention here, as she specifically calls for a return to the maternal.[39] Offering a lacerating and sharp critique that the psychoanalytic turning away from the maternal and the feminine (flesh) is itself a product of patriarchal coloniality, Musser demonstrates that the specter of the lost mother haunts Black and brown fleshiness. Specifically, Musser takes the position that if the conditions of disappearance, violence, and severing of the mother tie are the result of global capitalism and its violent machinations of moving bodies, destroying kin, and exploiting bodies, then the brown mother, too, has been disappeared.[40] Musser cogently argues that global capitalism relies on Black and brown mothering as the material for reproduction, while denying maternal labor to Black and brown children (thinking here of the erasure of the mother to slave, maid, or domestic worker), and complicates the uneven, yet overlapping, genealogy of brown and Black mothers. Moreover, Musser points out that these conditions of brown maternity introduce melancholy into the maternal dynamic, not only through the psychoanalytic foreclosure of the mother that Kristeva and others argue (which is still the White mother) but also because the Black and brown mother is doubly repressed, first by psychoanalytic maneuvers, which dismiss or disavow her, and then by the conditions of global capitalism, which reduce her to fleshy excess who is nonetheless possessed.

This bending, twisting, and turning of feminist and psychoanalytic perspectives toward the racial materialities of the maternal subtend with my two key signs—my mother and her tongues. I position my mother in this chain of unprivileged subjects, as both an overdetermined and disappeared figure. I think of how my mother's tongues enact, release, and contain the tensions of psychoanalytic theories, even as her speaking in tongues is a key site of psychoanalytic failure. I extend Musser's figure of the doubly repressed brown mother to argue that this double repression produces a melancholic motherhood: mothering under the burden of patriarchy and racism; mothering through the excesses of tongues, through feminine hyperbole and illegible language; mothering with the dour determination to pass necrolessons on to children, even if all these lessons are truncated by the impossibility of wholeness, summation, totality, and the real. I see my brown mother and her tongue/s as ludic, dislocating, interstitial, deterritorializing, an assemblage that operates against Oedipal logics that constrain maternal life toward control, discipline, and dispossession. My mother's mothering was shaped by a necropolitical melancholy, one which resulted from living in these fleshy maternal states, distant from and excluded from both legible (white, middle-class) mothers and legible (postcolonial, cosmopolitan) brownness.

My mother, I learned, told (and still tells) stories to make sense of her own historical present, and, in so doing, her stories regularize the monumental into the intimate. Her polysemic and intertextual stories underscore what Jacqueline Rose called the "yet unsettled relations" between feminism, psychoanalysis, and affect studies.[41] I see psychoanalysis as the vocabulary and my mother as the analyst. Who then, a colleague and a friend, ask me, is the analysand? Perhaps, I respond, the analysand is my mother's affective response to colonial and postcolonial predicaments—the melancholy, the preoccupation, the fixation, the conspiracy theories, produced and proliferated by these predicaments. But just as I offer this psychoanalytic telos, I too understand that my mother's tongue is a marker so loaded with mythical value that its weight bears down on the pages I write. So, I remind myself, just as I am reminded by others, that the analysand can only lie: all she has is noise that fills the space of what she knows but cannot know yet or bear to know.

My mother has an abject tongue. She is what I would call obsessed with oppression. In a strange way, oppression and abjection were as much a tantalizing distraction as they were ordinary and bodily and bare life. They were the sum of her everyday life. In this way, her tongues reveal not extreme life but ordinary life and its affective cathexis. But just as her articulation of this abjection was part of the everyday, so too was the marking of her speech as improper, as made-up, as fake historical events; thus, all she spoke was understood (by those around her) to have been impossible or to not have "happened," or uncouth, low-brow, tawdry. Her stories occupied the location of the denigrated position, in the realm of illegitimacy, outside of respectability. Hers was a tongue of excess, a portal to a past to which no one wanted to return, and many did not think existed. But my mother was obsessed with this excess, and she was obsessed with surrendering (to it). It was through this obsession that she created a temporality of melancholic motherhood, an archival fixation with the past. Listening to her meant that I had to understand that the libidinal landscape of feminized flesh (its textures, perceptions, feelings, sensations, violations, etc.) was far more fundamental to how she understood being a brown mother than any kind of abstract or material institutionality, or lack thereof, in the political economy. The particular kind of stress my mother laid on the stories she told felt, in part, like an effort to shake them free of the embeddedness of the omnipresent male gaze and its many insidious logics and self-congratulatory traditions. Her stories made feminine adjustments to masculine time, maternal adjustments to paternal power, brown adjustments to white logics.

Abjection is my mother's archival fixation. Her archive is peopled with brown women, brown girls, and brown mothers. Men and boys are ancillary, even as they are necessary, even as she relied on them, even as she bore them. It is the only mode through which she understands her movement though space and time and land and water. It is a compulsion that holds space for consistent and frightening and unsavory measures of vulnerability and melancholy. The interpenetrative conditions that shape her relation to violence seep into one another, obscurely, opaquely, ambiguously, promiscuously. Hers is an archive that contains all sorts of debris and dirt, seen and unseen. Her relation to this dispossession is something she and I (through her, with her) have been processing for a lifetime. Yet our processing is inadequate. The gestures of deconstruction in which I have been trained are afflicted with failure. Her testimony falls outside the official, her witnessing outside the rational, her stories outside the documented—her memory insufficient, subjective, feminized, and racialized. Repressing such an archive is a key mechanism of patriarchal coloniality.

Jacques Derrida writes, "There is no political power without control of the archive, if not of memory."[42] So I route my mother's memory through queer of color critique and women of color feminisms to contest the affective normativities (i.e., forgetting, positivity, optimism) produced by supremacies, misogynies, violences. Such an approach to memory emerges from my mother's refusal to forget (Sara Ahmed's killjoy comes to mind), where forgetting is a political and an affective practice of hegemony. In refusing to forget, memory for women of color is decidedly antinormative. A dark cloud of illegitimacy was cast on my mother's stories. I orient myself toward this dark cloud, this brown tongue, this maternal archive, with its many dirty abimes, its accidental nuances, its casual violence, its indeterminate analysis, and its arbitrary tenderness. I have, as Derrida might say, archive fever.

Hers was an archive voluptuously overflowing with unusual inhabitants, strange sayings, violent stories, random tenderness. Her memories cohere around objects unpredictably, in ways that are fragmented and shaped by the logic of the unconscious. Nostalgia, personal memory, pain, and trauma are the constitutive elements that make up her stories—all partial, and somewhat destroyed. One moment I hear an achingly tender story about an old blind woman of whom my mother was very fond as a little girl, an old woman whom she would help cross the notoriously busy Harris Street in Karachi and who would delight her with stories, until they reached the corner bus stop. With delicate detail my mother describes her secret, preternatural attachment to this feeble, old, blind woman and their morning ritual of eleven months (just before she turned eight, my mother and her family left for Quetta). I struggled to understand the meaning, the significance of my mother's affection for this woman (an affection for random older brown women I observed my whole life, as if she knew them, as if she knew their secrets). And just as I would linger with this random memory, my mother would interrupt my silence with a perverse detail, stating how every morning her father woke her and her two sisters (but not her brothers) with a swift kick in the stomach, grunting, *Time to get to work.*

I think about what it means to take up these pieces without seeking out something authentic and complete, without needing to restore the fragments into a credible form. If culture is a litany of affective activity that isn't always legible to normative intelligible codes, then, as my mother described it, her intimate familial, national, class, gender, ethnoreligious culture was within and outside of the feminine excess of that which has been recorded, regarded, ritualized, and reckoned with. The collision of these poles filled in her real and imagined life story, assembling and reassembling, each moving across and through borders in ways both familiar and strange. In this way, my mother's memories were literally hard to grasp, slippery, vague, amorphous, embodied, even if, in rare moments, specific, factual, researchable. But without *her* memory, what is that which I would call *my* culture, *my* brownness?

The split subject that psychoanalysis posits was profoundly manifest in our conversations. While others moved into the fast-paced technological world, my mother stayed in her idiosyncratic, quasi-allegorical, slow, spread-out world. Being with my mother meant I had to come to embody her kind of sociality of slowness in the midst of my otherwise frenzied life. Her stories demanded a different temporality—one has to slow down for the imagery, the allusive clusters, the dense affect. In so many of our conversations, my mother repeated stories, over and over again, often asking (also over and over), "Did I ever tell you this...?" Repetition, memory loss and random epiphanies shaped our conversation. My mother deployed feminine vernaculars that were out of time, linguistic lyricism that disrupted anglophone and androcentric assumptions, lexical intimacies that arrested meaning, delving sometimes deeper, downward, into the underbelly, other times moving upward, vertically, diagonally. Sometimes the stories didn't change; at other times, significant details would change: an uncle would turn into a brother, a father into a grandfather; Dhaka would change to Chittagong, London to Atlanta. The weight of memory bearing down, breaking wholes into holes, totalities into remains. And sometimes, but not always, a second, third, or fourth retelling revealed a previously unspoken dynamic, fact, or emotion. Repetition for repetition's sake. Repetition for revelation's sake.

I had to learn to read my mother's stories, as Deborah Britzman says of slow reading, "a scene within a scene within a scene," or what Heather Love names, "not merely close, but too close, claustrophobic, even abject."[43] My mother's intertextual narrative practices revealed that subjectivity is who one wants to become in your/my eyes in this/that instance. But her fragmentariness presented a formidable challenge. It wasn't about sameness; it was instead a symptomatic sort, indicative of an encounter that couldn't be assimilated into our modern immigrant family, a refusal to submit to a temporal logic—or, better, the distortion of that logic by interference, by interruption, like a gravitational pull of some other, unrecognized force. I had to learn to write in tongues, as she spoke in tongues.

And truth be told, again and again, my conversations with my mother were interrupted by a break, by real ruptures, by exterior forces. The interruptions were themselves new ideas, which decentered sometimes, confirmed at other times, what my mother's tongue was offering. Here was another metaphor for theoretical work: theoretical work as domestic interruption. The interruption of life—illness, children, cooking, family, relationships, housework, emotional management, time itself—was specific and decisive, sometimes cruel, sometimes banal. But there were other interruptions—of stories within stories, of secrets and metaphors that snuck up on her and on me, of gazes met and lips sealed, of knowledge making within the work of mythmaking. It was ruptural. It reorganized her and me and the space between us in concrete ways. The change had consequences. My object—her tongue—changed in those moments, requiring both of us to reassemble, shift, bite down, or let go.

So when Derrida wrote that the mother tongue, even when inhabited, is un/inhabitable or when Andre Green writes that nothing can represent the maternal object, I respond by taking the position that language achieved through a separation from the mother is nothing but an accretion of lies.[44] I respond by saying that my mother's tongues linger with the haunting feminist and queer desire to name the mother, to foreground the deep intense desire for intimacy with the mother that gets replaced, in the modern world, for successful subjectification. The dialectical oscillation between the tongue as flesh (from which we must depart or which we can never inhabit, represent, embody) and the tongue as language (subject-formation) echoes the way the term itself is in a weird space of indeterminacy, where it is neither fully of body nor fully of self. I have stakes in this indeterminacy, this dizzying circuitousness. It takes me where I would otherwise not go. It takes me in, down, and through feminized, fleshy, maternal brownness. It takes me in, down, and through the remains, traces, or vestiges of the maternal element in one's tongues, the many, mutable, excessive, and uncontainable tongues (in my mouth and in hers). It takes me in, down, and through affect as analytic and demands that we think about how affect produces sociality, likeable and unlikeable brown mothers, good and difficult brown daughters. It takes me in, down, and through the limits of what can be uttered as queer, where queerness is informed by its historical specificity of sexual irregularities, where queerness liquefies all the stories that we have of maternity, of family, of learning to love and to lust, where queerness sheers normativity, where queerness is bodily and that which challenges the limits of what can be understood as a desirable body, where queerness is often vilified as cowardly or dirty, where queerness assumes the presence of queer desire despite the silence, where queerness names something of the uncapturable or unpredictable trajectory of an erotic life, and where queerness refuses the hegemonic disassociation from the mother, the feminine, and the femme and instead lingers with and makes love to the eggs, the breasts, the vulvas, and the tongues of the mother.

Reckoning with Brownness

Innocent as smashed night birds. . . .

—DIONNE BRAND, *THIRSTY*

One spring day in 2016, my mother and I were chatting over a cup of chai about an upcoming family wedding in Islamabad. My white Southern butch lover joined in our conversation and shared with my mother her plans to join me and my then-teenage daughter in Islamabad for the family wedding. My mother quietly smiled at Erin, who at this point she had known for several years, and advised her (and us) to "not be the gay" while we were there. While I understood that my mother's rejection of the discourse of gayness ("don't be the gay") was fundamentally about rebuffing a particular meaning of sexual discourse produced in the Global North (visibility, language, naming, etc.), confusion played on my lover's mouth. "Not be the gay?" she responded, probably thinking how impossible this was for her. My mother, at ease in this rhetorical mode, inclined to declarative sentences, repeated simply, "Yes, don't be the gay." As long as she followed this advice, said my mother, Erin would love Islamabad.

A few evenings later, my mother's warning to my white butch lover to re-frain from "being the gay" in Islamabad became an open and ongoing joke among my first-generation cousins, all of whom had gathered at our home for dinner. As members of the global diaspora living in the Global North and Global South, we were all in different ways products of varyingly wannabe elite, postcolonial institutions, socialized in the soft ethos of liberal feminism, antiracism, anti-Orientalism, and other mainstream sociocultural formations that tend to rule the terms of sentience and resistance. This elite pedagogy of resistance fueled our uproarious laughter at my mother's advice to Erin (and to me/us) and fed our smooth pleasure in defying the sovereign powers of historical heritage and the weight of external South Asian culture that daily bore down on us. My cousins and I had quickly absorbed her advice into that which we had come to see as the opposite of modern epistemologies and modern freedoms, precisely the opposite of that which can be taken se-riously. We were in the temporality of "now:" the new postcolonial diaspora emerging from under the available new global languages of becoming visible, valuable, legible, legitimate. If Orientalism is the cultural logic of the modern, the bourgeois West its exteriorized persona, then the educated, postcolonial South Asian diaspora is its wet dream.[45]

Buttressed by the provinciality of my mother's tongue, we had mastered another (colonial) tongue. At the threshold of her tongue, we felt we knew what was in her thoughts. But we were at the border of her tongue, and not inside it, and in that borderland of words, we mistook our liberal pleasure for radical knowledge. Our conceit at my mother's broken English and our gentle mockery of her backward injunction to Erin papered over the structuring matrix of violence that underwrote the means through which we came to be the educated diasporic elite cackling at a brown Pakistani mother's ill-informed convention. We couldn't see how my mother's rejection of the discursivity of "being the gay" versus, say, a rejection of queer being "don't be gay" (which is *not* what she advised) wrapped the language of visibility/identity in precarity. Her use of the definitive article *the*, even if erroneously used, announced gay as identity, as definition. To *be* (gay) versus to *be seen* (as gay)—one a mode of being in the world, the other a mode of articulation (of that being), one ontological, the other annunciatory and performative, one interesting, complex, a temporality of emergence, the other a liminal space subject to scrutiny, surveillance, and violence. The very epistemic and hermeneutic work of my mother's injunction (in that she both offered knowledge of oppression and a tool of survival, pleasure even) cast the line between sexuality and survival as simultaneously fluid (in that there are available furtive maneuvers) and hard (in that both furtivity and fugitivity are requirements of crossing, in this case, passing). My mother's "don't be the gay" was not an injunction to hide-as-ontological-disappearance but rather hiding as a veering-away, a skirting-from, a swerving-around the immanent violence of hegemonic heterosexual imperatives.

But her how-to-live and fierce urgency of hiding was lost on us. Hers was a pedagogy of how-to-disobey-without-being-visible-to-the-oppressor. The libidinal surplus in her story (on tongues), just as in her injunction ("don't be the gay"), was ritualized and rhythmic, hyperbolized, and carnal ("being the gay" gestured the body/sex even as it mandated the disappearance of both). She was the abject maternal figure, her tongue overflowing with the past, with myth, with femininized il/logics. So seduced were we by our ascendent, assimilated, grammared, and trained tongues that we could not see how our laughter masked the injury cathected to our sociality, how woundedly attached we were to our own violent worlds, how brutally and blindly we mobilized our own version of antibrown, antimaternal racial humor. We, like so many others, had internalized the racial hatred and sexist dismissal that is so often projected onto the brown domestic mother.

What hit me like a gut punch amid my own laughter was that my mother's feminism, a feminism that, as Sara Ahmed has written, "traveled to me,

growing up in the West, from the East," produced particular kinds of socialities, solidarities, intimacies, analytics that allowed my mother and other
brown mothers to live in and through violence, in and through a world not
of their own making. And as Sara Ahmed has argued, "where we find feminism matters; from whom we find feminism matters."[46] My mother's frames
of knowing took on a vernacular quality that produced a calculated and deliberate invisibilization (that, in part, meant hiding from the powers that could
destroy you). She rejected the normative feminist notion that "moving from
silence to speech" or "coming into voice" was necessarily empowering. My
complicity in laughing at my mother underscored what little *thought* work I
had done to excavate and understand her modes of being, thought, speech,
and knowledge—my mother's everyday commons, her (and my) brown commons, as Jose Muñoz has written, or, our undercommons, as Fred Moten and
Stefano Harney write.[47]

In company with my cousins (and perhaps to a certain degree for my cousins), I turned my mother's injunction into our evening comedy, and in so
doing, I, like so many others, betrayed her vocabularies, reconstructing and
deconstructing her speech acts, distancing myself from her subject formation to become my own subject, trying to grasp at modernity, cosmopolitan-
ism, independence, and individuality, and succeeding in perhaps nothing, or
little. Our laughter catalogued our failure, and when my laugh rolled into a
stone silence amid my still heartily laughing cousins, I realized that it was her
brownness—as abject maternal, as misery cognition, as conspiratorial
madness, as backward injunction, as domesticated interiority, as mother
tongue—that was queerer than my white butch lover holiday-ing in Islamabad.

This small moment, in all its laughter and play and cruelty, cracked open a
profound progression of questions. What is the meaning of (our) brownness
(both in this moment of our superiority over and against the brown maternal and in other moments of inferiority, insecurity, precarity)? What does the
brown maternal reveal about the liminality of brownness, or can it, or does it,
or does it really matter and, if so, to whom, and to what end? What concerns,
anxieties, facts, fictions animate (my) brown mother's speech? What modes
of dispossession distress her? What forms of livability does she take on with
deadly seriousness?

The everyday violence of being a brown, immigrant, and domesticated
mother, often illegible to those more modern and cosmopolitan around her, is,
in part, what intimately, intellectually, politically compelled me to my mother's
tongue. But by offering my mother's tongues as (bad) object (of inquiry), my
aim is not to examine tongues as a new metaphysical object or object-ontology.

Rather I am interested in how the object (tongue) is involved with the subject (mother) and how such an involvement gives insight into the conditions of brown life. Thus, part of answering these questions is reckoning with brownness and its curving, ambling relation to coloniality, immigration, precarity, vulnerability, violence, language, and the libidinal. And to be sure, such a reckoning is always and already simultaneously geographic, corporeal, and psychic.

In his posthumously published *The Sense of Brown*, Jose Muñoz offered brownness as a mode of being, as feeling, as sensation.[48] For Muñoz, brownness is not rooted in a central identity on which it may be mapped; it is neither a singularity nor an atomized being; instead brownness is "a being with, being alongside."[49] Muñoz coined the phrase, "brown affect" or "brown feeling," as a way to frame that sense of brown that is always outside normativity, in the shadow, in the whisper, in the haunting. Further and perhaps most crucial for this archive, Muñoz articulates brownness as an affect that gestures to paradigms of violence: "brownness is a value through negation"[50] This capacious conceptualizing of brownness as racialized affect always in asymmetrical relation to others, as a field of negation and as a possible brown commons, means that to feel brown is to feel "something else," "elsewhere, an other-wiseness, knowledge-beyond-knowing."[51]

Muñoz's *Sense of Brown* and, more broadly his oeuvre, offered brown feeling as an analytic, as a theoretical term that captured communal melancholia and sensation, conceptualizing brownness as that which is felt, sensuous, affective. Such a framing is important in my archive of tongues, where so much of how I understand the maternal is through brownness and so much of how I think of brownness is through and in the shadow of my mother. Writing brownness through the maternal and the maternal through brownness marks that something feminine, something brown that hovers over this archive. In suturing brownness to the maternal and the maternal to tongues, I consider how tongues, like brownness, shadows and foreshadows (maternal) knowledge, inheritance, and suffering. As a grammar of suffering that is recognizable, the brown maternal, at times, exposes a lucid, if inconvenient, ontic and at other times, a way of being that is far too messy, too polyvocal, too paranoid, and too feminine to be taken seriously.

Thinking of brown affect in the shadow and beyond, Jasbir Puar, in her book *Right to Maim*, writes that she works with *shadow terms*, or third terms, that hide behind two oppositional and binarized concepts.[52] In her work, Puar offers up the term *debility* as the shadow term of the disability/ability binary—debility as that which shadows, hides behind, even as it overlaps with and modulates the able/disabled body narrative in the Global North. As Puar develops it, if disability is identarian, then debility is a verb, an active means through which particular racialized populations are rendered disabled (but not dead). I turn to Puar because her description of *hiding* but overlapping concepts, those concepts which hide behind that which we openly and directly articulate is useful in my conceptualization of brown maternal secrets and the excavation of those secrets. I think of tongues in the shadow of our mouths, my mother's tongue in the shadow of my own tongue, my tongue in the shadow of my daughter's mouth.

I turn also to Puar because I think of the brown maternal as an always and already debilitated position. I say this because the maternal body of which I write is deliberately rendered abject—a body dismissed or dominated—consequently subject to varying disabling machinations of control, violence, and subjugation. Certainly, the relegation of mothers to the symbolic (over the material) is part of a patriarchal racist maneuver, and one that specifically tethers brown domestic/ated mothers to the immanent possibility of disability, injury, illness, brokenness, and slow life. I refer here to the particularities of how the brown maternal figure is *made sick* by the combined forces of heteropatriarchy, capitalism, and whiteness, and as the domesticated illiterate housewife/mother, is least in relation to the (occasional) rewards of these power formations. She is instead a figure always reduced to the body, the home, the husband, the in-laws, the children, to the shadow of others who are always (or mostly) the self. This reductive maneuver compounded by the way my mother's tongues made her a problem moved her (flesh) toward slow life/slow death—a shift that, while made to look as natural as aging and (bad) life choices, was in fact the deliberate debilitating of the brown maternal. The brown maternal, I argue then, is a specific site of negation, thus debility; therefore, both debility (make sick) and necropolitics (make die) also hover over this archive of tongues.

The laughter that followed my mother's injunction "don't be the gay" reveals how the conditions of global capitalism and residual coloniality produced my mother in one moment as self (through border mobility and heterosexual histories of class, capital, and masculine economies) and in another as negation (through brownness, through femininity, through language). My mother's early life was structured by the global capitalist, nationalist enamorment, and neocaste conditions of 1950s Pakistan, conditions which (often) produced daughters only to repel them; while the US neoliberal structures in which my mother mothered her brown children produced her as backward and stained with the past. Both the past (daughter) and the present (mother) were orchestrated and composed by the conditions of coloniality, capitalism, antibrownness, and the practices and intents of men. This metaphorical and literal stain on the brown maternal as simultaneously too much and not enough and the ethical indifference with which the brown maternal is produced only to be dismissed is a recurrent theme throughout my mother's life and life stories. My mother bore this stain affectively and sensorially; it shaped her life through an assemblage of discontinuous, lived experiences, formed by voluntary and involuntary memories, metaphors, and mutenesses, expressed through shifting registers of voice, affect, cadence, words, and analytics. The conviction that structured my mother's offering of (her) objects of attachment and survival (her advice to Erin) came through this vexed brown affect of having lived through assemblages that would, if they could see you, destroy you. Her fleshy tongue, then, becomes the less visible register, the shadow register, the secret register, from which I think about the intersections of biopolitics, geopolitics, and necropolitics.

To be racialized and gendered is to live in and through violent enfleshment. One of the consequences of living through these violences is the acquisition of years of trauma, years and years of negotiating the ways structures of racialization and oppression feel and sensate and the ways those feelings and sensations cohere around the histories, practices, ideologies, violences of race. Importantly and poignantly, then, brownness is always tied to and emerges from this relation of both violence and possibility, an epistemological disruption that moves, shakes, and vexes us toward another set of vocabularies. Such an understanding follows Amber Jamila Musser in *Sensual Excess: Queer Femininity and Brown Jouissance*, where she offers brown flesh as a way *in* to alternative knowledges. Musser asks: how does *brown* "move through the flesh to elsewhere?"[53] Developing the notion of brown jouissance, Musser argues that brown jouissance emerges through an insistence on keeping the mother at the center of political subjectivity. The figure of the mother returns us to both the feminine and the sensual; thus, Musser further probes, how might brownness invite us to think differently "with the flesh, with the sensual, an invitation to make new knowledge and new politics?"[54] In dialogue with Musser's rethinking of brownness and the maternal, I too offer brown flesh, embodied in my brown mother's tongue, as a way *in* to disobedience, as a way into diasporic im/modernity, as a piece of flesh that presses against modernity to expose another, unexpected field of being, knowing, feeling, and sociality. I write the brown maternal as an excessive form of femininity and melancholia, tied to a structure of negativity, a relation of fleshy difference. It is the lived experience of being inside and outside, on the side, on the other side, on the negative side.

Like Musser, I develop an understanding of brownness through women of color feminisms and queer of color critique, thus, a queerness and feminism that is always and already in relation to brownness. And this route to brownness versus other routes (say, W. E. B Du Bois's color line, Stuart Hall's floating signifier, Gayatri Spivak's subalternity) is another sort of reckoning. Thinking instead of brownness as shattering negation (Frantz Fanon), as deeply felt process (Zora Neal Hurston), as bridge (Gloria Anzaldúa), as feeling (Jose Muñoz), as new politics of knowledge (Amber Jamila Musser), as shadow term (Jasbir Puar), I frame brownness as the disturbing encounter of various modes of being—the brown maternal sucked dry by the excesses and ongoingness of historical violence—and the hermeneutic through which we might reorder that being, knowing, and feeling into livable spaces, where errant femininity, maternal melancholy and queer negativity shape world making. As a cluster of affects and a site of tactile anxiety, the brownness I write of is always in relation to femininity, abjection, and queerness. I stitch together that lexical gap between the brown maternal and queerness that for so long I, and still so many others, cannot, would not, will not see.

But just as I see brownness as a mode of confrontation, constituted both by the racial and ethnic abject, by historical particularity, and by queer modes of knowing and being, I understand that brownness is a particular encounter (and if I am to be honest, collusion) with colonialism and its contemporary iterations, and as such, brownness embodies and enacts deep tensions, antagonisms and violences with blackness (a point I dwell on in chapter 3). Thus, I frame brownness as a racial formation trapped in its own shifting specificities, even as it touches, slides into, converges with, remains aloof to, and diverges from the global and diasporic field of blackness. Eclipsed and accelerated by coloniality, brownness could spurn blackness, even as it stumbled in its own uncertainty, its own precarity. And this different genealogy of violence and survival and ascendency matters and is one that flickers and materializes in this brown archive. The general distancing of the South Asian (diasporic) subject from the provocative fleshly tasks of Black studies (with, of course, few exceptions) pits the immodesty of the transatlantic slave trade against the more modest and task-oriented colonial practices of the British in South Asia. Postcolonial and South Asian studies has been averse to think about the brown body and the brownness of our bodies. It is a particular and peculiar aversion and evasion. The British, we like to tell ourselves, were not consuming our flesh.

But I would like to propose that brown maternal flesh was being consumed, both symbolically and materially. This consumption of the brown mother—what my mother referred to as *ma ko chus le na* (suck the mother dry)—in the form of exploitation, absorption, erasure, violation, and defeat was the means through which brown fathers accomplished (some) mastery of self and the brown diaspora came to boast itself as modern and cosmopolitan. The reduction in perpetuity to feminine domesticity, maternal irrationality, immigrant illiteracy, sexual subjugation produced a subject and a sociality of madness embodied as brown maternal rubbish (my mother's advice, injunctions, sayings, stories, etc.). I take the position that such rubbish extracts a different kind of social material and demands a different sort of reckoning with our brown mothers' vernaculars of life making. Yes, the brown maternal body is (often) a domesticated body. But it, too, is (often) an unpredictable one.

To return, then, to Musser's provocation, how does brown "move through the flesh to elsewhere," I offer the brown mother and her (speaking in) tongues as flesh and figure evocative of burden, tethered to patriarchal violence, secured by capitalist exploitation, restrained by colonial constructions, wrought by heterosexual manipulation, bound to and bitter about the brutal violations which produce/d her. I offer brownness as a fixated analytic that breaks open my mother's fixations, and therefore, too, my fixations with her fixations.

To ruminate on my mother is also to ruminate on brownness, on brown feminine modes of world making. As part of the terrain of the unthought, brownness creates unsettlement, discomfort, tenderness, awkwardness, and discomposure. A brown/ed body, an affective fixation, a bad object, a furtive queerness, a dirty language, brownness is my errant, excessive, listless, promiscuous, insubordinate mother tongue. But to center the brown mother and her tongue isn't just to offer an anxiogenic tableau of objects; it is to epistemologically trouble, to underscore the insecure boundaries of self and *other* and mother, to deterritorialize the territorialized figure of the mother of color, to place in perpetuity the liminality of how we think about survival and the building of life worlds.

As a minor figure, my mother understood brownness as a burden and a benediction, exquisite and fraught and inescapable and clandestine in the midst of violent racialized and sexualized geographies. I take this brownness, turning it around and around in my hands, privileging some aspects, cutting others, mistaking parts for wholes and wholes for parts. I write brownness as a fraction. It is all I have: an odd, misshapen, porous archive of one brown mother. Regardless, I think, my mother's tongue, like time, holds multitudes; and as such, an archive of tongues is also an archive on temporality; and both have their own rhythm.

1
abject tongues

*A memory intruded into the present as if by
its own will. I was ready for the intrusion.*
—SARA AHMED, *LIVING A FEMINIST LIFE*

*We first arrived on the East Coast of America in October of 1977. My brother
was three, my sister was five, and my mother was still nursing me. For three
months we stayed with a friend of my father's whose wife and baby had died
in childbirth. The friend had returned to India to remarry, so we had his two-
bedroom house to ourselves. My father had taken a job in a security company
and had enrolled in a community college in the evenings. My mother was home
with the three of us, new to America, inexperienced in American ways. She felt
cold and strange and cautious even though she had desperately wanted to come
to America. The suburban America we arrived in was a place where everything
worked and was manicured and clean, with small, tight smiles on white faces,
wholly unlike the excess, density, animation and voluptuousness of Pakistan.
My mother had somehow managed to replace the dirt and lack of late 1970s
Karachi with the spotlessness and surplus of the American suburbs. But having
never owned the means of surplus, she found curious the assumed relationship
between surplus and happiness.*

But soon came her first glimpse. A white woman neighbor who had seen my mother nursing me offered her a free sample of Nestle infant formula, along with a no-nonsense statement, that it would change her life forever. With a newly talking toddler, a school-aged girl, a needy infant eating her time and her body like food, and a husband who came home late every night, also hungry for food and her body, my mother was ready for this magical powdery milk and promptly shook it up with hot boiled water. But, unfortunately for her, I was a stubborn baby, refusing, rejecting, spitting out the American formula, and insisting, out of habit, out of history, on her flesh. My tongue's refusal to digest the powdery thickness of American nourishment bound me to her body and her to mine longer than she wanted, as weeks and months passed with unsuccessful attempts to replace breast with bottle. But one day, tired of the everyday labor, frustrated by the strangeness of this new life, saddened by the solitude, my mother reached into my half-open mouth, which was animally moving down her body, pinched my tongue between her fingers, and whispered into my ear, "I will train your tongue for Angrezi doodh (English milk) if it's the last thing I do."

And with an agility true to its accord, she disciplined my tongue. She denied me her body and instead gave me the tactile plasticity of American latex. She trained my mouth to its easy shape, its accessibility, its mimicry of flesh. She trained my tongue to accept another mode of sustenance, another way of being. She worlded my tongue away from her, pulsing it with the simulation of sustenance. And, yes, I came to fancy this American milk. Its sticky, thick sweetness became familiar and nourishing over time. But like the sand that darkens and congeals at contact with water, feeling at one with the sea, only to lighten and fragment seconds later when it departs, the residue of her body and the taste of her flesh had already been absorbed in my tongue, eclipsed, perverted, peculiar.

The Utterable

My mother was her mother's third daughter, initially named Mano by her grandfather, who waited in anticipation for a grandson after two granddaughters—my mother's older sister and another girl who died of smallpox at the age of three. Eventually, from Mano, she was named *Mehru*, short for *Maher Banu*. Depending on the pronunciation and the historico-religious context, *Maher* means expert or highly skilled; or a mandatory payment, in the form of money or possessions promised by a groom, or by a groom's father, to the bride at the time of marriage, which legally becomes her property in the event of a divorce. When we asked my mother the meaning of her name, she mentioned neither of these meanings. Instead, my mother told us that *Maher* refers to the small wooden part of Islamic prayer beads (*tasbih*) that connects the tassel to the beads. It was considered symbolically, she said, as the bridge to Allah. Others confirmed that *Maher* also meant the bridge to Allah. Soon after my mother was born, everyone began saying she was a bridge to good luck for the family, for almost immediately after her first birthday, her mother gave birth to her first son, and then two more sons, each sixteen months apart.

According to her American traveling papers, which were drawn up by my father in the fall of 1977, when he sponsored her for a US visa, my mother was born in 1946, one year before the India-Pakistan Partition, in Limbri, India, a small village in the state of Gujrat. All her younger siblings were born in the territory that, less than a year later, was formed into Pakistan. My mother unequivocally says that her birth year of 1946 is false, that instead she was born a few years earlier, maybe 1943 or 1944, because her older sister's birth date is also written as 1946 and because everyone's dates were changed when India changed and records and land and families and memories were burned to the ground, and she remembers this change, this changing, alluding to and dismissing a vague if twisted memory of Partition. According to her "official" birth year of 1946, she would have been too young to remember the British-enforced India-Pakistan Partition in mid-August 1947. The logics of time and age and memory and colonial archiving indicate that the drama of mass death and mass rape would have been over by the time she could form full sentences.

My mother tells me it is difficult to narrate the course of events in her life because no single memory fully describes what she remembers and what she shouldn't know at all. She tells me she remembers trucks that rolled through their streets, piled with bodies. Her older sister said the trucks were full of tired workers, slumped down, exhausted, motionless, their bodies mangled together, their mouths open. My mother remembers one day when she stood out in the street in front of their apartments, mesmerized by the trucks driving by and the strange waft of air they brought with them, when her mother snapped her out of her reverie by roughly covering her eyes with the palm of her hand and grabbing her tunic by the tail to pull her inside. Later she would learn how terrified her mother was of Hindu soldiers' bestial rapes and mutilations of Muslim women and girls, often openly enacted on the streets on which they roamed, rapes which her mother (my mother's grandmother who was a midwife) had firsthand helped heal and, in many cases, had helped abort the subsequent pregnancies. Later she would also learn that this vague visual memory of piled-up bodies on trucks that drove through small colonies of flats, around government buildings, through the slums of the poor and the shops of the working class in the filth-thick air, with guns pressed against the bones of their streets, was not spectacular at all. It was simply extreme life seeping into ordinary life. But just as her memory of those trucks function in the genealogy of the deathscapes that made Pakistan, these same post/colonial geographies, economies, and politics would determine her migrations. They would also bleed into her archival tongues.

I learned early in this project that I would have to read my mother's relations, affections, memories through a different grammar, a different register. Many fragments, even with my probing analysis and deconstruction and excavation, remained a mystery. But these fragments commanded more attention than any other logical or ordered fact, if only because they could be named. There were things I knew (as fact). I knew that her father worked for the State Bank of Pakistan and that his job required constant reassignment, so they moved every few years. Quetta for two years. Then Karachi. Peshawar for four years. Then back to Karachi. Later Chittagong and Dhaka, then Lahore. Finally, and for what felt like one permanent moment, Karachi. Each city, for my mother manifested as temporal and episodic, and her memory traced them as such. I could depend neither on linearity nor on continuity.

I know that my mother was part of a postpartition, postcolonial, capitalist class that had access to homes, low-paid help (the result of the deeply embedded and little-disputed remnant of the Hindu caste system), cars, drivers, quasi-elite postcolonial educational institutions (embodied often in Catholic schools), and border mobility. This capitalist class community came into being at the historical juncture of a new imagining of the Pakistani state that needed loyal government servants to set up the financial and capital infrastructures in the newly forming East/West Pakistan. My mother's father in warring India was a small-town banker who got noticed by traveling government teams pursuing male Muslim workers whose identities and ambitions were deeply rooted in both class mobility and Islam. He was selected and quickly began his training in (and climb up) the world of state finance.

My mother benefited from this postpartition Pakistani diasporic expansion, which resulted unevenly in a class consciousness formed through a de facto acceptance of informal and caste-based domestic workers, discourses on colonial and nationalized meritocracy, values, and ambitions of modern and modernizing lifestyles, including cars, homes, and a fluency in the English language (even if English was rarely spoken in these homes). The homes her family lived in announced status: they often lived in large homes previously occupied by the British. But when they lived in these homes, they often took up only two rooms, leaving the rest of the home to its quiet echoes and English ghosts. They were accustomed to living in close quarters, in proximity with other familial bodies. In these large homes, then, much of the space went unused, as did much of the furniture, as food was always set on a large, white sheet on the floor and eating was always done with their hands. Their life and their attachments had little to do with actual wealth accumulation, just enough food to feed a family, just a little bit of gold to marry off the daughters. My mother and her siblings often wore the same *shalwar kameez* (loose pants and tunic), her and her sisters washing everything nightly to wear again the next day. Nothing in the houses in which they lived belonged to them, not even, as my mother says, a single dish. My mother would say, *We came with our relationships and our clothes and left with the clothes that still fit and most of these relationships still intact.* But stratified labor practices were deeply embedded in their lives. Every home—from Quetta to Karachi to Lahore to Dhaka—came fully staffed with domestic help, working-class women and girls and boys and men looking for work; residual coloniality now mashed up with what Arundhati Roy calls the "cesspit of the Indian caste system."[1]

I knew also that, like so many other women born in the 1920s, my mother's mother, my grandmother, was fourteen when she married her husband, who was seventeen. And like so many other mothers in the 1940s, my grandmother had more births than children, more infants than grown children. She gave birth to nine children, all born in her own mother's house, who worked as a midwife and who delivered all nine of her grandchildren, one a stillborn and two who died of smallpox before the age of four. Six survived into adulthood, five into late adulthood. My mother, in a deeply tender but circumscribed description, tells me her mother *was a weak and servile woman, a woman who did the same mundane domestic tasks every day, with little change. Cities changed; the number of children and elders in the house changed; time and politics and nations changed. But she didn't change. Spineless, docile, illiterate, no tongue in her mouth*: these were the words used to describe my grandmother. *I couldn't save her, not from others or herself.* According to my mother, it wasn't until 1962 that her mother learned to write her name. This was the everyday ordinary; they all shared a naturalized commitment to the mundane and monotonous repetition and reproduction of life.

As a young girl, then, my mother was instead infatuated with her *dadi*, her paternal grandmother, who lived with them until my mother turned fifteen, at which point she moved to Taif, Saudi Arabia, where she died shortly after, in the care of another son. My mother described her *dadi* as a dark-skinned, very religious woman, who would sit in the corner of their small apartment every day, on the floor, cross-legged, *a tasbih* in hand and, from sunrise to sundown, pray. As a young girl, my mother was fascinated by her grandmother's disciplined ability to pray nonstop for hours, unmoving, undistracted, rapt. In my mother's words, her *dadi would just go inside God every morning. No matter what was happening around her, she just went inside God*. For my mother, her *dadi* was sublime. When her prayers ended in the evening, she would call out to my mother, "Mehru, make something spicy with our *chai* today." As it turned out, even then my mother was skilled at cooking the spiciest of dishes and would delightedly prepare crispy, spicy snacks for her grandmother, who seemed to depart from prayer only for food. Threaded together by their daily ritual, my mother held her grandmother's daylong prayers in such earnest reverence that she convinced herself that the profundity of an elder's daily spiritual practice would, by mere presence, transfer to the young.

Later I learned that this story was shaped by a single profound lacuna, revealed to my mother by her maternal aunt after her *dadi*'s death. After her grandmother died in 1967, my mother would carry on and on about how much she missed her, extolling praise after praise on her grandmother's spirit. The words my mom often used to describe her *dadi* were simple: *a simple woman she was; she could do no harm*. After many grumbles and eye rolls, my mother's aunt muttered: *She tried to poison your mom. She poured acid into her bathwater. But your mother never used that water; by chance she threw it out*. After a long silence, my mother finally asked why, but her aunt's answer didn't advance the story. She simply said, *We all saw each other as destroyable*.

I was about one year into writing this book when my mother and I were sitting together at her home and were on the speakerphone with her younger sister, my maternal aunt. My mother and I had been talking about her *dadi* when my aunt called. After our initial excitement about being on the phone together (we are both very close to my aunt, who ten years younger than my mother, lived at the time in Karachi), my mother disclosed this story about their *dadi*'s attempted poisoning of their mother. My aunt responded—a shade too quickly, as though she did not want to dwell on even the idea of this violent scenario: "There was never a woman like our *dadi*. She was virtuous." After a moment of awkward silence, she spoke up again, "But life was hard, and people hurt each other. Nobody is pure. Don't be so negative." My aunt said this with a tone of finality. I looked at my mother, sitting across from me at the kitchen table. She hesitated for a minute, this strange entanglement of violence, femininity, and brownness flickering in her eyes. *Yes*, my mom finally said, *there are many ways to interpret this story*. Her eyes searched mine as she said this, and I knew she was wondering if I believed her.

I think about how one naked fact can elicit such a different range of feelings—some of anger, others of discipline, and even others of secrecy, of tenderness. My great grandmother tried to poison my grandmother, her daughter-in-law, my mother's mother. My grandmother survived by the odd chance of throwing the poisoned bathwater out, instead of bathing in it as she was expected to do. Maybe she was particularly tired that day. Or too cold that winter day to get in the cold water. Maybe just when she was about to bathe, someone demanded her time. Maybe she sensed something different about the bathwater. Whatever her reasons, my grandmother wasn't meant to die that winter at the hands of her mother-in-law. Instead, her mother-in-law would live on, exalted as a spiritual and disciplined woman by her own daughter, no less, and my grandmother would cross oceans to die in a cold American winter. My mother's maternal aunt discloses this moment of violence. My maternal aunt forecloses this moment of violence.

I hear the echo of my aunt's words: *Life is hard. No one is pure. Don't be so negative.* I hear the difference in each utterance, a subtle, but crucial, internal alteration. *Life is hard*, a phrase we heard often while growing up, functioned as a blanket alibi for repressed interpretations of power and violence. It was paired with its oft-circulated cousin phrase: *woman means pain. Life is hard* referenced, even as it refused power. *No one is pure.* The impossibility of purity meant that pollution was superlative. But my aunt's charge, *Don't be so negative*, had multiple targets, directed at her maternal aunt for directly interpolating another history onto my mother for recalling and reciting this history, and onto me for rendering public a moment of private past violence. Negation is a time-honored episteme in brown maternal thought, yet it too is just as seductive to turn away from. My mother's recourse was to reclaim the multiplicity of interpretation. Her rhetorical use of *many interpretations*—even as she offered none—mollified the fractures in both sisters' idealized love and romantic memory of their grandmother. My aunt anchors her love in a contemporary refusal of the past, through a silence that stretches across the techno-mediated oceanic phone call, mapping distance with time and difference and disavowal.

I think now that my aunt is right, in a most ironic and painful way. Her statement writes out a shared historical violence among and between women, and part of her disavowal has to do with brown women being neither ready nor able to face the painful legacy of how they consumed violence against them to construct violence between them. So many powerful unexamined emotions—love, desire, jealousy, and need—undergird the historical relationship between these women. Given the formations of power that threaded through these women's relations, the unquestioned characterization of their grandmother as deeply religious functioned less as a reflection of actual history than as the occlusion of it. Love is a powerful motivator toward disavowal, toward delusion. Their love for their *dadi* was out of time, against time, cutting through and cutting out violence, just as, too, my tarrying with the negative cut their optic, their optimism. Indeed, all three of us have fatal affinities.

My mother tells me that the first fourteen years of her life were very isolated. She and her older sister were always expected to be in the house, doing housework or schoolwork. They were not allowed to leave the house under any circumstances and never unaccompanied. And when men, including male relatives, were in the house, they were confined to their bedroom. But on or about the 1960s, this changed. They began living in what were called colonies, a cluster of buildings with flats and common areas, instead of large, gated, secluded estates abandoned by the British. The colonies were communities of small flats, often, but not wholly, organized by religious sects. Unlike the isolation of the large gated homes, the colonies were different, full of life and debris and disorder and density and world making and sensation; the smell of food, the odor of bodies, the noises of children, the gossip of women abound. The shift from large homes to small flats may have felt like a demotion to my grandfather, but for my mother and her older sister and her mother, the shift meant an end to social isolation, which came with both idealizations and costs.

In the spring of 1961, my mother was fifteen and living in Chittagong, East Pakistan (now Bangladesh). They lived on the third floor of a small somewhat exclusive colony reserved for government servants and their families. My mother spent her days disdainfully doing housework with her older sister or taking care of her four younger siblings. Schoolwork was neither here nor there; by this age she had internalized how little education was valued for the women in her family. It was a random weekend morning (she knew it was the weekend because the men were home) when she looked out from her window and saw a young girl who worked for another family, curled on the cement floor of the courtyard, crying. Peering closer, she saw that the young girl, who wasn't much older than her, was holding a dead baby, wrapped in white sheet. Shocked, my mother rushed down the stairs and outside to the young girl. All the older women—mothers, grandmothers, aunties, and housekeepers—were busy tending to their flats and domestic duties; no one paid attention to the young girl and the dead baby in her arms. Asking the girl what had happened, the girl simply explained, "My baby died, and I need to bury him." My mother sat down on the hard cement and hugged the girl. She knew that she couldn't ask an adult to help the young girl—the remnant caste system would keep any self-respecting middle-class person from assisting the girl and her dead baby. Indeed, the distance between my mother and the young girl was much more than the three stories that separated them; histories of casteism, classism, colonialism, and colorism shuddered between them. The young, weeping girl held her dead baby, desperately repeating over and over her need to bury him. Wanting worriedly to help the young girl but unsure of where they would bury the baby's body and what would happen if they were caught by any of the adults, my mother decided to wave down a street vendor, who was selling caps and toys, to help dig a hole. The street vendor (who likely had seen more than he had bargained for from his perch outside the government flats) handed my mother a garden spade and awkwardly returned to his cart. The girls drifted to a small garden in the courtyard of government homes, and setting down the dead baby, they dug a hole and buried the baby, a small Islamic prayer humming on their lips. How or why or when the baby died or who delivered the baby or who fathered the baby, my mother never knew, and she never asked. She knew only what was available in that moment, the extreme desperation of the young girl, no more than a few years older than fifteen, needing to bury her six-day-old baby. Any other context or background would have been extraneous. The silence of the girl and secrecy of the burial made clear what couldn't and wouldn't be spoken. Eventually, the young girl returned to work, my mother to her chores, and the random hot spring afternoon, when two young girls buried a dead six-day-old baby boy in the cool grass of a government-allotted colony, never reached the heights of being inked into record; instead, this moment quietly swelled like a tumor in the recesses of both girls' psyches.

For months after the burial, the girls exchanged sad glances and secret nods, but these were placebos, a pretend cure for an irreparable injury and a connection that could never be cultivated. Eventually the young girl disappeared. Her baby was dead, but the hegemony overcasting her life was anything but dead. Weeks went by, with neither a furtive glance nor a nod of intimacy, no sliding touch, as they passed each other at the gates. The bourgeois privacy of my mother's life versus the working-class spectacle of the young mother meant that no more intimate relations passed between the girls, and the haunting bond the girls had forged was utterly uncultivatable. She never knew what happened to the young girl or the conditions which led to that strange day. The shock of learning death so intimately and so secretly gathered into a chronotropic space of disillusionment and decay, creating, dreamlike, a slippery field of the everyday necropolitical as natural. The dead baby, the desperate maid, the deceit of a morning when two young girls buried a baby introduced only the beginning of many necropolitical secrets my mother would intimately encounter in her migration toward the West, toward the North.

I think of how so much of my mother's life was about these double and triple gestures of secrecy, wherein young girls learned the mechanisms and survival strategies which older women hid obsessively and necessarily and which could render them vulnerable—their sexualities, their desires, their secrets, their babies. The significance of class difference between my mother and the young girl (or for that matter of the social differences between my mother and the street vendor whose help was hailed) underscores the nuances and messy textures of social class in postcolonial South Asia. The intertextuality of (postcolonial) class crossings with (excess) sex crossings in this moment exposes the structural and paradigmatic violence that shaped the two young girls' intimate interaction, indexing the broader field of hetero-capitalist coloniality, where class, color, and bodies are given value by external cognitive interventions, including modes of discipline and death. My mother was complicit in the class structure that allowed this baby to die, just as she tried to stitch the relation by helping, even as she was rapidly learning that the social and economic positions of some women depended on the exploitation and immiseration of others. The momentary relation between the two young girls in newly emerging/ed East Pakistan, while not easily articulable, reveals that the alchemy of class/caste is made up of eruptions and immediacies and breakages, just as they are marked by feminine and maternal retreats and secrets and deviances. The young maid's burial of her dead baby tracks her complete alienation: no lover/husband to accompany her in the burial, no aunt or mother to heal her after birth, no community to pray over the death of her baby. The young girl is named in this encounter both by my mother (and me) through a set of class, labor, and sexual socialities, no matter how much we (I more than my mother) try to soften the blade of class disparity with affective words. But the facts of the burial are present in the encounter, as are the tangible class positions, even as the story is shaped more by abject flesh and feminine feeling than mere recitation of event. At the age of fifteen, my mother couldn't fully understand the conditions of the young maid's abjection, but what she did know then was that there were things that women just handled in secrecy—sexual violence, beatings, abortions, sickness, and the dead. It was an early pedagogy in the complex and shaky class and patriarchal structure she inhabited that spit women and girls out like the brown juices of chewing tobacco. Her time in Chittagong became an affective and temporal reminder of just that. In fact, my mother's stories of her four years in Bangladesh, two in Dhaka following the two in Chittagong, are all thick with mythic, mystic, misogynistic descriptions of both her relations and the material conditions of life around her in these cities.

One year later, in 1962, my mother passed her metric exams in Chittagong, and the family moved to Dhaka. The elders in the family had also begun the talk of marriage for my mother and her older sister, and with each passing month, my mother hoped to hold off this inevitability (even as she fantasized about leaving her father's rule). In 1965, they left Dhaka and moved to Lahore, where my mother briefly attended Kinnaird College, a well-known women's college whose reputation oscillated between its deep feminist and lesbian lineages to preparing Pakistani women for marriage. But eight months later, they returned to Karachi, and my mother never entered a classroom again. Leaving Lahore for Karachi in 1966 was the last leg of my mother's internal migration under the auspices of her father's home. It was also the year her older sister was married off to a Pakistani immigrant living in Sydney, Australia, a man notorious for both his good looks and his compulsive gambling. With two gold necklaces and a set of eight gold bangles, my mother's older sister left Karachi for Sydney with a philandering, but handsome, husband.

My mother and her sisters were trained in both servitude and suspicion, developing both over time as a hermeneutic of survival. So, too, was her mother and the many women of that generational moment, where the global order around gender was shifting but the chasms playing out over the earth just barely caused a bristle under their feet. My mother was part of a certain global transition where women were going to college and university, sometimes even abroad, but often not to completion (neither my mother nor her sisters completed college, while all three of her brothers completed undergraduate degrees in the United States). Women like my mother were scattering to a series of short-term jobs—tellers at banks, primary school teachers, and secretaries, while they studied for a short period of time after matriculation. Once their studies were over, they were expected to get married and settle into the affective cultures of extended family life, into the habitual structures of the domestic, marriage, and reproduction. The silent task of this generation of newly middle-class women was to navigate the contradictions of their own interior desires within exterior structures of desire that hadn't quite caught up with what women, globally, were actually doing, thinking. The challenge was to grasp that years of surplus education didn't necessarily indicate less servitude or violence or domination. Moreover, she was part of a generational moment of women who (mostly) stayed in these habitual structures, surviving, recreating, and living out the very tapestry that forms the provincial, the everyday, the twists and turns of the brown domestic and diasporic world. It is this certain habitus that she reveals and brings forth.

In 1967, my mother's marriage was arranged to a young electrical engineer, and three short months later, the engagement was broken off. My mother's father had decided that the young working-class engineer he had chosen for his daughter was frugal and incapable of financial independence, evidenced in his many requests for money and his assumption that my mother's family would pay for the wedding. He was ruled by money-grubbing women in his life, said my mother's father. Within a month of the broken engagement, my mother's ex-fiancé ended his life with a bottle of sleeping pills. The broken engagement followed by suicide caused a web of scandal and gossip, with my mother at the center. The news of his death cast a grimy shadow on my mother. It was hard for her to imagine that the same man whose hand shook when he tried to touch her would so boldly end his life. Predictably, my mother emerged in the storied scandal as a vixen, a woman who lured men toward destruction, even as she had no say in either the engagement or the dissolution of that engagement. Desperately wanting to escape the salacious gossip, my mother pleaded with her father to allow her to study banking, as he had, but in London. Her father, a man shaped by many gendered and class anxieties, wanted her gone, and her request made everything simpler. She would leave Karachi to study in London, and the cacophony of gossip around her broken engagement would, like her fiancé, die with her departure.

It was the winter of 1967 when my mother was released from the grip of gossip and into the loneliness of London. There she took up a room in the house of a young Pakistani couple, spending her days working as a teller in Habib Bank, part of a Pakistani-owned conglomerate with global operations, and spending her evenings studying for a banking degree. London was an electric city, swarming around her with the sort of sociality that could consume all (her) old ways of being. But my mother barely understood the world around her. She was, instead, overwhelmed with feelings of isolation. She was staying with a friend of her father's—a Mr. Kumail, who worked for a shipping company, and his wife—to whom she paid a rent of five pounds (of her fifteen pounds salary) every week. Mr. Kumail's wife was a sweet but self-effacing housewife, who was nostalgic about Karachi, a Karachi that for my mother didn't exist. Mr. Kumail was a cocky, presumptuous, wannabe Englishman who made many moves on my mother. His seductive tactics included telling my mother his wife would never find out, insisting that she didn't know what she was missing, rubbing her legs under the dinner table with his feet, and begging repeatedly for *just one night*. Despite his blunt, unwanted flirtations, my mother was intrigued by his worldliness, and over evening dinners, she listened to him talk endlessly in Urdu, offering his analysis of national politics, international finance, the logics of English wealth accumulation, English ways, English racist ways, all wholly dipped in fraudulent Pakistani patriotism. It would take another decade of listening to men discuss and praise Pakistan with feverish nationalism for her to conclude that all nationalisms were nothing more than overly played out, passionate, masculine parodies.

But in London, English had been thrust upon her, like a border, a regime, a frontier—fluid and flowing for those who had been trained in the queen's tongue but broken and awkward and funny for others, like my mother. So listening to her host brought her back to the familiarity and lyricism of Urdu, the poetics of the language softening the energy between them. Unsurprisingly, he interpreted her engaged listening as invitation and would enter her room so freely and so late at night that at some point she moved the heavy wooden dresser against the bedroom door. She managed to ward off all his advances, but a paranoia had set in about men. Mr. Kumail held both her job and the keys to her bedroom in his hand. In her two years of living in London, my mother changed houses three times, each time living with married men and their wives, each time moving furniture to block the door, each time learning that because she was a young woman living on her own, to them she was also a whore.

By the winter of 1969, my mother had been living in London for almost two years and was trying to renew her visa for a third year. It was for this reason that her father came to stay with her for one month. He was doing some work for the State Bank of Pakistan and was offered a small office in the Habib Bank. And even though her father was a cold, cruel and controlling patriarch, with a quick fist and a sharp tongue, my mother welcomed his familiar presence. Her father's companionship softened the edge of her loneliness, and it kept her third male host from knocking on her door every night. But one evening, when she and her father were walking home from dinner, they were approached by a "rich Englishman" who offered her father "a good amount of pounds" in exchange for one night with her. After they hurriedly returned to the house, my grandfather furiously relayed this story to my mother's third host, who looked dutifully appalled, repressing his own presumptuous and aggressive overtures toward my mom. The two quasi-elite Pakistani men heatedly and eagerly destroyed the Englishman in their Urdu vernacular, grumping and waxing philosophical about the pomposity of white men and the conceit of the Orientalist gaze to read him as a pimp and his daughter as a whore, scrutinizing and dissecting the prevalent Orientalists' fantasies of the time, a process that allowed the men's egos to return to their rightful swollen status, their tongues wet with the drool of their homemade cocktail of nationalized masculinity, sexual greed, religious paternalism, and emotional fraud. But for my mother, indignant, shamed, there was no return to dignity or integrity. No invitation to share her fury, her fear. The rage on her face and the words on her tongue were short-circuited by the odious look of disgust she saw on her father's face, in the flicker of his judgmental eyes when he met her gaze. His look immutable, accusatory, stuck, glaring. It was a look she knew well, affectively, sensorially, and specifically.

Shortly after her engagement had broken off and before leaving Karachi for London, my mother had attended a wedding with her mother, her grandmother, and her sisters. When the women returned home, a little late but happy, henna glowing from their hands under the streetlights, her father awaited them. He immediately walked straight to his own mother and slapped her across the face. My grandfather's matter-of-fact slapping of his own mother reflected the filiarchal power structure in which all these women lived, but even so his audacity to hit his own mother shocked and silenced the other women. My mother and her two sisters instinctively swung their bodies downward to hold their toes (a common punishment), as the rest of her father's rage was spent on my mother's mother; his own mother having fallen from the slap. I grew up hearing about my grandfather as the man who slapped his own mother. A slap that was commonplace and extraordinary, foolish to not anticipate it, foolish to accept it. It was that look from a man, any man, that severed my mother from active rage and into a space of feminized shame. It was a look that codified her body as burden, something quickly to wash one's hands of. Her rage, in neither that moment nor the other, could reside on the surface. It floated in an unmappable elsewhere. This was a moment of casual dispossession, rendering her disciplinable, thus possessable.

Just a few weeks later, after her father returned to Karachi from London, my mother received a letter detailing a soon-to-be-divorced father of five living in the United States, looking to remarry. Within weeks of the letter, my mother had a visitor in London—a flirtatious, charming Indian man who spoke flawless English. He was also a father of five, his ex-wife a white woman who had been in and out of psychiatric institutions in the northern part of the States. In the grip of both discourses—one that demanded subjugation to marriage and the other that razed her as a whore—she succumbed to the pathos of a necessary failed resistance, to the antidote to shame, to the esteemed web of paternal and marital sanction. She had swallowed whole the formulated binaries and dictums offered to her around her body and sexuality. She saw no evidence pointing to an otherwise. So, in the winter of 1969, after two years of living in London, with a rejected British visa, my mother returned to Karachi. In so doing, she was quickly engaged to that charming Indian man and father of five who had been selected by her father as the perfect match for my mother. In October of 1970, my mother married my father, readying herself to enter into a family notorious for wife beating, rape, racketeering, forgery, and money laundering, readying herself to marry a man whose ex-wife was redolent of Jane Eyre's madwoman in the attic.

My mother relates to her memories as she relates to the land of her biological birth. No matter how long she stays away from them, no matter how much a comparative edge makes her look at them critically, sometimes with a vengeance, she is nonetheless always attached to them. In them, she finds something equivalent to the unique mixture that makes up her psychic, social, and fleshy formation; in them, she finds something that is always at the same time transparent and deceiving, gratifying and frustrating, promising and ominous. I think of Toni Morrison's practice of "rememory," in which the past erupts into the present, assembling together pieces of the body, the family, the people of the past.[2] Or of James Clifford who wrote that we need stories (and theories) that are just big enough to gather up the complexities, even as they keep the edges open and greedy for surprising new and old connections.[3] Marylyn Frye once wrote that if stories stayed where they are, we would get nowhere.[4] And, indeed, for decades my mother's stories stayed with her, in her. I feel this containment and spatiality in my mother's stories. I think of how understanding the politics of locations means observing how we look at the center, and knowing that the farther we move, the center becomes smaller, even as it perhaps becomes ideologically grander. I try and step back, to see the web, the matrices, the labyrinth, the interruptions and not just one lovely or loathsome silk thread.

Interruption

....

To tell my mother's life story, in her words, in my words, is, to a certain extent, to acknowledge how integrally tied her life was to my father, her husband, and that who she is and what she experienced and how she moved through the world with little or with much, with ego or with shame, with fear or with clarity, was in part a sociality that emerged from this relation. But just as I acknowledge this, I see my father as both sustenance and interruption, as necessity and extraneous. I mean this in both literal and figurative terms. My father is present—and is tied to my mother in ways noted throughout this book—just as my mother is restlessly and intimately and uncomfortably and multifariously entangled in and attached to this dependent relation. The registers of difference between my father and my mother, their modes of retelling and performing the past, reveal the heavy hand of the gender-sex-race-capital matrix that shaped their everyday sociality. Indeed, my father was enamored by my mother's lovely and poetic Urdu tongue, but perhaps this was the only tongue of hers he enjoyed. I witnessed his lifelong effort to silence or dismiss or disavow her (stories), sometimes through patriarchal benevolence, other times through middle-class humor, and on more than one occasion through masculine aggression. That said, I do not doubt that there is deep love between my parents, but love, to paraphrase Toni Morrison, is no more superior or purer than the lover, and that which we call love is tightly entangled with care, dependency, familiarity, fear, comfort, warmth, desire, and subordination. Veritably then, I think he must have known: if his voice effectively silenced my mother; my mother's tongue, if mobilized at will, could have destroyed my father.

....

My father's mother was born in 1911. She was fifteen when she married a nineteen-year-old young man, whose family was in the bone-charring industry. My father proudly describes his mother as a devout Muslim woman. What I exact from this is that she imparted that religiosity to my father in two ways. For one, she dreamed of leaving India for (a) Pakistan. For her and many others, Pakistan was not merely a space on a map. It symbolized a distinct imagination of Muslim-ness, one that was emanating and spreading through the popular consciousness of (some) people, even as it too was the strategic cartographic architecture of both colonizers and the national bourgeoise. In 1940, when the Muslim League endorsed the idea of a separate state for India's Muslims and after the 1940 resolution that recognized Pakistan as a political goal, discrimination against Muslims began to mount into daily practices of exclusion, bias, and violence, especially at the level of the government. At that time, my paternal grandmother was the mother of five children (she would have a total of nine). Her dream of leaving India for the *idea* of Pakistan intensified daily, and she talked of it with anyone who would listen. Religious belonging was like a fetish for her, a fantasy-like longing of possibility operating through a series of other signifiers. It made sense, then, that my paternal grandmother credited her survival of anti-Muslim hatred by Hindu Indians to the tight-knit loyal kinship of the Charania men. Like my mother's father, my father's mother loved men and maleness. She disavowed the egregious adultery of her husband who throughout their marriage had unapologetically slept with girl servants, the violent misogyny of her two youngest sons who had notoriously beaten women in ways too cruel to describe, the perpetual black-market dealings of her older son whose reputation had followed him across seas, and she turned her other cheek to the cock and malice and greed of her four daughters (three of whom ironically eloped with Hindu men). And to be clear, these were open cruelties, as not much was or could be hidden in the small 400-square-foot flat shared by all thirteen family members in Bombay. My father inherited this blind love and faith in his family, unseeing the violence the men and women enacted on others, the violence they enacted, once they married, on my mother. His mother's dream of living in Pakistan was hammered into my father, but it would take him thirty-three years to fulfil his mother's migration dream. In 1974, five years after his mother's death, my father's family migrated to Karachi, Pakistan, a migration expedited and legitimized through my father's marriage to my mother.

But the real temporal turn for my father was 1961. In the same year my mother helped bury a young maid's dead baby in Chittagong, my father left Bombay for Alpena, Michigan. In the picture taken to mark his departure, my father stands, his face cleanly shaven and his tight, curly hair freshly cut, dressed in black slacks, a white shirt, and a large, brown winter coat in preparation for the wintered America into which he was arriving. Three, long, white rose garlands hung around his neck down to his waist, a proud anticipatory smile set on his lips and a large brown curvaceous ship in the hazy backdrop. In 1961, there were twelve thousand Indian-born immigrants living in the United States. My father became one of them. He was nineteen and ambitious, with big plans to study engineering. He had been admitted into Alpena Community College and joined his childhood friend who was also studying engineering there. Not wanting to be alone in a big US city, my father delayed his admission to UCLA and chose this small American town to begin his studies.

Two young brown men in the small, rural Michigan town of Alpena in the 1960s certainly set off the racist chatter. Unable to make friends or build any kind of community, they stuck to each other, grateful for their friendship and utterly isolated in freezing temperatures that neither had ever experienced before. Nobody had warned them how cold America could be. On Fridays, both young men would venture out to a nightclub, where younger college students would socialize and dance. My father, Bollywood in his blood, loved to dance and excitedly attended every Friday. And every Friday, he was snubbed, ignored, rejected. Both young men stood at the side of the dance floor, dejectedly watching the White college students in this White college town dance to pop music. After months of exclusion, my father grew tired of both the rejection and the subsequent inability to just *dance*. Determinedly, one night, he got on the dance floor and began dancing, combining his Indian/Bollywood swagger with new American pop moves. My father, true to this day, is quite the dancer and tends to take up the dance floor, garnering so much attention that other dancers and bystanders often encircle him, clapping and swaying to the music. This might have been the night his lifelong love of dance became the life of every party he would attend. This was also the night he met his first love—a local, White Catholic girl.

Her name was J. She was fifteen the night my father met her, although she told him she was sixteen. Shortly after, my father and J. became lovers, and for months, they secretly dated. Eventually, J. invited my father to her home, in what became a weekly ritual of dinner, described by my father as a bland American meal flavored with her mother's anti-Indian xenophobia, her father's Orientalized fascination, his own meritocratic Indian nationalism, and J.'s hungry adolescent love. The racist and nativist fervor that shaped his weekly dinners with J.'s White family were undergirded by US histories of White control/expulsion of the *other*, the increasing economic disparity between the Black and brown diaspora in the United States, and the new, but small, trend of interracial families. The 1911 US and Immigration Commission, which identified South Asians as the "least desirable race of immigrants thus far admitted to the United States," renewed by the 1923 Bhagat Singh case that barred South Asians from naturalization, had just fifteen years earlier been replaced by the 1946 Luce-Celler Act that allowed South Asians to apply for and become naturalized as US citizens. The South Asians that "made it" buttressed the promise of freedom that contoured the American Dream and calcified bootstrap class imaginaries around "hard work." My father was early on this path, having internalized this meritocratic thesis far before the 1965 Immigration and Nationality Act and the known entity of the South Asian entrepreneur that came to constitute the future imagination of the model minority Indian. Thus, even as he was submerged in the racism and fetishism that contoured his weekly dinners and shaped his new romance, my father benefited from the 1960s paradigmatic shift that was beginning to render South Asians legible and desirable model immigrants.

My father's arrival in the United States and his relationship with J. were caught up in all these jurisprudential-cultural-historic, postcolonial, and capitalist formations, as well as the settler-native-settled-slave-refugee-alien-migrant matrices. But nonetheless, his arrival and his ability to stay in the United States involved the deliberation, thought, intent, ambition, and planning that came to be expected of young brown men who were the sons of businessmen and who had (some) access to both the West/North and the English language. It meant convincing his father that he would acquire an engineering degree in the United States; it meant managing his older brother's greed and insecurities; it meant promising his mother that he wouldn't fall in love with a White woman while living in America. He broke every promise.

As the months passed, the young lovers became more and more infatuated with each other, but J.'s mother couldn't stand the sight of my dark-skinned father. She forbade her daughter to see my father, but J.—naïve and unstable and passionate—wasn't easily reigned in. To her, my dad was perfectly marriageable; he was outgoing and a good dancer. He was the right age, right size, right looks, just the wrong color. So when my father learned from J.'s cousin that she was threatening to run away, he snuck her out of her bedroom window, and drove her across state lines to Illinois, where they entered a US courthouse and married. He was shy of twenty, an immigrant, a student; she was sixteen, in love and pregnant. It was 1962, five years before Loving v. Virginia. Their marriage would end by 1969, just after the death of his mother, his acquisition of US citizenship, and the birth of their fifth child.

My father's first job was as a dishwasher in a small restaurant in Alpena for $1.25 per hour. After he and J. eloped, they drove directly to Los Angeles, a city they heard was accepting of interracial couples and immigrant men. My father took his second job at a company that tested aircraft equipment, again for $1.25 an hour. But in six months, after five different promotions, he was earning five times that hourly rate. The company manager came to be very fond of my young father, now twenty, with a wife and a young baby girl. Impressed with my father's aptitude for engineering (despite his never completing his degree), the manager offered my father a long-term contract of five years, under the condition that he would be able to pass the test for the California state security clearance. The test cost $5,000. Hungry for stability and anxious to please his now-pregnant (again) wife, my father pleaded with his boss to pay the fees for state clearance. His boss agreed; my father passed his clearance exam and began bringing home an unexpectedly high salary. Within months of the birth of her son, J. was pregnant again, this time with twins.

I do not want to paint a simple picture of my father, as he is, indeed, one iteration of brownness. He is a man, like so many other immigrant men crossing oceans to build a different life, full of dreams and desires to do the right thing. He, like other immigrant men, negotiated his way through the American world. He was a dark-skinned boy from India who had developed a diasporic way of seeing the world, who was attached to being in, but not of, America. He was an interloper in a world, thus subject to many forms of racial and imperial humiliation, some of which I witnessed, others of which I did not. My father, too, is a religious and loyal man, devout in his own particular way to the organized and faith-based life of Shia-Ismaili Muslims and committed to his family. His success in America was both serendipitous and intricately tied to the racial and gender genealogies of that temporal moment. It was an age of possibility. When he arrived in America in the 1960s, he wasn't sure what was greater: his ambition to become an educated someone who could financially support his family back in India or his commitment to his mother to avoid the seduction of White women. His failure was inevitable. So was his optimism.

When my father recounts this time in his life, there are many holes, particularly in the years from 1962 through 1969. How did my father, a young, dark-skinned, immigrant Indian man, navigate the racial-ethno-gender regimes of the United States in the 1960s, accompanied by his young and insecure White wife, whose devotion to him opened the door to his (and later, our) citizenship? He recalls with trepidation the first and only time J. accompanied him to Bombay. J. enthusiastically fell in love with the famous Indian mangos. She was so enamored by their sweetness that she would eat a dozen or so every day. Predictably, she ended up sick and in the hospital for two weeks. When she returned to the United States, she went directly to her mother's home in Alpena, too thin and weak to care for herself or her children. Her mother convinced her that it wasn't the mangos that had made her sick but that my father and his Indian family had tried to poison her. Paranoid and unstable, J. was easily convinced. When my father returned to her two weeks later, she had him locked out of the house and called the police on him, who, to their credit, just escorted him off her mother's property. It took weeks for my father to convince J. that nobody had poisoned her, and eventually, after many long nights of phone conversations, J. returned to him with the children. Two months later, she was pregnant again, with their fifth child.

As part of what Sara Ahmed calls the "useful class"—the postcolonial and later the globalized transnational mobile class—my father came to experience the temporal and identitarian designations of South Asian, Pakistani, Indian, brown, Muslim, Immigrant as simultaneous sites of attachment, precarity, and crisis. He shared relations to work and to violence with other immigrants, with Black and brown people, yet he managed to produce a sense of crisis that was deeply personal, essentialized, and mostly, although not completely, apolitical; a sense of crisis that fundamentally magnetized attachments, attunements, affects to South Asian minoritized groups, while corroding the same to other racial groups. The privilege of masculinity and class allowed my father the ability to move quite literally through the world, but what encounters made him stop, summon courage, slow his heart, and think about his power/lessness? An avid storyteller, my father always had a story, a quip, or a random political fact to offer about his early years in America. His stories were structured and dramatic; he knew when to pause, when to speed up, when to inflect, when to await re-action. His lengthy letters to us over the years and to his siblings when afar and his beautiful handwriting (reminiscent that of Marie Antoinette) betrayed what could have been another life. But, so too, were his stories and memories shaped by androcentric structures of belief—linearity, reason, triumph, optimism, and promise. To get at the dirt was difficult, but every now and then I hear the despair in his voice. He carries what he sees as his transgressions daily, and as he ages, his words and his gaze linger on the past, his voice heavy, his memories remorseful, his posture pouring down toward the earth.

....

It was October of 1970 when my mother moved out of her parent's home in customary tears and into a three-bedroom Karachi flat occupied by her husband, her father-in-law, and her older brother-in-law's family of seven. In one flat over, lived her two younger brothers-in-law, her three sisters-in-law (one had by then eloped with her Hindu lover). Within a month of their marriage, my father began traveling weekly, some south-to-south travel and some south-to-north. His traveling kept him away from home three weeks out of each month. He would leave on a Sunday and return on the following Saturday, only to leave again the following evening or, if delayed, Monday morning. For the first eight years of their marriage, my father traveled eight months out of the year. My mother's days and evenings, then, were spent with in-laws, deeply ensconced in the customary structure of domesticated servitude. The labor of cooking, cleaning, and caretaking fell to my mother, as the new bride, and to one hired domestic worker, a young Muslim boy from the Northern Pakistani border town of Chitral, M. M. was part of a small migration of Chitrali men and boys who had arrived in Karachi, which at the time was a hub for migratory labor, particularly for men and boys from various parts of Northern Pakistan. Many of these Chitrali men and boys entered into domestic work, given the embedded caste/class arrangements, which, on the one hand, gave them a safe site of continuous labor and access to certain middle-class lifestyles, while, on the other hand, complicated, in sometimes irreparable ways, their own kin and domestic relations. Our early childhood in Karachi was heavily shaped by M., who was the only person we ever saw helping our mother in an ongoing list of domestic chores. My mother's older sister-in-law, a proud woman entitled by the hierarchy that shaped their relationship, did the bare minimum. My father's sisters also took great pleasure in exploiting the labor of his new young wife.

My mother's abiding recollection of those years—1970 to 1977—was of ongoing, unacknowledged, endless domestic work and exploitation, and in the murkiness of memory, of watching other women/girls get exploited. She always said the best part of being married to my father was going to the cinema, something she had never experienced and could never experience in her father's home. This was a small but significant joy. Cinema enchanted my mother; it made the world beautiful to her, intriguing and vast and transfixing, just as it also affirmed the familiarity of melancholia, betrayal, and human fallibility. Conversely marriage, for my mother, was like an alienated planet, living with others with whom she could make little connection but who were nonetheless part of her everyday life. The separation between the feminized space of domestic work and the masculine world of money was something my mother had completely internalized. Yet despite this regulative ideal shaped by duty, respectability, and servitude, my mother saw both realms as calculated battles.

She observed quickly that her father-in-law made nightly visits to his young maid, a girl not older than seventeen. She learned promptly the art of stoking the egos of her sisters-in-law, while politely ignoring the libido of her brothers-in-law. She had to practice daily not to internalize the mean-spiritedness of her new family, who trafficked in gendered social cruelties and petty power plays. She constantly found herself at the receiving end of a particular kind of cruelty that centered around the body, viciously and comically exposing her fragility and precariousness on a daily basis. My father's sisters were self-willed, haughty, undisciplined, arbitrary, and severe. If my mother cooked a dish poorly, she would be forced to eat it, while they laughed until they became bored. If she folded her youngest sister-in-law's clothes with the slightest unevenness, she was forced to touch and kiss her feet in apology. At the time, this particular sister-in-law was fourteen years old, and my mother says she cannot count the number of times she bent down to kiss the young girl's feet, who would look down at my mother's bent, lowered body with triumphant arrogance. At other moments, her sisters-in-law would open the bathroom door on her (a door which opened to the family room), laughing because she squatted (instead of sat) on their proudly owned English toilet. They mocked her Urdu (they were a Hindi-speaking family), compared her to J. (whom they had all met only once and never liked), and threatened constantly to send her back to her mother's home. In one particularly egregious memory, they put my infant brother into a basket and loosely hung the basket from their second-floor apartment balcony with a makeshift rope, threatening a fatal fall. My mother was cleaning the dishes at the time, and one of the younger kids came to tell her that the basket in which her son was sleeping was unstably hanging from the balcony. When my mother confronted her sisters-in-law, they denied everything and laughingly placed the blame on their teenage daughters, who also were quickly learning to emulate their mothers' brazen cruelties and greed. Indeed, so self-righteous they were in their greed that my father's sisters would drink water only after it had been boiled with one gold coin, a piece of copper jewelry, and a small piece of silver. To them, drinking water distilled in these high-valued metals meant good health and beauty.

The young boys were a different kind of target for these gendered cruelties, whether my brother or the sons of my mother's oldest and widowed sister-in-law. My mother's father-in-law, a lecherous drunk with jaw cancer, would pour my brother brandy when he was a young kid, would watch until he drank the brandy to its dregs, and would laugh hard, as he and the other boys subjected to forced drinking would, as my mother described it, *jhoom* (slosh drunkenly) around the house. My mother felt helpless in these daily taunts and humiliations and dangers while my father was gone, and when he returned, they would change colors and treat her with such sugary sweetness that he dismissed her litany of stories. It was not that my mother had not experienced cruelty or even violence in her life, but it all had stemmed from one figure—her father. Here, in her new married home, cruelty was rhizomatic; it came from everyone and everywhere, in small ways and large ways, significant and insignificant, petty and grand.

My father's brothers were another story. Not interested in (but silently fully supportive of) the petty tactics of their sisters, they enjoyed making my mother squirm, making sure that she understood that they, like my father, had (some) sexual access to her. Lewd comments on her body were daily grammars, along with behaviors like ogling, sitting too close, rubbing up against her, massaging her shoulders with their fingertips spilling toward her breasts, lying in her lap when she was too pregnant to wiggle her way out from under their weight, nestling their heads on her swollen stomach, on her swollen breasts, insistently knocking on her door late at night when my father was away. And on and on goes the list of domestic social humiliations and harms and harassments that made my head spin as a young girl. My father worshipped his brothers and sisters. He could not see their wrongs. Theirs was the iron will of the house. For my mother, a small sliver of perspective came from observing their treatment of her oldest and widowed sister-in-law, whose working-class roots from Bhavnagar, India, combined with her widow status (of the oldest son, no less), put her in such precarity (including multiple attempts at sexual assault from her father-in-law and her brothers-in-law) that even her suicide attempts appeared to be a momentary gift of life. Comparison by extreme was a consolation. And when that wore off, my mother added a new prayer to her nightly pleas, imploring *Allah: if he wanted to grant her in-laws heaven, she would gladly go to hell.*

All my mother could do to communicate her existence was have babies— obedient light-brown babies. Becoming a mother was about feeling relevant in my father's life; it made her, ironically, feel less isolated, less alien, more visible. She was naïve enough to think that motherhood made her a "real" woman and shrewd enough to know that having children meant she contributed to the family legacy (*if J. could give her husband five children, she could at least give three*). That motherhood was its own form of silencing, dispossession, abjection, she would learn much later. That motherhood would also be the most electric relationality she would experience (far more than lovers and husbands) was also to come later.

In 1977, my father's traveling came to an end, and he decided that the deteriorating social, economic, political, and environmental conditions in Karachi were the perfect incentive to return to America. He remained deeply attached to the fantasy of the good life in America. The very cracks and vulnerabilities in this ideological program that he had experienced, he quickly brushed off. My mother was more skeptical about what she had been told about that dreamy place called America, overflowing with the modern and the good life. But after seven years of living with a family of lecherous men and cruel women, she desperately wanted to leave Karachi. What she had come to understand, in the midst of all these other characters, was that her husband was *good enough*, despite his willful ignorance, his swift temper, his stubborn unseeing, his compulsory optimisms, and his enamoring of White America. My mother often described my father through a classic Urdu expression, *keecher mey kamal*—a flower in shit, a phrase which allowed her to distinguish him from the Charania clan. And indeed, compared to his brothers, my father was mild, just, and reasonable in his patriarchy. He was ashamed of the public-facing cruelties that followed his name and was determined to be good and do better. His attachments and his inheritances often made this difficult, but for my mother intent went a long way toward forgiveness. Leaving Pakistan with him, even if shaped by insecurity, loss, and the unknown, was doable, imaginable. "No one leaves home unless / home is the mouth of a shark," writes poet Warsan Shire.[5] So, in October of 1977, twenty-five days after Pakistani Prime Minister Zulfiqar Ali Bhutto was thrown into a four-by-six cell and twenty-one days before my mother's youngest sister married an elite publishing tycoon, my parents left Karachi to arrive on the East Coast of the United States, in a small suburban town in New Jersey, named Cherry Hill.

....

My mother landed in America not so much with intention but in the folds of compulsory heterosexuality, capital, and fantasy that moved bodies, like my mother's and many, many others, in every epoch, with varying degrees of sub-jugation and brutality, as well as agency and desire. Her arrival in the United States with my father's newly established citizenship and shaky middle-class status and connections relied on this history of unequal social investment, although it was framed as earning and hard work. For both my parents, the North and the West were beautiful and abstract signifiers of freedom and mobility, but they were also yoked to danger, fear, insecurity, and a perpetual outside status. Thus, the triad of arrival-migrant-diasporic subject mapped out for my mother differently than my father, as the gendering of life, mobil-ity, autonomy, diaspora, space, time, and identity was cast over her life like a second layer of skin.

But it is also true that immigration, for both my parents, was innately a conservative framework. It trafficked in an ensemble of their desires. It blocked them against radical thinking. It blocked them from intra- and interracial solidarity. It blocked them against fashioning an antination discourse, yet it appeared to be the most radical access that they (and others) had to border crossing and dissolution. My parents, like so many others, had learned to rely on and display class, merit, financial capital, real estate, in both visible and invisible ways, through sedimented and intractable patterns that taught them the management and reproduction of life (and violence) as we know it. All their advantages in the United States were built on modes of racial, class, and colonial extraction in the country and in the world around them. Through their movement (toward middle-class America), they became part of the colonial power—still intruders and interlopers but now benefiting from a small, but significant, accumulation of wealth.

For my mother, class was mere fact—unavoidable, tragic, superimposed, sometimes interesting, sometimes joy killing, sometimes protecting. The class influences that collectively accumulated and traveled with my mother were primarily the consequences of male economic supremacies, as brown immigrant women's wealth (especially if they are mothers) has always been unevenly sutured to their male counterparts. It was at her father's discretion that she held and practiced border mobility, living with middle-class diasporic Pakistani bankers and their wives. It was at my father's discretion that my mother received her monthly allowance to cover household and child-rearing expenses. She lacked any formal relation to the economy. She lacked any formal education, as she had never completed any degree program. She lacked proper documentation that would have allowed her to work, as she was undocumented for her first thirteen years in America. She was fundamentally estranged from the means through which she could feed, clothe, and shelter herself and her kids in America. So, for my mother, class was the only logic of protection, built through the world of patriarchy. Whatever was outside of the home was worse than that which was inside, and of this she was convinced.

My mother's material isolation from the world of commerce meant that her class was unstable and indeterminate, or stable and determinate only through the familiar stranglehold of patriarchy and nationalized colonialism, first through her father, later through her husband, now through her children. The multiple vertices of identity and social reality that shaped my mother and the multiple forces that acted upon her and the encounters that she acted within are entangled with capitalist modernity, its subsequent labor practices, its ability to contour desire and shape knowledge. Overlaid with the politics of gender, violence, immigration, even within the context of a capitalist class that had border mobility, complicated and collapsed any determinism of class status or the primacy of capital in my mother's life. Certainly, capital shaped the conditions of possibility in my mother's life, but to say that this was fixed permanently to a particular class is antithetical to what we now know about the very nature of language and discourse; it would overlook how multiple identifications play out through existing power structures; it would efface the unmapped genealogy of sex/nation/colonialism that haunt capital itself. The messy enterprise of class in the context of post/neo/coloniality demands seeing class as a moving analytic and a moving experience. The simplistic "class politics" that Marxism allows or the "good life" that the model minority myth promised both fail to capture the way my mother's stories didactically and phantasmically offered a small and important nuance of intersection.[6]

In 1980, three years after my parents migrated to the United States, my grandfather sent my father his profits from the sale of his Indian bone char factory—where charring animal bones produced the decolorizing filter to produce white sugar. My grandfather's health was failing, and he was ready to retire in America. Ever the entrepreneur, my father channeled the money into the restrained asset-building characteristic of the older diasporic generation. Specifically, my grandfather's money landed in the southern geographies of US real estate, where my father became the owner of two manageable twenty-room airport motels in Atlanta, Georgia. He ran the front desk, and my mother cleaned the rooms. My uncle and his family of seven soon became the owners and operators of the second motel. I had begun kindergarten at a small school close to the motel, called the Raggedy Ann and Andy School. We lived in one of the motel rooms, and my uncle's family of seven lived in another two. We had also found a small community of Shiite Ismaili Muslims and a *Jamatkhanna* (a Shiite Ismaili congregational prayer hall), which we began attending regularly on Friday evenings as a family, and on Saturdays, all of us children for Islamic studies. For two years, both brothers ran the motels family-style, with their wives and older children all working in the everyday mundane labor of the hospitality industry. Owning these small motels only slightly separated us from the working class and struggling poor immigrants, as it allowed my father to give small jobs and small loans to arriving families from South Asia. It made him and thus us the respectable working middle class. But economic stability did not translate into social capital. For even as we had (sometimes) abundant food and shelter, the questions of where we lived, how much money we had, how good our English was, how much money we needed to keep earning and saving, were constant.

And there were other South Asians, mostly the ones who had migrated from Uganda after Idi Amin's 1972 expulsion of Indians and Pakistanis from the country, who were far wealthier, far more educated, and didn't hesitate to display their wealth and education. In the decade from 1972 through 1982, these light-skinned South Asians had accumulated a significant amount of material wealth, grand homes, and advanced degrees. They saw themselves as superior, White-adjacent Muslim immigrants, faith-based, but also worldly, sophisticated, cosmopolitan. They notoriously looked down on Pakistani immigrants, and neither my dark brown Indian father nor my lighter brown Pakistani mother were exempt from their classism or racism. Paki-bashing was their treasured pastime, and colorism was pervasive. Moreover, even as new landowners in the Southern United States, we could not escape the dirty histories of our family reputation, which had followed us across the Indian and Atlantic oceans into the gossip networks of the small South Asian and East African immigrant communities to which we belonged.

At the end of our second year of living in and operating the motels, in a move so clandestine that no one saw it coming, my uncle ousted my father from the family business. Overnight, he manipulated the motel deeds into his name, forged my father's name (until the day this brother-in-law died, my mother feared his masterful ability to forge signatures), drained their joint bank account, and transferred the money to an offshore account. An old friend of my father's who worked in the local bank had called up my father to inquire why he was emptying his bank accounts into his brother's. The violent fight between the two brothers over the motel properties produced no results for my father. His money was gone, and so was his name from the property. As my mother described it, if our family had one American dollar, my uncle took seventy-five cents and distributed the remaining quarter among his living eight siblings. But my father, trapped in stupefied deference to his brother and in blind loyalty to the family bloodline and hierarchy, no longer had any fight in him. My uncle watched over us smugly, as my mother packed our things. There was talk that we would return to Karachi, or maybe even Bombay; that we could start over there; that there was support and family there, unlike the isolation and betrayal here; that the American dollar translated to more rupees. My father debated the next steps in a trip our family took to Bombay, staying at an old friend's flat in Bandra and escaping to Mount Abu, a hill station near the border of Gujrat in Rajasthan. But despite the peace of the hill station excursion and the community of old friends in Bandra, my father saw returning as failure. So after three months, we returned to Cherry Hill, where he had applied for a job and would again try to pursue his engineering degree. But this also would not last, as my father quickly relearned that sustaining life for five people in US dollars was a devastating challenge, especially without the financial backing of real estate, access to some liquid wealth, and multiple bodies to labor. Money problems and too many mouths to feed and isolation and duplicity from extended family and day-long visits to the welfare office meant that stress, anger, and pain were daily occurrences. To make matters worse, once we had returned to the North, three of my father's white sons came to live with us, increasing the number of mouths my father had to feed and giving way to another layer of violence, for which my mother was unprepared and to which she never fully submitted. My mother learned quickly that the everydayness of extended immigrant family life in the United States was compounded with other vectors of disenfranchisement, exploited feminine labor, maternal fear, gendered violence, and masculine regeneration of life.

The Aggregations

I tell them it ain't me lying. It's memory lying.
—GAYL JONES, *EVA'S MAN*

My mother has an endless preoccupation with the past. Like the drag of melancholy, my mother's narratives of the past encumber the present, shaping her affective daily performance, cultivating a perverse absence of the now. As she would say, *Now is always then or before; now is the other* (perhaps, conversely, the past is the *self*). Over time I learned that her present was itself a living archive, stopping time, making time, saturating her living, temporalizing that which is gone, cocooning it in the shelter of her thoughts, organizing her survival. Her countertraumatic structure of paying attention to the past impoverished the threat of the now, sensorializing, grafting the past onto the present. Unlike others who were drawn to the past, my mother interrogated the past, drew it forward to the present, not under the gravitational pull of nostalgia but through the most miniscule scrutiny of power, violence, asymmetry, coercion. Jose Muñoz once described the present as "a prison house of the here and now."[7] But for my mother, recognizing the present as an enclosure didn't necessitate a turning to the future as a longing, as a mode of fugitivity (as Muñoz describes), but rather the enclosure of the present meant turning backward and inward to the stories held in the body. Her fixation resounds against the coloniality of time, teaching me that political time intervenes into maternal time, as time, like space and subjects, is a psychopathology of coloniality.

In the deep groove of our Pakistani diasporic familial cocoon, my mother was often called a conspiracy theorist. Everything, anything, was suspect. In our family, almost everyone found her stories frustrating, sometimes comical in their ridiculousness, but always solipsistic. I came to be fascinated by the elaborate plots, twists, intentions, and dialogues she experienced, imagined, and uttered to anyone who would listen and with absolute seriousness. Her stories were a magnificent mix of suppressed rage, expressed bitterness, nihilistic crudeness, and they cared nothing for the optimistic strain. Her stories were historiographic excess. The deep constitutive relationship between my mother and these conspiracy theories reveals an archive that is always and already a feminized and racialized construction—abject, mad, contradictory. I see her conspiracy theories as one mode of witnessing and surviving the grief, the melancholy, the perversity, even as it meant that she came to embody each of them daily. I conceptualize her conspiratorial fixations as countertraumatic. I conceptualize her conspiracy theories as a site of alternative knowledge.

Hélène Cixous once encouraged women to write in the ink made of mother's milk. Cixous was referring to the importance of women rewriting culture through the birth of a woman-centered language, what Irigiray called a female language.[8] But Cixous's point of writing in the ink of our mother's milk is also a reference to our mother's breasts, to her body and her/our tongue as an archive through which we must move (and not avoid). My own nagging refusal to leave my mother's breast, to drain from her the peculiar and perverse ink through which I write this archive has not escaped me. So regardless of what my mother bequeaths to me, I listen, I transcribe, I translate, I write into this soft, wet, appealing text.

A knife was inserted into her vagina. That's what my sister-in-law, M., told me. She was the third wife of your father's younger brother. It was a butter knife, not a sharp knife. His violence was carefully choreographed in this way, methodical and precise. It wasn't blood that excited him. It was fear. Cold fear. This was his third wife. The other wives drew the line at other places, but always farther than where you can imagine a woman can take it, will take it. His first wife took the cigarette butts being put out on her inner thighs and on her breasts but left after a beating so brutal that she landed in a wheelchair. The second wife took the black eyes and bloody noses and bruised arms but left after such a vile moment of violence during her pregnancy that she had her own father perform a third-term abortion. This was your dad's younger brother, who would knock incessantly at my door, every night your dad was in America. The first seven years of my marriage, your dad traveled all the time, for weeks, sometimes, months at a time. I listened to his knock, until it sounded, not like a knock, but like the moaning of a feral hungry animal. The knock had tones, from polite to cocky to desperate to angry, but I didn't open the door. I never opened the door. If I did, I knew that anything after that would have been my fault.

My mother told me this story when I was nine, maybe ten. *He kept knocking on my door.* I knew even then that knocking was a labyrinthian, maze-like, muddled verb, an active syntax, a verb that, as Dionne Brand writes, is "a tragedy, a bleeding."[9] *He kept knocking on my door.* She meant I wasn't raped. She meant I'm weighing my words and I might not be telling you the truth. She meant I might have been raped. She meant that knocking was the sonic scape for a rape that was imminent. *He kept knocking on my door.* She meant there is something unutterable lying beneath this verb. She meant he just did enough to scare her without breaking the family code as he understood it. She meant that her memory, like her sense of safety, is scrambled and that this was not the beginning of that scrambling. She meant trauma scrambles time. She meant that he had deniability. She meant that not much happened. *He kept knocking.* She meant this is anything but inconsequential to the machinations of patriarchal power of the everyday. *Knocking.* She meant she was immured in and inured to his force, to the shared space of shame, confinement, intimacy, desire, violence, and terror. *Knocking.* She meant she knew intimately the banal violence that people generally acknowledge and discount all in one blow. She meant life is a story structured around banal moments of dispossession. *Knocking.* She meant she knew his desire was contoured with violence. She meant: What desire did not involve a taking over, a taking from?

It is only now as I write out these words that this *knocking* overwhelms my memory, overwhelms this story. It would take years of hearing this story for me to understand this knocking, *his knocking* as rhizomatic—a stem of violence that had no root, no linearity, no end, but was instead part of a pattern of emergence, of decadence, of virility and longevity that apprehends the multiplicities of everyday male hegemonies. The pitch of the word *knocking* in the sentence never failed to sound. It was a reverberation that contained predatory value. *Knocking* was the verb used to nod to misogyny, the grammar that kept a woman like my mother always alert. It was a sonic formation that foreshadowed dispossession, foreshadowed the way femme bodies and femme tongues are in a state of always watching, always waiting, for what poet Andrea Abi-Karam calls the "signature injury."[10]

My father denies my mother's memory. He says he would have known if his brother sexually intimidated his wife or, for that matter, if he was sexually interested in his wife. Although he now admits, at the age of eighty, that this same brother initiated the gang rape of the thirteen-year-old daughter of their Karachi housekeeper. He now acknowledges that after that gang rape, this same unscrupulous brother set his eyes on that thirteen-year-old girl's younger eight-year-old sister, waiting, just barely for her body to be available, enjoyable for sex/rape. He also earnestly reminds me that it is through this unfortunate relation (of sexual captivity) that the younger sister became his brother's fourth wife and gained US citizenship. Focus, he tells me, on the positive.

Here again, I found myself in the familiar position of trying to work through this cold prohibition of negativity, his (but not only his) compulsory optimisms. I wanted to offer my father an alternative cartography of these two brown sisters, one that cracks open another form of knowledge and, in so doing, rejects this silver lining, this ends-justify-the-means discourse. I wanted to offer my authority as a scholar and speak to him of the histories of bodies and subjects moving across land, water, life for a myriad of reasons, including traps, dependencies, brutalities. I wanted to say, yes, the younger sister eventually gained US citizenship, something we all learned to deeply treasure, but the means through which both the United States and US citizenship became available to her meant subjection to daily class and sexualized hegemony coupled now with White supremacy, menial working-class conditions, and amplified by neoliberal alienation. I wanted to tell him that subaltern subjects are also geographic subjects—crossing, making, surviving, resisting colonial geographies—as they travel through the Anglophone Ocean; that moving is not about reproducing (even if and when reproduction is a consequence of moving).[11] This complicated, complex, vexing, and violent geography is what these women know most intimately, most dangerously. To a certain extent, my father knows this also. But denial and optimism are seductive libidinal enterprises of thought, and my father always fell into their outstretched arms. Your mother's memory, he tells me, always pivots on the negative, the unbelievable, the unverifiable, the dead. His statement confirms that brown maternal memory and brown feminine memory, even by those who bear witness to that same history and certainly by those who don't, are seen as nothing but dead pieces of knowledge. My mother's memories, whether dead or whether I can give them the circulatory life of signs, of words, of the present, are regardless deadened by the men who hear her, my father and her father, her brothers and his brothers.

Like the vibration that remained after the persistent *knocking*, I find this memory equally dreadful and disturbing. Like others, this maternal memory gives primacy to violence, a maneuver that involves a rejection of pragmatics or facts or dates or rationales, a maneuver through which perhaps, possibly, we access another ontology. It is, too, a memory that gives primacy to feminized flesh, thus to feminized and maternal perception, the maternal as repetition, as infinite reiteration, as vertiginous. When I was a young girl, this story constructed my bodily comportment and conditioned the way I learned to move through the spaces of our home/s and among the family when men were present. I learned to observe which men sat too close, which men's eyes were shifty or lingering, which men hugged too tight, too long, which men loitered at the thresholds of bathrooms and bedrooms and closets, or which men looked hungry and which looked placated.

I knew these girls. I still know one of the women. Familiarity is (often) ground for solidarity. I trace my finger back to the metaphor of tongues, overlaid with the metaphor of the body, superimposed by the unconscious, trapped by conditions of its existence. I trace my finger back to these speech acts of flesh. Without, I hope, "committing further violence in my own act of narration," I tell this particular story.[12] I find myself incompetent to capture it, to analyze it. I am insufficient. But, still, I work to do what's necessary: speak to the mother, speak to my mother.

Two sisters tangled in an archive of violence: one survives in and on to a life in America, where her work never ends; the other passes into death. *Do you remember playing with N. on the roof of our house and underneath the charpai? You were the youngest and always in the way. N. was thirteen, so she could watch you and her younger sister, D., while you played ghar-ghar (house-house). N. used to oil and braid your hair. In those days, we didn't just have children because we wanted them and loved them but because having children was having help, having hands. But, one day, N. didn't come to the house. Her mother didn't come either. Your dad's younger brother, M., at the time was in his third marriage. His wife, A., was Hindu and British and beautiful. They had two babies already, and A. was pregnant with her third. Your father's brother was notorious for being a drunk and a wife beater. Everyone knew he beat his wife senseless, and before her, two other wives, not to mention all his lovers and girlfriends. Everyone knew he got off on it. This third wife, A., openly spoke about it. She was a blunt, educated, modern woman, not like us. But she had eloped with M., sneaking out in the middle of the night, leaving her well-to-do British-Hindu family to live in Karachi, in an extended Muslim family with all of us. He was a charmer, that one. He knew how to move his mouth and his hands, and the women went crazy—eyes-closed, they followed him. M. had three friends visiting from Bombay. The young men sweet-talked N. to an ice cream stand. N.'s mom was powerless to argue with the men and took D. and went home. When A. came home from her office job, pregnant, swollen, and tired, she told me she saw the end of the rape. One friend was mounted on N.'s scrawny body; the other men stood around and watched with lusty eyes, drool in their mouths, M. zipping his pants. N. got pregnant from that rape. A. took her to the doctor for the abortion, but because she was a lower-caste girl, the doctors in Clifton Hospital wouldn't touch her. N.'s mom and A. performed the abortion themselves, with A. aggressively massaging N's stomach with her fists and the full weight of her own pregnant body to help expunge the fetus.*

I hear my mother's words, and Ismat Chughtai's short story, "Mutti Maalish" ("Fist Massage") swirls through my head.[13] In Chughtai's story, a hospital maid named Ratti Bai describes to an upper-class patient two methods of abortion used by poor women in India. One entails standing on the woman's belly and massaging it with your feet; the other, more brutal method involves yanking the fetus out with your hand. So obscene is Ratti Bai's telling that the patient throws up.

My mother couldn't break the silence, but the next day, when A., in a small corner of their kitchen, told her everything, she went to check on N. She had learned early in her marriage that for her husband's brothers, cruelty was a form of sociality, as arbitrary cruelties punctuated the day-to-day of work-eat-sleep. In the early evening, my mother returned to us, saying over and over that girls weren't safe in our family. And later that night, in her own home, N. began to hemorrhage. Her small adolescent body, overcome by the violence of rape and the miasma of masculinity, gave way to death. That same night, N.'s mother, whose patience with violence and poverty was weak and worn, drank a small bottle of poison and died, leaving eight-year-old D.

A year passed, with no consequence for M., who now freely set his eyes on D., who, like all of us girls, was growing up visibly fast, but, unlike us girls, was a motherless poor maid. A vicious set of sexual politics produced these elite men's access to free sex and impunity for violence, effectively transforming class antagonisms into a direct antagonism against proletariat women (i.e., the practice of an uncriminalized rape as long as the women are working class or poor). N. was fungible, replaceable. But her spirit resided in her younger sister, D., who would not die from rape, but instead would survive many years of sexual violence. Daily rapes resulted in a settled relation of sexual captivity, unspeakable physical violence, and childrearing for M. and A.'s three small children. D.'s ability to labor for my uncle was divided by her availability to be used for sexual pleasure by him or his friends, the sum of which was violent excess, or, in the case of her older sister, N., a kind of necropedophilia.

M.'s wife had left him, shortly after N.'s death and the birth of their third child, fed up with the extreme physical violence that filled her marriage and his sick, sexualized, unpunished violence toward working-class girls and middle-class wives. Too much violence to stay, she said, merciless, gratuitous, endless. But the consequences of leaving M. were brutal. Drunk on power, impunity, and money in early 1980s Karachi, M. threatened to kill their children if she tried to take them out of Pakistan. Better dead than with you in England, he threatened. Terrified and stupefied, A. returned to her parents in London, and her three young children—two sons and a daughter—stayed in Karachi with their father, raised by D. When my father sponsored his younger brother for US citizenship in the late- 1980s, he migrated to the United States with his three children and D., eventually marrying her and getting her US citizenship. They lived with us in a new home my father had purchased in the suburbs of Atlanta. For one year, we bore witness to their relationship—one of complicated bondage, violent, volatile, brutal, dependent, dirty, and normal. D.'s servitude was visceral, her abject position was one to which she wholly submitted, even to the unlearned eye. Eventually, M. took D. and his three children and moved to Miami, a city with no family, no witnesses. Twenty-two years later, after seven abortions, countless hospital visits for assault, two attempts to poison M., and one son of her own, D. left her rapist.

When my mother reminds me of these two sisters (one of whom I call my aunt), I think of how some women live with death and some women die. I think of the architecture of domination, how it is composed of many small but significant parts, small but significant misogynies: class antagonism, the gendering/sexualizing of the working class, the eruption of sexual violence on the poor, poor health care, structures of caste/class, the fraternarchy (rule of the brothers), the wife as the figure of perpetual patience, and the abject brown mother. And if we think about misogyny as the rationalized, uneven distribution of subordination/violence/death, we see how each of these were symbiotic with death-making capacities. But to us, these men, our uncles, represented the extreme patriarchal fantasy of viability, a familial dissymmetry that was at once extraordinary and precisely most common. There were no alternative frames available within this fraternal-patriarchal dissymmetry, no way for these men, my uncles, to put themselves into the shoes of these young girls, to see a mirror of their own faces, forcing upon them violence and/as sex. They were immune until they arrived in the United States and White male supremacy and economic precarity clashed with the brown masculine supremacy that they had so naturally internalized and for which they would never stop fighting.

For N. and her mother, death was and is the only antieconomy. But D.'s suffering was what Audre Lorde might call "the deaths we are forced to live"—chronic, cruddy, ordinary, rather than sublime.[14] Indeed, despite all that happened to these girls, it never, as my mother said, rose to the level of an event, let alone a crisis. By definition, crisis is exception and exceptional. Tied to temporality, crisis is not meant to last. But this was something else. These girls' suffering—or life-as-suffering or woman-as-pain—drifts across and through my mother's own life into a form of life that never quite gets verified as event or eventful. This was merely the everyday of subalternity. It was what they talked about over chai; it was what they learned to laugh about together, even if the laughter was heavily shadowed by fear, by anxiety. Violence for these women was inescapable; it was no different than breathing or breeding. They were all already in the hands of the others, bound up with others so much—whether as witness or victim, as mother or maid—that who they were, who my mother is, is this living relation.

The violent lives of D. and N. are preserved in my mother's memories, as my mother was required by patriarchy to live within its violence, somewhat distanced and protected, even as it inscribed her psyche and domestically contained her body. These were the psychic dimensions of sexual survival, transferring trauma, like blood, from mother to daughter, sister to sister. The working-class conditions combined with caste-driven misogyny facilitated pedonecrophiliac practices and even, arguably, the murderous bio-necro-politics of letting die (N.) and making live (D.). For D. and N. there was liter-ally no enclosure from violence (i.e., the ability to refuse to open the bedroom door); these girls' bodies were as physically available—indeed they had no bedroom until they entered the bedroom of their rapist—as they were sym-bolically available.

This difference between the wife and the maid is tremendous. Both could be violated, the maid at free will, anytime and anyplace, and the wife at any moment of deviance, no matter how minor or miniscule; a capacious inter-pretive field of deviance which was completely produced at the discretion of men—naively making oneself available (i.e., opening the knocked-on door gave men deniability); wearing revealing or fitted clothing (i.e., a sari blouse too tight, too low, too bright, too noticeable); being amorous in speech or free in movement (i.e., talking too much, or too long, or too interestedly with men or when men were around); wearing red or magenta or scarlet or maroon (i.e., only loose women wore red); and on and on went the list of everyday femi-nine policing. So for my mother the conditions of biopolitical and postcolo-nial modernity meant that she was *allowed to* live and thus experienced life as always shadowed by violence, rape, and surveillance. The layers of power performed in this ongoing moment of violence against two sisters constituted the slow, consolidating education of my mother.

My mother's ongoing ruminations on abjection and my father's refusal of those same abjections produced a litany of speech acts that entered into almost every conversation. In my mother's stories, I heard over and over again the intimate proximity between death and women's imaginations. I learned over and over again that heterosexual technologies of domination are always and already technologies of death. I discovered, and thus studied, repeatedly what others considered the lack in her stories—lacking legibility, lacking intelligibil-ity, lacking reason, lacking civility, lacking politeness, lacking readability, lack-ing, lacking, lacking. She rubbed her abject words on unwilling participants. Burning words. Wasting words. These were her words. Stark. Naked. Brown.

2

forked tongues

———

"Did the same God that made her make me?"

"Yes."

"Well, then, I don't like him."

"Why not?"

"Because he made her white, and me black.
Why didn't he made us both white?"
—HARRIET E. WILSON, *OUR NIG*

There is a song I grew up hearing. It comes from the 1978 Bollywood film Satyam Shivam Sunduram (Truth Godliness Beauty).[1] *In true Bollywood fashion, the film features several songs, but there is one in particular that resonates with the racial pedagogy of my childhood. The song, sung as devotional song in a temple, is titled "Yashomati Maya"—a reference to the maternal goddess Yashoda (Mangeshkar, 3.17).[2] Yashoda Ma, known for fostering the god Krishna, represents the sacred and the sacrificial maternal—Yashomati Maya functions in the song as an endearing call to his mother.[3] The song is a mythical dialogue* between the young Krishna and Yashoda Ma, with the quizzical refrain, "Why is Radha (the goddess Radha was the god Krishna's beloved) gori and I'm so kala?" The word kala, which literally translates as "Black," is a common pejorative term to reference both brown and Black skin, and it has different syntax registers, such as kali (feminine), kala (masculine) and kaley (plural). The word gori, literally translates as "White," although the word gori also has multiple referent points, "light-skinned" or "beautiful," on the one hand, or "foreigner," "colonizer," or "White person," on the other. The lyrics trace the story of Yashoda Ma being asked, repeatedly and earnestly by the young god Krishna, "Why is Radha so gori and I'm so kala?" In response to the refrain, Yashoda Ma offers two tender, amorous, fabulative explanations to Krishna for his dark skin. As the lyrics go, the mother smiles at her child and explains: "Oh, sweet child, you were born in the middle of a dark stormy night, and the darkness of the night cocooned your skin like a blanket, coating in its color, making you kala." The child, dissatisfied by this answer, again asks: "Why, ma, is Radha so gori and I am so kala?" Yashoda Ma again lovingly responds to her child: "My dear child, yes, beautiful Radha was born with very fair skin, but she also had very dark eyes, and with her dark eyes, she cast a magic spell on your skin, and that's why you are kala."

....

My mother has always been candid about our impotence against whiteness. She raised us on this impotence, simultaneously exaggerating our brownness as determinant, just as she inflected it with specialness. White men inherited the world, we were told. Race, she would then say, is outside of us, an American problem. But, also, our living breathing brownness is a problem for America and Americans. *They don't like our color*, she would openly observe. And then a few minutes later came her enamoring of whiteness. With a deep rhythmic melancholy, she would talk about fair skin, beauty, happiness, success, and power, folding each one into the other, until her words held no difference between them. Her adoration of whiteness was a site of tactile anxiety, lodged in sensation. So, too, was her loathing of it. I found myself seduced by her words, eating her contradictions like tasty morsels of food. It took three decades to dissolve my longing for ascendance to every texture, every dimension, every facet of whiteness—ontological and epistemological, semiotic and philosophic, corporeal and affective; three decades of this rhythmic rehearsal to depart from whiteness, to release the burden of this inheritance. Instead, for years and years and years, I daily reached for the face cream that lightened my skin a few shades, convinced that with it, I, too, looked *gori*.

....

The first time my mother met my father's children was in the winter of 1977, a month or so after arriving in America. The oldest, and only, daughter was fifteen years old, followed by a thirteen-year-old boy, two twelve-year-old twin boys, and the youngest, a nine-year-old boy. My siblings and I were all younger than five. My mother was nervous to meet them. Trained in the norms of hetero-envy now cocktailed with the supremacy of whiteness, she felt jealousy wash over her when she laid her eyes on the kids and their White/r complexion. Her first thought was that, other than their dark thick hair, they were much lighter than she had expected. Her very dark, brown-skinned husband clearly had weak genes. The children's much-lighter skin meant, to my mother, that they resembled all the dark-headed Whites my mother had previously met and did not, in any way, resemble our father. As far as my mother was concerned, he may as well have plucked five random children from the closest suburban mall and called them his children. As far as my mother was concerned, their whiteness/lightness amplified her (and our) brownness.

They were equally suspicious of her, side-eyeing her as the other woman next to whom their mother was confined to hopelessness, condemned to no return. Their brown father had returned to the United States with a new brown wife and three small brown children, who, with flat round eyes, stared at them. In the seven years my parents had been married, my father had traveled to the United States several times to see his other children, and, properly inculcated in middle-class ethos, he would bring them generic presents—a small check, and platitudes on Pakistan—before disappearing again for months at a time. In this way, their father was, in kind, a stranger. But my mother, in her strangeness, was seen as cagey, the domestic and domesticated *other* whose proximity could not be avoided.

This group of children (who called themselves White and whom my mother saw as White) scaffolded whiteness around us. My mother's insistence on seeing my father's first five children as White and their insistence on seeing us as brown/er mapped out empirically (as an object in the world), imaginarily (as an ideological site of power), and as a mode of subject formation (the practice, comportment, etiquette, or ethos of living whiteness). Their presence in that moment and in every subsequent moment interpellated whiteness (the proverbial Althusserian "hey you"), restoring a white body politic that encircled the brownness of our bodies. My mother felt that interpellation as a charge in the body, shaped by and shaping the textures of her felt relations to self, other, space, and place. It was a fresh, awkward, and messy encounter. My father stood there, somewhere in the crooked center, unevenly between his past and present, between his studiously acquired white proximity and his nationalized Indian brownness. His optimism, a trait for which my father is notorious, spilled out, thinking the envy in everyone's gaze could be bracketed. But had he looked closer in either direction, he would have seen that the trouble stewing would quickly and summarily dislodge this bracket.

For my mother, the experience of crossing international borders only to find that she was *browned* demanded a different cognition from her. Gender, she understood completely. And sexuality. Nation and class, too. Around these, she had developed a number of modes, vernaculars, riddles, figures of speech, and metaphors that resignified her relations to self and others. But race, in its US-American iterations, was vile, strange, and unpredictable. Race, of course, is deep in South Asia, even as its linguistic and material expressions and experiences vary. Having moved internally through East and West Pakistan and across the borders of India, Pakistan, and England meant that my mother was also deeply schooled in religious-ethnic-class-caste politics. Words like *gori* and *kali* and their accompanying value system were deeply entrenched in her and in our lexicon. In fact, in the Pakistani context, my mother was often called *gori*, as she was lighter-skinned than both her sisters and her husband. However, her entry into America felt like a sudden, unexpected interpellation into being a hyperracialized subject, dipped in brownness, caught up in the hyperbole of whiteness abound.

Everywhere she looked, whiteness was threaded through and through with beauty, education, likeability. Her two years in London had not prepared her for the particularity of US antibrownness, its blunt force, its nakedness, its conceit. Her dislike of England and English nationalism (which she got a healthy dose of among the quasi-elite Pakistani diaspora and white Englanders) was visceral and historically rooted. But her movement through southern and northern United States life was differently circumscribed by the fraught and fractured matrix of race, class, gender, sex, and nation. If in England she was immersed within a Pakistani diaspora, only briefly encountering white Englanders, in the southern United States, there was no ethnic enclave among whom she/we could hide or disappear. Of course, there were always *others* in the US South, some of whom were cast closer to whites, others cast alongside Blacks, but the South in which my mother was immersed in the garishly racist eighties was marked most heavily by the Black and White divide, in policy, in culture, in education, and in historical memory. The foreignness of American whiteness was part of her everyday life, which meant that, more than being seen as Pakistani, she was simply seen as brown. So it didn't take long for my mother to learn that *it was our brownness Whites didn't like.*

My mother's relation to brownness and whiteness took on very different forms from those of my father, who worked closely with Whites, under the auspices of capitalist logics, model minority sensibilities, and the coveting of the American Dream. The racial humiliations he experienced were coded in the deep lines in his forehead after an endless week of work, exhaled in the long drag of his after-dinner cigarette in our small living room, discharged in folded fists when our grades were poor or spoons were misplaced or the kitchen was unkept, or released at night on my mother. My mother, conversely, only worked in whatever business her husband owned, doing the feminized labor—primarily working as a maid in the small motels he owned. She held only one job outside of her husband's business. In the early nineties, she took a position at a White suburban daycare center. We encouraged her by offering her our own internalized vision of independent American women. We told her that American women work and that she should too (introducing the concept of work as though it was alien to her). We reminded her of the importance of excelling in English—that if she stopped practicing, she would lose it altogether (laughing meanwhile at her pronunciations, confusing our ego for education). We assured her that the children would love her because we loved her (hiding from her our embarrassment at parent-teacher conferences, where the White teachers couldn't hide their smirks at her use of their prized English). We advised her, *Isn't this why we came to America, so we can all make someone of ourselves, including you?* By then our move from respectable working class to middle-class sociality had whetted our appetite for more, even if tainted by histories of dirty men and dirty money. A false calculus of abundance formally positioned my family as middle-class immigrants, with a working father as sole breadwinner and a stay-at-home mother. This was the American Dream, we thought, wages in our mother's hands. We had yet to realize that our neoliberal assimilated tongues would hit the surface of our mother's body and shrivel up like prunes. The greed lurking in us would take a few decades to discover.

My mother, perhaps more or less naively, was fascinated by the idea of care as paid labor. This she could do. Care is, above all, a practice that produces (meaningful) relations. Her primary identity as mother, daughter, aunt, older sister meant that if she could do nothing else, she could always take care of

children, even White children. Motherhood without race. A raceless economy of care. Our youthful ardor and her essentialist naivete bled into each
other. Our romance with America paralleled her romance with motherhood.
Also, and perhaps more importantly, she loved money. Not money that she
could eat or with which she could feed her children. But money she could pile,
fold, and hide, as she licked her fingers and counted it in the secrecy of her
bedroom.

Soon after she began working in the daycare center, the complaints began.
The kids jeered at her, turned their noses up, and turned her into all sorts
of unrecognizable caricatures. When she set down rules, they broke them.
If she touched them, they cringed. If she walked by them, they told her she
smelled. When she read to them, they collapsed into giggles at her English,
only to eventually be joined by her, which would cause their laughter to stop
dead in its tracks. They wanted to laugh at her. She tried to laugh with them.
Her brownness excluded her from the symbolics of their pleasure, for within
their youthful White elite formulations, my mother could not be part of their
laughter. The triumph was theirs. The shame was hers.

The repetition of her effort may have eventually produced a partial embrace, but two months into the job, after only one measly paycheck, she was
called into the administrator's office. The older White man, his tightly shirted
belly pouring out of his belted pants, asked her, "Do you wear deodorant?
The children say that you smell." He laid on her a barrage of questions, each
one more humiliating than the other, each one embedded in a ritual of racial
dismissal and feminine failure. Each question encircled her, as in that moment she was produced as and reduced to the overly embodied ethnic abject
and the dirty brown maternal body. She was in a lose-lose situation, unable
to make even the most harmless of Whites (children) happy—much less the
leering older man whose gaze was weighted with the historical disgust for
brownness and the particular contempt and control directed at brown immigrant mothers. That day, my mother was fired because the White children
said she smelled.

Marked by this racial defilement, but one up for revision, my mother
learned plainly and quickly the conscriptions of whiteness. She learned how
to wear a generous amount of deodorant, wear breathable American fabrics
and not the georgette maxis and tunics from her Karachi days. She trained
her tongue to perfect a few English sentences, practiced and perfected a quiet,
wry smile (a gesture she knew gave everyone the impression that she had no
tongue in her mouth), and she quietly accepted her fate that she would not
and could not be an independent American woman. In another version, this

event was hers to shoulder—she wanted to be a housewife; she chose to be subordinate to her husband; she was the one convinced that the domestic was refuge; thus, she was too scared to go out into "real" world. Working outside the home in the formal and profit-oriented economy was the key metric for the hardworking immigrant. Her failure to remain in that economy marked her as a kept woman, securing the impression that the concept of *work* was alien to her.

For my mother, the logic of both colonialism and patriarchy meant that she understood her body and her place as naturally subordinate to whiteness and masculinity. There was no attempt to escape from race and ethnicity or other various identifications (a critique often directed at the postcolonial bourgeoise), but neither did she systematically assemble around it. Rather, she saw whiteness as ubiquitous, sometimes seductive, other times scathing, always controlling. Whiteness, like masculinity, was a living, breathing, active, and coercive formation of power in her life, and to it, she appeared to prostrate.

We had arrived in the United States as a family of five but were quickly joined by my father's brother's family of seven, by my father's father, by his younger brother, and, soon thereafter, by three of my father's White children. There were seventeen of us living in a four-bedroom suburban house, first in Cherry Hill, New Jersey (a home my father had purchased), and later in Atlanta, Georgia (in a home his brother had purchased with the profits of two airport motels he owned and operated). We lived together in joint family formations in both cities, where multiple generations live under the same roof, and thus, where adult secrets and scandal operated in plain sight. So we all soon came to know our uncle was fucking a white woman, G., his White lover, was always at our house. She had dinner with us often, after which she would retreat to another private room in the house with both of the brothers, while my mother and aunt would clean up. G.'s intimacy with our family—our very brown, very immigrant family—felt both flattering and intrusive.

She was always there. She brought banal treats for us when she would travel. She learned a few Urdu words that she would awkwardly pronounce with her deep southern drawl, and we would obligingly laugh, as she turned our language into lampoon. She was physically a domineering woman, standing close to six-feet tall, with a big blonde mane, bright gaudy jewelry, and large breasts revealed in tightly fitted clothes with low-hanging necklines. In comparison, both my mother and my aunt looked like small brown mice—shrunken, shy, stupid, and mute. This is not to say they were these things. G. was, in every conversation between those two women, and they both had a magnificent and imaginative foul mouth. Her robust, White female sexuality, her southern brashness, her financial perspicacity, her ability to take over a room, her adeptness at getting the men, including the young boys, to stare at her with lust in their eyes, was all grated into piles of powdery fetish or ambivalent dissonance, every moment possible. But the gap between their script and her body was too wide to fill, so they developed an approach to her that was economical, even if retaliatory, graceful, even if disingenuous. What remained despite these tactics was the lesson of questioning their own skin and abjuring their own feminine bodies, even as they, in each of their own ways, abjured hers.

My aunt never stood up to her openly philandering husband; his flat, open palm and menacing words were enough to keep most of us cowering. My mother was terrified of him. He was the oldest of all my father's living siblings, controlled the family income, and had a cruel temper and a mean laugh. Both my mother and my aunt had expertly perfected two English phrases when they addressed him: *I'm sorry* and *I'm wrong*. In fact, this was often the only time my mother and aunt spoke English. When the men, especially my uncle, were present, these phrases circulated in our house like carbon dioxide, sometimes up to ten times a minute. But even the boldest of us crumbled at the sight of him. His open affair with G. was but one of his smaller cruelties. The one and only time my aunt stood up to her husband, he responded to her swiftly and viciously, saying if she ever tried to leave him, he would hire "five *kaley* [Blacks] to rape her."

When my mother told me this, I had entered my teens. We no longer lived in a joint family, and G. had exited our life. I, along with my older sister, uncomfortably swallowed this story, its viscerality coating our skin. We forced it deep down in the recesses of our psyche, not knowing, not understanding what to do with this epistemic-linguistic-racist sexual violence. What we did know then was that we didn't really like our aunt. She was a mean-spirited and intensely competitive woman who exploited our mother's labor, mocked her silence, made heartless comments about our height, speech, hair, incessantly compared us to her smarter, taller, fairer-skinned children, and told us as often as she could that we would never amount to anything. She used my mother to gain leverage, and my mother, who was both spellbound and scared of her sister-in-law's elaborate wit and cunning, let her. It is also true that despite these observations, the two women had the ease and comfort of old friends. They found relief in each other's oppressions. Theirs was a relation composed of conflicted feelings of tenderness and hostility. So when my aunt told my mother and my mother told us, I felt strangely sorry for her, even as I felt the onerous burn of this cruel racist rape threat whose terms I didn't quite yet understand. And as is true to my mother's style, I heard this story not once or twice, but over and over again, and with each iteration, meanings arose to me sharply, angrily, unpredictably.

Years later I would study the genealogies of enmity between Black and brown people. I would come to understand how the eighteenth-century colonial project spectacularly resounded in twentieth-century South Asian identity making. I would realize that the settler logics of seizure, elimination, and assimilation would come to be so entrenched in our sociality that we would learn daily and deeply the ways to ward off blackness, that we would all be marked most by White class and White social formations. I would come to know that my uncle's statement was a tacit and unsurprising normalization of the psychic installation of global antiblackness and White supremacy's stunning ability to sustain relations of intimacy across great distances. I would become conscious of the well-rehearsed fact that antiblackness is a prerequisite for world making, even at most levels of abstraction.[4] Blackness as an object always traversed or ruined by the abusive truths of whiteness reverberates in this violent mess of brown-borrowed, white supremacist constructions of Black rapists-for-hire, the subjugation of brown women, the rapture of white women, and the domestic banality of it all. As Tiffany King writes, each form of colonial violence has "its own way of contaminating, haunting, touching, caressing, and whispering to the other."[5]

The historic racial schema lying beneath this tactile and visceral threat mobilized, just as it recoded, that particular moment of South Asian colonial patriarchy. My uncle's menacing and racist words reveal how brown diasporic success and the rising global middle class depended upon naming the brown body at once a register of oppression and a site of diasporic antiblackness. Certainly, the project of immigrants has always been a project of figuring out how to distinguish themselves from Black Americans; and South Asians have, at different historical moments, been mobilized as a normative index to which to compare Black pathology.[6] Constructed as inexhaustibly revisable, moving with racial logics and geopolitics across time and space, brown is what can be exploited and maintained for a facile multiculturalism to inhere—the fixed "dread" of blackness providing the ground against which the figure of a more complex brown possibility/revision unfolds.[7] This is the Fanonian predicament that underwrites racial discourse: the subhuman is invited to become human on terms that require anti-Black sentiment.

Living in the southern United States in the 1980s, we learned quickly that blackness was something from which we should distance ourselves. Black was different than brown. South Asian colorism and its obsessive fixations with being *gori* merged organically with US antiblackness, neither necessarily with any real material benefits, but both layered with ordinary pragmatism and an ideological gloat that sometimes served us and other times wrought us toward our own destruction. We all failed and succeeded at this differently. In part, because there was a way in which we delineated ourselves from that which we understood as American, particularly white, but also Black and other immigrants; through language, food, song, prayer, and dance, we came to think of ourselves as unique. We also tailored our brownness to be as *less* brown as possible—we learned the fashion, memorized the pop songs, refined our English, chastened our gaudiness, absorbed their sociality, and even pretended our achievements weren't impressive, *just ordinary*. This kept our shame and our insecurities manageable. But all this performance was engaged and perfected in the company of other Muslim immigrants: Pakistanis, Indians, Bangladeshis, Somalians, and Ethiopians. We did not socialize with Whites, as both intimacy and sociality were marked by brownness. This well-rehearsed mode of being externally one way and internally another afforded my immigrant family a certain safety, one that while not static, conditioned our relation to both blackness and whiteness. The messiness and uneven-ness of immigrant White adjacency threw into relief the semiotics of violence and animated expectations of class. Anxious speculation and insecurity atrophied the language of intrasolidarity, of intersubjectivity, and of intimacy, even as we ironically lived in what was fast becoming a Black middle-class suburban neighborhood. We were still mostly oblivious to the fact that our revisable selves were integrally tethered to the agonizing and violent texture of anti-blackness, one to which we, too, could on the unfortunate, the regrettable, or the right/wrong day be subject. Produced and pitted against and through each other, there was little-to-no inherited ground for racial empathy.

This was the affective and cognitive field in which I came to hear of my uncle's threat to my aunt. It simultaneously revealed his delirious Manichean commitment to a psycho-sexual-colonial dyadic mode of thinking (masculinity/femininity, subject/object/thing, rapeable/rapist, brown/Black/White/yellow), just as it also exposed the recalcitrant racism that shaped and continues to shape so many diasporic communities. His use of Black men as myth (as already rapists) and metaphor (the worst of rapists) against the fiction of the defenselessness brown woman (as always abject, thus, rapeable) pulled together multiple refusals. It refused collective thinking about violence against Black and brown peoples; it denied the intersubjectivity of blackness and brownness as racialized modes of being; it disavowed the psychic life of his internalized antibrownness. But the elasticity of his threat lay in the way it tied misogyny and antiblackness together; the way it produced both Black men and brown women as subjects who can be controlled and puppeteered by money and violence; and the way it unflinchingly exposed how brown diasporic patriarchal families antagonized and conspired with the normative investments of whiteness, man, and money.

Antiblackness is, of course, not installed in the United States, but it gets deepened in the United States in specific and peculiar ways.[8] In the Pakistani context, Black/*kala*/*kali*/*kaley* is a slur mediated through the language of coloniality, class, ethnicity, religion, and caste, as much as through aesthetics, colorism, morality, and sexuality. And indeed, the phrase my uncle used in his threat was "*paanch kaley*," which translates to "five blacks"—a dehumanizing grammatical move of replacing adjective with noun, as noun. My uncle's use of *kaley* was certainly, in part, derived from the particularity of US colonialism, where Black male sexuality is perceived as simultaneously knowable and perverse, and thus can be wielded for control and violation of another disobedient *other* (the brown mother). The historical specification of this deployment of blackness is tied to the reduction of blackness to nothingness (blackness as nonbeing) that can thus be taken up as one pleases.[9] On the other hand, the articulation of this threat didn't necessarily require the temporal and geographic location of the 1980s southern United States, as a more complex transnational history of race reveals how this use of *kaley*, like so many other untold moments of racialized linguistic violence in the private spaces of brown immigrant homes in the United States and elsewhere, is an assemblage of racial formations not yet examined, including extralegal violence against brown bodies, claims about (Black) excess, and the biopolitical erotics of racialization. The historicity of my uncle's threat and the specificity of his racialized language (in Urdu, no less) indicates that there is already an entanglement that has happened, even as that entanglement doesn't mitigate the violence of the encounter.

My uncle's racial fantasy of blackness facilitated his sexual fantasy of violence against his wife and his sexual fantasy of and with White women. Whiteness is a body that has time, a subject that moves with time. Blackness is historical fixture, a timeless body, which can be called upon again and again as a means to mark both the progress of the White self and the emerging brown male subject (but not the brown maternal), even as we know brown diasporic relations with whiteness are ontologically vulnerable. Who else but a brown moneyed man, whose psychosexual landscape accedes carte blanche to these colonial pathologies of brown women and Black men, would dare utter such words? What was being worked out in my uncle's sexuality via his brown wife, his white mistress, and his mythic Black rapists? How many other times did he wield the Black phallus with his wife, or perhaps even with his white mistress, or his own brown phallus in a way that was threatening, violent, coercive? Did he see Indian Muslim male sexuality as subsidiary to Black male virility, having deeply internalized the British stereotype of the desexualized Indian man? How had the figure of the priapic Black heterosexual male and the domesticated brown mother become so important to brown male immigrant time, space, sex, and success?

In wielding the Black phallus, my uncle revealed the psychic anxiety he faced with his phallic authority. His statement annexes the violence of his own brown phallus and replaces it with the prescriptive order of patriarchal and anti-Black colonial logics: the paradigm of the Black penis, subtracted from both the phallus (as organizer of self) and nothingness (its delusional plentitude).[10] Literally, in this moment, the Black penis and the brown vulva become objects of desire, demonization, and discipline, while the brown phallus is marginalized as active enabler or distant observer. Figuratively, both subjects—the Black rapist and the brown mother—are constructed as unsovereign, tawdry, and predictable. The latent grammar in this statement is that both figures are gluttonous animals that require ritual watching—one disciplined by the act of rape, the other commissioned for the sport of rape. His invocation of Black male sexuality as a violent, undomesticated commodity he could access to discipline his domesticated brown wife (also a commodity) effectively combines the resilience of anti-Black logic and misogyny to render primal the everyday dense "erotic life of racism."[11] To have admitted that the brown penis is as overdetermined by the West and whiteness would have involved him in a contradiction that his antiblackness and misogyny could not reconcile, could not abide. Conversely, the puzzle my aunt was left with was to reconcile the threat of rape as one that exists outside the patriarch (a myth, certainly in her life) and to aggregate the level of sexual insecurity her husband expressed around his always and already flaccid brown masculinity (erected only by White women). My uncle's sexual history with White women—before, during, and long after this comment—and his violent control of his brown wife (and other brown women, including my mother) reveals his own psychic desire to control his brownness through the acquisition of both the phallus and capital.

Brown male heterosexuality gains its discursive power through marking itself as *not Black* (just as it loses power by being marked as *brown*). The deployment of the pathological Black heterosexual and the nonpathological White mistress tightens the link between white supremacy and racialized heteronormativity, just as it absorbs the pain of Black and brown mothers, who live lives circumscribed by violence from every angle of White logic. This calculated threat operated as an intimate pedagogical moment for my aunt, effectively enacting the violence of (gang) rape without ever delivering on it, effectively cutting off the tongue of the brown mother (my aunt's and my mother's). His threat cunningly absents him from the sexual violence itself, even as we all knew my uncle was a man skilled in many violences, likely including raping his own wife. This was, after all, the same man who, shortly after they arrived in America, told my father that he would teach him how to hit a woman (a skill he thought my father lacked), and who told my mother soon after she married my father in Karachi that women are like bones: suck out what's good and then toss out the rest.

By the time I was a teenager, I already knew the world my family inhabited together demanded a certain violence, a certain control, a naked intimacy with brutality. Needless to say, I also learned that violence had many expressions. The history of whiteness hardened into my mother's life, and regardless of her knowledge of whiteness, she was not prepared for the bearing of whiteness, neither its Southern nor Northern iterations. Her desperation to leave Karachi and to come to America was shaped by the fact that she felt she was running out of ways to survive. But her arrival in the United States meant a physical departure and dispossession from and through the formation of a new home/land and where she discovered, in very specific ways, what James Baldwin called, "the weight of white people in the world."[12] She had moved from one colonial geography to another, initially from the Global South to the Global North, then from the whiteness of US Northerners to the whiteness of US Southerners—so most permanently from one South to another South. She observed quickly that both Souths were peopled with oppressed figures and that both Souths brought with them all sorts of betrayals, violences, erasures, alienations, dismissals, and lies.[13] But I would be lying if I didn't say that by this point, we had all created some fantasy with whiteness (and thus also with or against blackness) of which our desired ascendency wouldn't let us be robbed.

The peculiar quality of the suburbs in Cherry Hill, New Jersey, in the late 1970s, sweet and irritating, falsely leisurely, while intensely laborious, meant that my mother had to develop a sociality with whiteness that was unfamiliar, awkward, and ill-fitting. And even with a brown female majority, White supremacist brown patriarchy took up a cozy space in our home. Two men ruled the house, my father and my uncle, and both were men who loved white women and who, without consideration, bought them to our house to socialize over cheap whiskey, cards, cigarettes, and sex. Unfaithfulness, like violence, were ordinary occurrences of domestic life. But betrayal was further intensified when my father's white kids arrived to live with us, as in those moments the intimate transaction between mothering and race entered an uneven battle, one that was at once cultural, religious, national, and financial.

In the strange circumstances of life with and against whiteness and patriarchy, economic anxiety led my mother to hide money whenever she could get her hands on it. With dollar bills rolled up in old, frayed socks, my mother learned, over time, the craft of subterfuge. The men, characteristic of Global South economic styles, stockpiled cash at home for varying reasons, for *Jamatkhanna* donations (for the Philadelphia *Jamatkhanna* we attended every Friday), for poker games, for whores, and for long-term mistresses. *Cash was king*, my father would say, and my mother believed him completely. But just as these men controlled the wealth and hid the cash in bedroom drawers, they were careless and self-absorbed, and hid the neatly piled bills in plain sight and rarely counted it down to the dollar. It was not a long step to theft, as my mother's skilled furtivity and the men's injudiciousness merged into feminine opportunity. *One day*, she would whisper, as I watched her lick her fingers and focus her eyelids to the stack of cash on her lap, *we might need this*. Her theft lightened her burden.

One random January afternoon, my mother brought me upstairs with her. She had an instinct to count her money whenever she had a rare moment of privacy, and as the youngest always clinging to my mom, I excitedly knew that I was part of her secret. But that day, before we cocooned ourselves in the back of her closet to her secret stash, my mother noticed my father's drawer was ajar. Yanking it open, she saw that my father's money was gone. She turned to me immediately, whom did I tell about this money? No one. Never. This was our secret. I savored our secrets. I relished that I was secretly a part of something that was secretly part of her. I saw fear wash over her face. When we went downstairs to the living room, my uncle, my aunt, and their older children were immersed in the banality of American middle-class leisure, watching White and Black families on TV and laughing as though they belonged in the sphere of American cultural joy.

My father was outside smoking a cigarette. My mother gestured him to come into the kitchen. *Your drawer was open. Money is missing. I looked everywhere. Where could it be? Your boys, E., N., and R.?* My father's three teenagers had come to stay with us. *They had gone out in the morning, their voices confident, their pockets fat....* Her words were replaced with a thundering slap across her mouth. My father's thick gold ring with a large red ruby flashed back and forth. Her words collapsed into a gargle. His children would never steal from him. The red stone flashed back and forth again. Impossible. Again. The blood red stone now bouncing like a laser beam. How dare she? Red darted through the air. Her head jerked to the side. She swallowed more of her words.

My uncle entered the kitchen. When he saw what was causing the commotion, he nodded his head critically, coolly stating, *You don't even know how to hit a woman; let me show you.* With his characteristic malicious smile, my uncle opened and closed his palm to form a fist, performing his violence before laying the first punch. My father averted his head, and for a split second he looked away, as though suddenly tired from his patriarchal duties of disciplining women, earning money, sharing money, saving money, worrying about money. My mother had slid her hand out of mine at the first slap. But I stood there and watched them. I did not doubt for one second that these two things—loving and beating—were conjoined. I had learned early the secrets of beating these men who beat my mother and loved my mother. In the precocious way of children, I shared her stress and learned her doubleness; my understanding emulated the semiotic of our family before it had fully emerged.

But, for my mother, it was one thing to take an open-palm slapping from her husband and another thing altogether to take a closed-fist beating from her brother-in-law. In her eyes, he was the brute of the house, ruling all of us with his iron fist. My mother closed her eyes, anticipating the weight of her brother-in-law's heavy fist. But to his credit, my father, as though suddenly emerging from deep thought, stepped in and derailed his brother's swing. My mother limped away. The men went out for a cigarette. Hours later, a note was found. E., N., and R. had taken the money in the dresser drawer and had returned to their mother in Alpena, Michigan. My father's money was gone. And so were his White children.

....

suffer with me tonight . . . in my native hue . . .
—FRED MOTEN, *B. JENKINS*

My father's children returned to live with us sporadically through the 1980s and the 1990s. Each arrival was shaped (often) by either the threat of violence or the event itself. My mother was convinced they were untrustworthy. She had been set up to take the fall for their actions not once, not twice, not thrice, but time and time again. She was sure they held deep resentments toward her specifically and us children more generally (and to a certain extent, she fully understood the emotional ecologies of *why*). But, in those days, she didn't know the word *racism*, she would just say, *These kids don't like our color.* She was full of conspiracy theories. She was convinced that these children saw her as a domestic and domesticated fool. Her ease in the kitchen, her song-like tongue, her seamless brown femininity impressed in others that she was docile, dumb, defenseless—thus easy to take advantage of, to be made a fool. *Be careful*, she would warn me, her gaze always on the lookout. Theirs, she would caution, was a forked tongue, which I came to understand as different from what she called a sharp tongue. Forked tongues were duplicitous and disloyal, even if they were likable; they were disingenuous in their very loquaciousness, and loquacious these kids were.[14] Sharp tongues, conversely, were a feminine mode of survival; sharpening soft flesh was one way flesh and femininity could be (secretly) disobedient. *Meethi chori*, she called this, which translated as "sweet knife." The constant and concealed furtive practices that she developed were revealed only to a few. This for her, was a simple fact: there was a world of difference between duplicity and disobedience.

And so, with the arrival of the White children, she became more vigilant, cognizant, alert, peering out from the corner of her eye, making sure she didn't miss anything. Their difference was a threat. She didn't trust them, but she also pitied them: abandoned by their mother, only occasionally raised by their/my father, trained to hate brown people by their maternal family, yet themselves colored by their/my father—unclear borders, ambiguous belongings. Their own mother, my father's first wife, was never overtly mentioned, but it was an open secret that J., shortly after the birth of her fifth child and their divorce, lived much of her life institutionalized and that she eventually died painfully of uterine cancer.

Shortly after we had settled in Cherry Hill, my father received a letter from his oldest daughter saying that their mother had been checked into a psychiatric institution. Social Services had arrived at their home in Alpena and had called him, suggesting he take full custody of all five kids. But my father reasoned that J. wouldn't want to come to back to an empty house. So he took custody of three, the youngest son, one of the twin boys, and the oldest son. He thought his oldest daughter could care for her younger brother, neither of them alone nor J.'s house empty. After a few months, J. was released and convinced her sons to steal money from their father and return to her. That moment in which (their) theft was folded into violence (against my mother), in which she came to understand that violence in her life was sprawling and vast and included other male actors, tethered my mother even more seriously and secretively to her furtive maneuvers of survival.

In practicality, then, my mother had no control over when the children came to stay with us. My father made that decision and in a particularly methodical order. First, he would receive several mechanical letters from each of the kids requesting to visit. The letters, especially from his sons, were often just a few sentences, sometimes even just one sentence, repeated two or three times. The repetition of the letters and the poor writing would trigger my father's guilt at abandoning his kids. How could his English writing and speaking skills be better than that of his (White) children? He would respond by telling them to come as soon as their mother allowed. The letters came; my father arranged travel; my mother bartered time.

But truth be told, my father didn't always arrange travel; their mother didn't always grant permission; and my mother didn't always have time. Many times, the kids, sometimes collectively and other times individually, would hitchhike from Alpena to Atlanta, getting rides from random strangers to get away from a volatile and erratic mother and to come live with their estranged father. A loud knock on the door, and the sociality of my mother's home transmogrified. And once they arrived, it was clear that my father's residual anxiety at having lived through his marriage to J. and his liberal hunger for self-improvement would effectively motivate the firmness he took with my mother and the laissez-faire approach he took with them.

When the children came, they took over the house. They spoke loudly, laughed loudly, took up space loudly. Their comfort was her discomfort. Unlike her small frame and the smallness of her younger children, these children were big—big-boned, big-bodied, big-voiced, big-personalitied. So their sociality was her silence. But it was still my mother who dealt with their schedules, talked with them, advised them, and prepared food for them. She was generous, just as she was reserved and reluctant. These kids were dependent upon my mom's labor to consolidate and to support them and their relation to our brown immigrant world, which included everyday practices like food, prayer, trips to Kmart, thrift stores, *Jamatkhanna*, extended family, and the minute-by-minute language translation. To them, our culture was fun and funny—accessible, enjoyable, humorous, and easily forgotten. But if culture could be fetishized and enjoyed as a collection of objects (food, clothing, language), religion, conversely, was serious and inflexible, and in this, my father wanted his children completely inculcated. We prayed every evening as a family, sitting in a circle on the carpeted floor, Arabic prayers rolling off our tongues, undulating and inflecting in unison, hanging in the air, blessing—so said my father—our home. When my father's white children lived with us, they were expected to participate in this evening ritual; if their visit coincided with Ramadan, they were expected to fast; and when we went to the *Jamat-Khanna* on Fridays, they were expected to join. My father's expectations of religious commitment were nothing short of unrealistic, for us or for them. There were times they tried to resist my father's religions dogma—they were Christian, they said, not Muslim; white Americans, they said, not brown immigrants. On this, my mother commiserated with them. Through no fault of their own, they were awkward, self-conscious, tongue-tied, gauche. Their race privilege rested on the gesture of distancing themselves from his religious-racial identity. The paternal demand to *be* Muslim negatively interfaced with the loyalty they had to the father line. It produced a strain, a tension, an antagonism. This friction (with the father) meant a turning toward my mother, and in her, they would confide the complicated range of feelings, loyalties, confusions that suffused their experience in our home. Their disorientation demanded her (racialized/feminine) consolation. And in the space of that solace, perhaps they, too, came to care for her.

In these rare moments, my brother, sister, and I would stand outside the room when this happened, lined up against the faded cream wall of our middle-class suburban home, eavesdropping, the gulf between us and them exaggerated by the structure of a physical division and the secrets that appeared to be dispensed on the other side. What I could make out in the conversation was how my mother, despite her disaffection, was somehow sensitized to their emotions. I had repeatedly seen her disaffection, which I understood as an index of her ambivalence, her discomfort, her dissonance, her negativity. So when their affection loosened my mother in the way that love loosens the body, she tightened up, pushed back, gathered the three of us, and poured on us all the love the other children had let loose in her. She deliciously fussed over us, and we enjoyed every second of it. She saved her love for the three of us in a way that was electric.

I came to be fascinated with how my mother held onto the negativity of (their) whiteness. The ordinary ease with which she reiterated White as *other*, the casualness with which she dismantled the infinite specificity of whiteness was nothing short of mesmerizing.[15] I came to accept this as fact, even as this was disputed by my father and his family, for whom it was simply about the fact of patrilineality—or more simply, science. But my mother, accustomed to falling out of the brackets of legibility, was not interested in either the men or science. To her, these children were not her creation. They did not contain her history. Shared sperm did not make them siblings. She would search in vain for any reflection of herself and would return to herself empty, void of any connection, except the occasional pity, contoured by the fact of whiteness—the fact of their whiteness. Whiteness was not a detail to be passed over. Whiteness betrays. It controls. It unravels our cohesiveness. It is the outside/r that sees no b/order of entry. Whiteness can always come inside.

I have chosen to utilize and, to a certain extent, to reproduce my mother's account of these children as White (regardless of whether or not these children are White, or, for that matter, passable as White), in order to call attention to the ways whiteness was always a disturbing encounter that confronted my mother (and more broadly the brown maternal) with various modes of being incomplete, contradictory, and out of control. Her insistence on their whiteness, at the least, was an absolute evasion of the neat and rational logic of both the sacrosanct blood family and the ontological Law of the Father. For her, kin/blood/skin and being/feeling were always and already fragmented, incomplete, porous, penetrable, broken, veering out. These were as unpredictable as they were a necessary interpretive grid.

Constituted through her melancholic introjections, my mother's articulation of these children as White meant that whiteness was a crisis-intensified intimacy in her (thus my) life, both metaphorically and literally intertwined in her everyday, fragmenting her mothering, distorting her intimacies, softening the patriarchal injunction with racist forces. Neither "master" nor "disavowal" are adequate names for the affective work my mother did (and taught us to do) around whiteness. Her shifting allegiances for and against whiteness and Americanness are fascinating to me because of how they sustained her and her critical practices of and with survival. Pragmatically, these relations were shaped simultaneously by the hyperpresence of whiteness and by the calm, but ominous, absence of whiteness (because whiteness is never truly absent). This was a material relation that was always disjointed; one minute these children were fully her responsibility, taking up and taking over space around her and us, and the next they were off in their White mother's world—and months, sometimes a year, would pass without a single word. I think now of how these children's differences structured my mother's compulsion to see them as White and how that then dramatized a whole host of relations and affects.

The governing logics hailed by society and my father certainly beg us to understand these children as mixed race. But constituted as she was through displacements, exclusions, and erasures, my mother had a contradictory relationship to these rationalizing forces. She found reason futile at most times, and at other times, more a myth than myth itself (reason as a mythical undertaking). She was much more interested in feeling and gut, perception and insight, the body and flesh. So, in refusing them race (where race is always the *other* of whiteness), I came to see my mother's affective negation of their brownness as an un/conscious challenge to dominant articulations of patri-lineality and biochromatic racial and familial rationalizations. If, for most, their problem was that they had a brown father, for my mother, their (real) problem was that they had a White mother.

Of course, for my mother, naming the kids as White was pejorative, just as it was a way of naming them as outside of her inside/s. That everyone wrestled her on this conviction only further convinced her that she was right. Naming their whiteness over and over, she discovered a way of changing their relation to us and to her. If science and logic were establishing their patrilinear brown-ness, my mother was searching for another world, a world of mother-right. Her refusal to use their whiteness as a means to get closer to the "happy object" of White adjacency and assimilation, alongside her routinized refusal to see patrilineality as racial enclosure/inclusion, led to consequences.[16] Conversely, these kids never failed to broadcast their whiteness, which was also tied up with their American-ness. My mother saw them as clannish and bitter, carry-ing on, showing off, speed-talking in English. They spared no detail, reveling in the fine points that made them legible subjects outside of (our) race and into the American nation, setting aside their brown hair and sandpaper skin.

By 1986, my father's twin sons. N. and L., had enlisted in the US military. Both sons had taken on a love of country, uniform, and guns. One might argue that this was an inevitable horizon for them. It was what they under-stood. The White working-class Northern ethos of their maternal family had instilled a deep nationalist loyalty, one that lined up with their muscular sub-jectivities, despite the brown immigrant sociality to which they were also ir-regularly tethered. My father had realized that of his first five children, not a one was interested in college, and thus he proudly accepted their enlistment as a bootstraps effort to build a quality adult life. My mother, suspicious and ambivalent about masculinity and militarized patriotism, came to realize that even as adults, the patriarchal-colonial tableau of the whiteness of her hus-band's children, his sons in particular, would continue to suffuse her home.

Shortly after N.'s enlistment, he came to visit us in full military attire. I was ten. My mother served my father and his now-grown son, as they both indulged each other in the romance of a father-son catch up. My mother was listening in on their conversation, her ear to the wall, her finger pressed against her lips, shushing me, her eyes wide with focus. She heard N. bragging about guns he had in his possession. My father raised his eyebrow but appeared mostly unfazed by this comment. But my mother knew better. While N. con-tinued to entertain my father with patriotic stories, my mother called me to the top of the stairs and told me to stand watch. I could see her as she opened his luggage, moved around his clothes, and found two guns—a small pistol and another one, a little larger, more elaborate, and complicated-looking. She hesitated, her face filled with dread, her eyes scheming. She could hear the men still talking. Finally, she walked over to the bathroom garbage can and threw both guns in the trash. She then went into her own bathroom, returned with her trashcan, and emptied it in the trashcan with the guns, now covered in toilet tissue and other waste. As she walked away from the now-overflowing trashcan, power, like agency, gathered in her. The sight of his guns and his cavalier boasting about them triggered for my mother a litany of violences, from the India-Pakistan Partition to the Bangladesh Liberation War to the militarization of Karachi streets under Zia's regime in the early 1980s to her younger brother-in-law's love of guns to every evening news channel documenting American men's right to guns. Her brown femininity formed in relation to this masculine militarization and phallic nation making. Disposing of the guns, if for only a short moment, infused in her a sense of control and confidence.

It was early evening when N. discovered that his suitcase had been tampered with. He came flying down the stairs, red-faced, eyes-bulging, veins popping, exploding with rage. He stood in front of my mother in his military uniform, shouting until his voice gave out, words like *fool, illiterate, dumb immigrant, and stupid woman* sputtering off his tongue. His red face against his White skin and greenish-brown uniform literalized my mother's warnings, moving terror from feminine paranoia to material event. She received his words in stone silence. When N. stopped to take a breath, my mother quickly put the three of us in the car, drove to a nearby McDonald's, where we sat outside at a curved table in the play area. My mother's stare was blank, and her hands shook, as she held a Styrofoam cup. We had sat at many McDonalds during our American childhood. It was cheap and had a play area, where we galloped around, easily pleased by the bright yellow-and-red colors, the dusty slides, the company of carefree children, oblivious to the bleak look in everyone's eyes, or our own. The bright colors reflected in her eyes; they glazed over. Her head throbbed. Feelings of rebellion stirred and subsided. The fantasy of departure could not hold. She had no money, no papers, only a driver's license, no family that wasn't also an in-law. She was completely and utterly reliant on my father. Without him, we had nothing.

When we returned home, my father and N. were still sitting in the living room. N. immediately broke into raucous laughter, gesturing, of course, to my mother's stupidity (*who throws guns away?*), because, of course, he had found them, and, of course, what belonged in the trash were not his guns but her meek attempt at authority. My father, eager to please his now soldier-son, awkwardly joined N. But as he opened his mouth to laugh, all that he could muster was big open-mouth exaggerated smile. The image of my father's failed laughter, my mother turning her back on the men, and the three of us holding onto some part of her body emblematized multiple and complex failures. N.'s militarized posture, my father's artificially engineered joy, their masculine solidarity, and my mother's feminine resignation symbolized the inheritance of the historical violence of whiteness. It revealed how the hydraulics of whiteness and masculinity imposed themselves on every scale of abstraction. I could interpret the very failure of my father's laughter, or his failure to deliver laughter to his son, as perhaps his own woundedness, his own ambivalence with the White nationalized Americanness of his children. Over the years, the letters from his children got longer, more detailed, pages and pages relating to their father what he was missing from their lives, what they were missing about his life. How many hours and years did he spend trying to reconcile the impossible, both his absence and their presence?

When I think back on that time, I realize that my mother ultimately conditioned us toward a servile identification, to better play the role of both less than and greater than. When I would point this out to my mother, she always responded by saying, *When you live in the ocean, you can't make enemies with the sharks.* Whiteness's capacity to inure her to pain by virtue of its materiality, its almost theatrical power, and its uncertain proximity as kin resulted in a precariousness of empathy. She had to live with it, even take care of it, just as she was cautious, watchful, weary, and paranoid. If the particularity of hurt as a racialized, sexualized, and gendered phenomenon is a historical inheritance, to recall Frederic Jameson's "history is what hurts," then my mother's intuitive saying on living in the ocean with the sharks is the work of history visceralized through the personal.[17] She marked whiteness in each "hurt," specifically in each of my father's children, and that marking served as a means to simultaneously contain the attempted hegemony in her life and to resist the heterogeneous forms of disembodied whiteness (my father's investment in his White children). The uncertain line between them (as White children) and her (as brown mother) animated a history which refused to disappear.

The aesthetic, economic, sexual, and racial forces of whiteness that tightened the varying links of subordination in her life could not be unhinged from the intimacies of whiteness in her home. And her strategic and symbolic efforts to dismantle whiteness from its iconic status were a far cry from the geopolitical power for which whiteness stands. Paying attention to the regimes of her everyday life meant acknowledging the routine reminders of her subordination. My mother's impulse to see and to articulate her husband's children as White was a reaction to that abjection. If whiteness is what catches you and catches up with you, then whiteness is always and already related to the possibility of violence and the instrumentality of a racial landscape; to learn this is not the same as racial violence.

This instance of N.'s guns, arrogance, rage, and laughter in our living room is, of course, full of contradictions. When my mother recounts this moment, she comes down neither on the side of the loyalty she enacts nor on that of the racial/gender essentialism she reproduces. Instead, she traverses what she conceives of as the impossible space of the brown maternal when it interfaces with race, power, violence, and masculinity. The symbolic power that penetrated our home when my father's White children were in it was enough to make my mother cautious, tepid, strategic (but not weak or powerless or stupid, as she was often interpreted). My father, conversely, focused on the individuality of his White children. For him, his White children's likeability was enamoring; they were witty, confident, interesting, and enjoyable (even if a little too loud and rambunctious). That these children could be likeable was not relevant to my mother. She saw (White) likeability as one style of White defense. For her, their likeability doubled down on the order of difference that it intended to transcend. It made them whiter. Even as she was tasked with lubricating their emotional and social world, her language and their language was incommensurate, like translation, always a failure waiting to be revealed. For her, there was only the impossibility of intersubjectivity, unavailable either through the color reductionism, white mimicry, or a happy multiculturalism.

Their whiteness was, of course, a fiction of that which they would never be, sullied by the stain of my father's brownness. That my father's children became White in relation to my mother then reveals something about the political significance of the mother. Fatherhood is perceived as the legitimate procedure of cultural inheritance (except of course in feminist scholarship, which routinely sides with the mother). The rationalizing forces of patriarchy, capitalism, and colonialism all centralize and solidify the figure of the father, the father's name, the father's law: the father as the legitimate progenitor and producer of relations. Socialized in this structure of legitimacy, my mother should have subscribed to the (bi) raciality of these children. But instead she was protective of the maternal (both hers and others), and thus brought to bear another gamble, the heritage of the mother.

For my mother, the "whiteness" of her husband's children had an equivalent in the categorical essentialism that sees the mother as an end in herself. But my mother took a phantasmic leap beyond the failure of essentialism to the peculiar and actual position of mothers of color. She refused to parse the racial details of these children. She adjudicated (to us and to anyone who would listen) the firmness of whiteness, overruling its elasticity, overturning its disciplinary mechanisms, and tightening its borders against the logics of assimilation, adjacency, ascendency. She could not and would not dematerialize these children from their mother. The mother for her was, as Laura Doyle has written, the "maker and marker of boundaries."[18] I think about my mother's insistence on the whiteness of these kids as an unavoidable anticipation, a passionate utterance against the doubleness of possession, that response to the fraught moment of motherhood and the race of her children. In this way, I saw my mother as refusing the patronymic, patrifocal, patrilinear and patriarchal b/order that would have codified these children as half-brown. Hers was a matrilinear view that functioned as an act of disobedience: it erased the father. And in so doing, my mother symbolically returned these children to their (White) mother, and such a hermeneutic, one that centers mothers of color, inevitably also re/values the white mother. For my mother, the maternal realm was the essence of the material realm. I learned through this that my mother's mark, not my father's, determined my fate. No amount of talk of fathers could suture the wound of brute facts. To me, for me, the patronymic became an empty category, a blank parody. I belonged solely to my mother.

....

I wondered if whiteness were contagious.
If it were, then surely I had caught it.
—DANZY SENZA, *CAUCASIA*

The structures of discontinuity embedded in the threat of whiteness visceralized for my mother a collection of negativities. Her ontic modality to be present in the world while stealing herself into slow unnoticeability was most difficult (and most essential) when my father's children were around. Her experience with raising these White children was so routinely degrading and required so much extra labor that it amplified her brownness in an already intensely racist order. She felt her brownness tumbling around in an eddy of meanings and symbols and affects, whispering, hissing, cursing, shushing, sighing, making, and unmaking her. Being a brown undocumented mother brought her closer to, not further away from, the kinds of despised subjects who continually face devastation and death as a result of their abject status. Motherhood like, other forms of abjection, made her (more) vulnerable. But motherhood was what she had and what she knew and where her power lay, just as it also was a patriarchal trap that presumed the universal mothering potential of women. The violence of disappointment was inevitable. So, too, was a reckoning.

What emerged, then, was a deeper unconscious practice of cloaking power-lessness in stories, metaphors, silence, and lies. And so my mother became a liar over time. It was but one "among a variety of the depressing options in the cornucopia of absolutist thinking about race and ethnicity."[19] Her everyday life and labor is inseparable from her experience of violence. Patrolling her affect around whiteness and masculinity felt like a second skin. In this revised frame, a certain stillness took over my mother—a stillness made visible by a repertoire of implements, from the fantastic and marginal to the actual and material that splintered both herself and her perception of and by others. This furtivity had a double, self-consumptive edge—the pathological drive of the pathologist. The deployment of herself is also the deployment of her brown-ness. Her internalization of White superiority is a violent and cruel rerouting—a rerouting that is almost anything but spontaneous. A long slow motion of improvisation, hers was a movement toward slow life and slow death. Long and slow, but over the years, it acquires alacrity, efficacy, and a silky fatalism. It entered every room with her. It shaped her silence and contoured her speech. It stiffened her body and loosened her tongue.

I saw this mastered improvisation that brought sense to senselessness, this lyrical lie that applied cohesion to chaos, manifest one day: thirty-eight years after arriving in the United States, the summer of 2015, when my mother first met my White Southern butch lover's parents, in a meeting my lover and I had naively orchestrated after moving into our new home. Leaning on her cane, my mother walked into our new home, where my lover's parents, S. and G., were already sitting at the dining table. She looked at them in dis-dain, a slightly grotesque look on her face. She's miserable in the company of whiteness that has produced a gender nonconforming body, which is how she sees Erin's parents. This misery cognition recognizes only that which is familiar, familial—intimate oppressions and intimate violences. She has pro-duced a whole cluster of affects magnetized to whiteness. I see them register on her face—the visibility of whiteness (or the lack thereof); the "emptiness" of whiteness; whiteness as a structural privilege; whiteness as a harbinger of violence; whiteness as a site of colonization. This working-class White queer Southern-ness—itself a form of fugitive living—produced in my mother an extramoral obligation that she meets with eagerness. She is either inferior, or she is superior. Her frames are limited. She has completely internalized this hierarchy. In this moment, she held out for superiority, exploiting this false ideological invitation, basking in its glory. I could see it in her eyes: the thrill of destroying what destroys you.

The antidote to whiteness was postcolonial class. Provoked by the incommunicability of racial and sexual difference, my mother leaned on her leverage. She spoke only once, proudly sharing the high levels of education her children have accomplished, a soft jab at my lover, who had dropped out of college after she lost her softball scholarship because of an injury. I felt Erin's hurt across the table. But Erin's mother, despite my mother's spite, was loquacious. Her gregariousness offered up a communicability that my mother does not see, does not hear. My mother was mute. She just heard the noise of talk, white noise. Conversely, Erin's mother could not hear my mother's silence. A certain fragility emerged, a certain limit, and an uncertain position. Whiteness abounding, insecurity enveloped my mother. She retaliated with cultural capital. She's vicious and judgmental—an elite Karachiite looking disdainfully at the White American working-class couple in her educated brown daughter's living room. S.'s sticky-sweet Southern tongue offers no consolation. My mother doesn't know this tongue. Its unreserved drawl reserves my mother's tongue. She has no speech here, except to repeat how educated her children are. Her pride spilled out, over and against Erin and her parents. She was immodest and gratified, completely, and utterly pleased with herself. She had raised better White children than the White woman sitting across from her.

3

promiscuous tongues

I can't say anything but lies.
—JEAN GENET, *FRAGMENTS OF THE ARTWORK*

When my mother was ten years old, her family moved to Peshawar, where they lived in a large estate house, formerly one of the residences of the English. Close to the Afghanistan border, my mother describes Peshawar as a devout Muslim city, rural, religious, and conservative. It was 1956. Shortly after the move, my mother got her first period, which, in 1950s Northwest Pakistan, brought with it the expectation of wearing the burqa. Careless and carefree, however, she often forgot to oblige, and since they had arrived from the urban center of Karachi and were only loosely religious (so loosely as to not be), no one in her family really enforced it. Their driver, however, a sweet Peshawari man in his forties, was uncomfortable with my mother's noticeable preadolescent femininity and with my grandmother's laissez-faire approach to covering, and he began keeping a collection of burqas in the car for the forgetful young Karachi girls. *This was not Karachi*, he would gently remind my mother and her older sister.

One day, the driver arrived at their home with a young teenage girl. Offering a rushed and blunt explanation, he introduced thirteen-year-old Jamila, whom he called "ugly and unmarriageable." She was the only daughter in her family and desperately needed work. After this explanation, he awkwardly scurried off, leaving Jamila at the doorstep. My grandmother, who believed the right age for marriage was significantly older than thirteen and with an eye toward preserving this young girl's respectability, told Jamila to grab her bag and move in. She would help around the house and stay in the room with the girls.

My mother quickly came to be infatuated with Jamila. As my mother describes her, she was tall for her age, had light-brown coloring, thick braided hair, a quiet face with dark spots from old and new acne, and deep, large eyes. Bewildered by the description of her as ugly and unmarriageable, my mother conversely thought Jamila lovely and companionable. The girls quickly became fast friends. Each day, when she returned home from school, my mother, normally disdainful of housework, enthusiastically joined Jamila in her household chores. Jamila, too, would strategically save the collaborative work, such as folding laundry or making *rotis* for the afternoon so that the two girls could work together. Meanwhile, in every passing minute she spent with Jamila, my mother's intimacy intensified, and she began working up the courage to confess her own small, controversial secret.

Jamila had been with their family for four months when my mother decided she could no longer hold in her secret. Both girls were folding clothes in the bedroom. The air heavy with trepidation, my mother reached over and hugged Jamila. The girls had a friendly and affectionate friendship, so Jamila returned the hug, kissed my mother on the cheek, and then turned back to the clothes. My mother further implored her, hesitant, childlike, curious. Her affection was growing toward Jamila, whose body my mother intriguingly saw as more womanly than her own. She kissed Jamila on her lips. Affection for my mother softened Jamila's reaction, and for a moment, the girls lingered in not one, not two, but three warm, secret, shameful, and delicious kisses. The rumblings of desire brewed slowly, but never materialized. Jamila's sense/s quickly shifted. She recoiled. Seething, shocked, she declared this was wrong, a sin, against Islam and despite my mother's stammering shame-filled pleas for forgiveness, Jamila stated that she would have to tell her mother. The warmth between the girls had gone cold. Filled with fear, my mother watched Jamila leave the room and head toward the kitchen. In a moment of quick impulse, my mother rushed back to her mother before Jamila could and with an absolutely straight face told her that Jamila *tried to touch her*. As quickly as the words came out of my mother's mouth, she regretted them. But it was too late. Jamila was immediately rushed out of the house and sent back to her family. Jamila begged my grandmother to not make her leave, saying that she desperately needed this work, that she didn't do anything, that she was the only person working in her family. But my grandmother, filled with the anxiety my mother had planted, sat Jamila in the back seat of the car and ordered the driver to take her back. The damage had been done. My grandmother and mother never spoke of Jamila again. No men were brought into this secret. But my mother, who later in life would become a stellar liar, had at the age of ten, told her first and most damaging lie and *ruined*, as she tells it now, Jamila's life and future forever.

Six decades later, this story achieved, as many of my mother's stories do, mythic and mystic proportions. I was sitting with my mother, and we were discussing the concept of *nazar*, which loosely translates as "gaze" and which is often used as the Urdu shorthand for the concept of the *evil eye*. My mother's belief in the *evil eye* is greater than any other of her religious or spiritual beliefs. To her, the evil eye, *nazar lag jayegi*, is both a powerful otherworldly force and one that can produce intergenerational inheritance, such as *lein dein*, another complicated Urdu expression that also alludes to inheritance. It must be deterred. Her advice on that day was directed at me and how she thought the way I dressed (and allowed my teenaged daughter to dress) would attract, not deter, the *evil eye*. We were deep in conversation, or rather debate, about what she perceived as my (and my then-teen daughter's) slutty clothing, her warnings against promiscuous clothing and promiscuous behavior on repeat, warning, always warning, about drawing attention to our bodies, our femininities. But she said, taking a small detour, sometimes, in rare moments, the *nazar* cannot be deterred; it is instead deserved; it is what you get for what you do. She began recounting this story, full of pith and moment: a childhood crush, a shared erotic moment, a moral rejection, an intense fear, all crusted over by a single but treacherous lie. By her own description, she was not innocent. She tells me, *It never occurred to me that Jamila might not be able to get work after that; that in the smallness of 1950s Peshawar, news of Jamila as (sexual) trouble would spread swiftly; that my mother, who was much more tender than any of the other women and the men in my family, would throw Jamila out. I never saw Jamila again. When you told me you are lesbian, it confirmed what I have always known about what happened between me and Jamila. I knew she had cursed me, given me the* nazar *and rightly so. I twisted her rejection of my desire into a false accusation that ruined Jamila's life, and Jamila cursed my blood with the lineage of lesbianism.*

Sixty years after my mother and Jamila kissed and my mother grafted a lie onto Jamila's character that resulted in, at a minimum, her losing her job, she became the figure through whom the crime of lesbianism was established in our blood. Jamila's fading silhouette became the placeholder for my lesbianism, the cause and punishment of my mother's wayward desire now running through my lesbian body. The pain and yearning inherent in my mother's desire and the shame of how Jamila was punished because of her outright lie moved my mother's understanding of lesbian sexuality from the material (desire as bodily) to the metaphorical (desire as symbol) to the mythic (desire as curse). For my mother, desire became something to bear, and the difficulty of bearing desire meant subsuming it to a deep interiority, unconnected to an outside, an exteriority. My mother's destructive lie was an antidote to her fear, and the bitter taste of both still scoured her tongue. Her desire for Jamila disturbed the order of things, her sexual dis/orientation produced social re/orientation. She had to make her desire, thus Jamila, strange.

This episode—particular and peculiar to the postcolonial Muslim, South Asian caste-class context—was one that, even with so much geographic, temporal, and psychic distance, insinuated itself into the composure of my mother's im/modern motherhood; her memory of her lie/hurt/destruction of a working-class girl became the narrative frame for my lesbianism. My mother's conviction of my lesbianism as a curse from a working-class girl whom she desired and subsequently (economically and possibly in other unknown ways) injured, and my subsequent living out of my lesbianism, perpetually expanded and enfolded her wound, rewound time and exhausted the modern idea of redress and subject formation.

Sara Ahmed once wrote, "Being a girl that wanted a girl troubled my mother, and the designation girl was already trouble. If women are already trouble, being a lesbian troubles trouble; double trouble, or at least, more trouble."[1] So the best outlet for the trouble of desire, for the stickiness of memory, for the fleeting moment of lesbianism, is mysticism. Held together by longing, fear, betrayal, disappointment, secrets, and lies, my mother layered her non-innocence with the mysticism of magic and blood, and, in so doing, she literalized class precarity as having the power to contaminate her/our maternal line. I realized in my mother's shamed retelling of this story that lesbian desire is the spectral presence at work in my mother's archive. Lesbian desire as apparitional, melancholic, mythopoetical. The notion of pernicious feminine desire held and moved with a rhythm, lucid and obscure, pastoral and futural, an inevitable lie and an archived haunting that could not be transcended. I think my mother's recourse to magic and to blood is a means to name and understand my lesbianism as both anathema and inevitable, intimate, and strange, foreign and familial. My mother's guilt and sorrow at hurting Jamila transmogrified class suffering and sexual deviance into magic, a kind of witchery, into a "touch across time."[2] Her matter-of-fact statement—*You are a lesbian because Jamila cursed me; her curse avenged my injury to her by transforming my lesbian desire for her into my daughter's lesbian inheritance.* Desire as inheritance. Desire transferred through time. Desire stolen across time. I now think of Jamila as my lesbian ghost. My mother's first crush. My mother's first destruction. Maybe she told me this story to heal. Maybe I excavated a wound. Maybe I am the wound.

....

It is difficult to narrate stories about sex in my mother's life because sex was both open and taboo, both a singularity and a multiplicity, the underbelly and the arc, the haunting and the subject. Such ubiquity meant that trying to parse out stories that were about sex exclusively was an impossibility. Yet as a young girl, and now, as a feminist theorist, I was and continue to be fascinated by my mother's relation to sex, her own mishmash, hodgepodge version of Freud's fort-da, fort-da.[3]

For my mother, sex was everywhere. Her eyes always undressed women, skimming their bodies, their hips, their mouths, their curves, their skin. She wasn't particularly subtle about it either. She looked without apology. She stared without hesitation. She gazed lingeringly, to the embarrassment of others. She smiled at women as though she knew their secrets. She looked at their bodies with deep approval, or, conversely, with terrible disdain. She damned women with her eyes. She caressed them with her gaze. I saw this my whole life. There was no neutral ground but a multiplicity of grids. Her frames for sex, unlike her frames for whiteness and masculinity, were ubiquitous, voluptuous, promiscuous. A bra strap, a pouring cleavage, an exposed back, a curved hip, a rounded ass always caught her eye. She didn't care much for legs, although a thigh would definitely catch her attention. A mischief would glaze over her eyes when she engaged such women. If the relation was intimate enough, she would look with slight reprimand, followed by a gentle pleased smile, and she would toss a nearby shawl over the exposed body part. This interplay of curiosity and connection, of approval and warning, of enticement and containment, of compliance and defiance fascinated me, confused me, empowered me. This sexuality—with its promiscuous web of salaciousness and secrets and structures and speech acts—is the centerpiece of this chapter.

My mother had a promiscuous tongue, overtelling overtold stories, in different, uncomfortable ways, making people feel ill at ease, causing awkward expressions, inspiring nausea, forcing unease. Her tongue was not one that could not be placated; it was volatile, unpredictable, and untimely. A single and unrelated question could lead to a cascade of unpleasant words strung together as a memory or a story, rolling rapidly and fatally off her tongue. The story of Jamila, for example, emerged not in the context of any direct discussion on sexuality, mine, or hers, or even in the context of this book or her childhood. Instead, her masochistic detour into Jamila emerged out of a reprimand on what she perceived as my revealing clothing and then slipped into a field of desire, punishment, and witchery.

For my mother, memory, sexuality, and morality are infinitely spinning together, what Julia Kristeva might refer to as "a fragile net stretched out over an abyss of incompatibilities, rejections, and abjections."[4] Sex, she tells me, is at best, a nuisance, a chore, but more often, it is worse: it is a loss, a trauma, a melancholy. Her disdainful, antagonistic relation to sex is not new to me. My mother tells stories about sex with an intensity and primarily through tropes, riddles, jokes, figures of speech, and metaphors, all of which are saturated with voluptuous materialities of abjection, shame, and humiliation. Sex is present, distant, enigmatic, banal, sublime, alluring, aversive; too much, too little, incoherent, and sensible. Sexuality endures, in her speech, as an irresolvable loss, what Anjali Arondhekar frames as a "poetics of melancholia."[5] These multiple vernaculars of desire and melancholia, suspicion and superstition, perception and paranoia, cleave my mother's tongue.

Like a pouring cleavage, her tongue was excessive, uncontainable, fleshy, embarrassing, and inconvenient. It forced those around her to sit in the miserable company of misogyny, class violence, the cruddy, the distasteful, and the dead; her tongue laid bare a kind of slowed, less spectacular mode of necropolitics. Men, of course, were her favorite subjects to make uncomfortable, but really anyone who valued reason and civility and optimism were deflowered by her tongue. Within the general atmosphere of brown immigrant precarity and the specific context of a model minority optimism and assimilation, my mother's tongue came to be characterized, at best, as "women's idle talk," and at worst, as anxious speech, negative speech, mad speech. Those in the company of her razing tongue would try to rid themselves of this unease and to restore, in some way, a mastery of self. But the promiscuity of her tongue prevailed. They couldn't walk away. She had done the work of killing their joy, as Sara Ahmed might say, or to paraphrase Tillie Olsen, of pouring vinegar on their honey.[6] Thus, one of the key tasks in taking on my mother's speech acts is to ask very directly: What (about them) made people in my family but really any listener (of whom there were many) so uncomfortable, and consequently, what are the stakes of writing from this uncomfortable margin, this discomfort zone?

I must confess that the words my mother used would have burned any self-respecting middle-class person's tongues clean off. Words like *randi* (whore), *churail* (witch), *visya* (whore), *chuth* (pussy), *bharwa*, (pimp), as well as linguistic figurations like *giriwi aurat* (fallen woman), *bahenchod* (sister fucker), *maderchod* (motherfucker), and *bosrini* (a whore's pussy or a stretched pussy), were everyday grammars, even as they each conjured violence against the feminine, feminine desire, feminine bodies. She (and other mothers) used these words promiscuously, masochistically, gesturing to the fact that her words had an orientation to pain, suffering, and the sexual abject, which was or, over time, became pleasurable and enjoyable.

This style of speech, I came to understand, was both radical gesture ("everything/one is suspect") and a tense parasitic enactment of and on her social and sexual world. Thus, if paranoia closed her (stories) in, I promiscuously open her (speech) up. By "promiscuously," I mean speaking with an intense orientation toward the body and the erotic and its attenuations of affect and abjection. I see promiscuity as constituting a way of centering the erotic in its multiple valences and as having philosophical value to exposing erotic nodes of connection, to understanding sex as a site of loss, suspicion, pleasure, and melancholia. My mother's assemblage of memories and her speculative history demands from me this promiscuity, this intense pull toward the inside of her affective and erotic economies. Her sensational and sweeping assessment of my lesbianism as a curse on her maternal line, thus on me, from a working-class girl on whom she had a crush and whom she subsequently got fired gestures to a sort of promiscuous thinking and speaking—a mode of speech and thought that tracks a series of contradictory desires, power relations, sexual complicities, and erotic thefts. To get at this promiscuity, I turn toward the queerness and the brownness of my mother's tongues, where both signify excess, sensuality, flesh, and feeling.

While I understand that promiscuity is primarily posited as a formation akin to sexuality and while I have stakes in this kinship, I want to also add another register, that of the promiscuity of speech, of precarity, and of passivity. My mother's original story on the tongue, for example, gestures toward this promiscuity, a maximal, fleshy, capricious theorizing—naked, erotic, affective, and unabashed. It is a story that resists the imperative of singularity, to one or the other binary, and is instead multifarious, unstable, and moving, just as it is intimate, erotic, promiscuous, and shameless. But just as this story centers sex and flesh, it also signals precarity and passivity. In this story, the tongue is precarious in that it is structured into its submission, and, as such, it produces and sustains sociality through taking everyday risks. In this way the tongue, too, signifies a site of passivity, as it has to remain in its material conditions, confined by the mouth, by the teeth, carefully, slowly, finding its way into speech. The tongue's passivity (to the mouth) and precarity (in the mouth) are certainly symbolic of oppression, but they are also the sites through which tongues enact a critical ethos (to speak) and labor (to move about). If precariousness is a condition of life that threatens it with death and if promiscuity is the capricious and senseless multiplication of sex and the erotic, then both are central to understanding my mother's tongues. Indeed, my mother's language, her medium of thought and ideological calculation, was always and already multiple, moving from literalism to allegory with every breath and orienting toward different affective interests—a tongue that could not be subdued. It was through these subversive speech acts that my mother developed her sharp tongue, while also beginning to formulate, fragment by tiny fragment, the disobedience that decades later would serve, not her, but me.

In this way, like my mother's promiscuous tongue, this chapter is a promiscuous archiving of her tongue that excessively, incessantly, unapologetically keeps the company of her speech. I spend this chapter following my mother's utterances and the certain kind of work these words did. I open up her old/er utterances to search for newer meaning, to expose what was subjugated in its hegemonic articulation, in its hegemonic circulation. I read my mother's speech acts slowly and closely, as a way into her history, dedicating a chapter to words she strung together to make meaning of life. To be clear, my mother opposed promiscuity root to branch, but it was in and through this entrenched opposition that she framed every conversation, story, thought, idea, memory. So in order to read promiscuously, I "do things" with my mother's words. My interpretive actions and analysis are a public act, for like promiscuity, there is no privacy to this *doing*. All promiscuities, even private ones, live in fear of being revealed and thus, reviled. I pull my mother out of her privacy, pretending all the while that a chapter on sex and the erotic is not an intrusion, not a grasp at her heart and body, not a desire to be close to whatever she was close to.

Four Speech Acts

....

*They talked and laughed loudly and
slapped each other on the back and had
developed a language all their own*
—BESSIE HEAD, *LIFE*

One

There is a joke that circulated among the women in my family. It was re-
cited often, over tea and food, in bedrooms where the women sat in long,
maxi nighties, in living rooms when they thought nobody was listening, at
weddings, engagements, baby showers, dinner parties, Eid parties, and even
inside the prayer hall of the mosque. There were actually many jokes, many
if not all dirty jokes, that had the women wildly laughing, wiping tears from
their eyes as they continued cackling, and joyfully high-fiving one another.
One after the other, the women would share these jokes, each one more satisfying than the previous. But there was one that was a group favorite. It goes
something like this:

A young man returns to his small rural town from the big city to marry.
He wants to marry an innocent, virgin girl, he says, since all the city
girls are loose and promiscuous. To his delight, his marriage is quickly
and smoothly arranged with a young woman—doe-eyed, fair skinned,
virginal. On their wedding night, the young man, excited to teach his
innocent wife the activity of sex, pulls out his penis and asks her, "What
do you think this is?" The young wife takes a long look and responds in
a songlike, innocent voice, "That? That is a mouse." The young groom
laughs at her innocence, correcting her gently, "No, no, darling, this is
called a penis." The bride again looks at his penis, and responds, "No,
no, that is a mouse." Agitated, but still gentle, the groom repeats, "No,
sweetheart, this is my penis." But the young bride keeps repeating, singsong, childlike, "That is mouse, that is a mouse, that is a. . . ." Finally,
the groom, frustrated at his bride's refusal to respond to his arousal and
at her childlike, singsong reference to his penis as a mouse, demands
to know why she insists on this reference. The virginal bride responds,
"What my uncle had was a penis, yours . . . yours is a mouse."

It was much later in life that I learned not to repeat this joke to feminist crowds. When I recounted this joke to select feminist and queer friends, they would curiously follow the body of the joke, only to look at me humorlessly at the punchline, often with a disapproving nod or a look of disgust. The joke's condensation and displacement, its implications and obscene underbelly, its use of metaphor and metonymy, its entire machinery, was not meant for particular audiences. In the hierarchy of speech genres, the joke certainly holds a low place, and a joke like this, even lower. It might be worth turning to Freud and his treatise on jokes, specifically the dirty joke and its many double entendres, but Freud, regardless of his provocative discussion on the processes of humor, never had female laughers in mind.[7] So what was it about this joke that had these brown mothers (and indeed it was the mothers and not the young unmarried or newly married aunts or older cousins) falling over in pleasure, a pleasure that couldn't be replicated in other audiences?

The slapstick sexuality of naming the husband's penis a *mouse* and doing so in a sweet singsong voice that is meant to emulate her not-yet-woman-girl-like status simultaneously produces the crisis of the joke, just as it holds together the groom's image of his bride's innocence. Indeed, the bride's smiling, singsong sweetness comes to enable the groom's participation in his own humiliation. The syntagma "that is a mouse" is the performative refrain of the joke. The zinger, of course, is that she knows the entire time what a penis is. But what's ghosted from the punch line (just as it is exposed) is the crisis of incestuous rape, the likelihood that the young woman's sexual knowledge was acquired in conditions not shaped by her consent. That her uncle had already fucked her with a penis that was not small, limp, timid, meek, timorous, shrinking, or *like a mouse*—uncovers the secret of family sexual violence, just as it also provides an escape valve that separates us from the fatality of that violence. The joke stages the open secret of family sexual violence, rendering it at once dirty and tender, tacit and intoned, patronizing and coexperienced.

But the point of this joke is not to rehearse misogynistic violence. The lubricant the joke provides—the young bride's persistent derision of her husband's penis as a mouse—indexes multiple pleasures: that the husband's penis is too small to be stimulating, that the virgin bride was actually no virgin at all, that men's assumption of women's virginity is itself laughable, that getting fucked constitutes a certain amount of sexual and worldly expertise, and that the urban groom is emasculated both by foolishly believing his rural wife is a virgin and for having a small penis. The joke, too, mocks the sentimentality of diasporic men who want to return to a fossilized homeland where sexuality is always predictable and orderly and where brides are always virgins, just as it also refuses to solicit pathos around incest and rape. The playful doubling of "mouse" as metaphor forms an important layer of the joke's opacity, as "metaphors reveal as much as they conceal."[8] Fundamentally, the audience decides what is revealed in the punch line: a survivor or a slut, a seductress or a victim, a desire for consent. or a fantasy of violence. At a meta level, like so much of my mother's speech, ambivalence is abound.

Regardless, what stuck was sex as a residue of patriarchal labor, sex as subtending with violence and the cold suture between these two phenomena in modern life. Colocating the comedic and the sexual, the joke exposes women's vexed relation to violence, coercion, and pleasure. The real opacity, then (thus, pleasure), is how the joke circles around the negative of/in sex. By centering abjection, this joke offers something larger, puts violence on the table, as a topic that has lost its secrecy, its prohibitive and unspeakable character, making its quotidian mapping, its everyday grotesque, something to talk about. But to be clear, this joke was by no means reparative. Instead, abjection sits in this joke, as it sits in the deep well of my mother's memory—unapproachable and intimate, repulsed and repulsive, extravagant and ordinary, laughable and horrible.

But if the *good times* of this joke was an index of misogyny's domination, what possibilities could these women's pleasure yield? I think of the texture of this joke and the polysemic satisfaction all these women had every time it was uttered, both the circulation of the joke and their subsequent laughter extra, excess, and promiscuous (much like the city girls the groom wanted to avoid). Their laughter at sexual violence, the regularity of it, the dailiness of it, the expected nature of it, the logic of it, the temporality and telos of it, was a partial understanding of being undone and of trying to regain control. It was a vexed and vexing affective terrain that could not be explained by a singularity.

Entrenched within circumstances charged with intimate violence and intimate need and overdetermined by the disregard of women's subjectivity and the always penetrated feminine, these women delineated something that Western sociologists might (not like to) call agency (if we think of agency as that which comes from the gap in the repetition of power exerted and power exercised). Darreik Scott's *fuckedness* as a location of both pain and redemptive possibility comes to mind, where he argues that if sexual abjection is that which makes blackness both Black and violable, then that very abjection also "endows its inheritors with a form of counter-intuitive power.[9] Following this, the young bride's *fuckedness* and her subsequent naming of her husband's penis as a mouse functions as a symbolic castration (perhaps with immediate material consequences, that is, the ability of the groom to perform the act of sex after being reduced to a mouse). The feminization of the groom (whose penis is visible but cannot be seen as such) versus the masculinization of the uncle (whose symbolic phallus, while unseen, is omnipresent) was one moment through which these women took back the terms of sexual violence, was one way to say no to the pleasure economy that interpellated women and femininity in a particular way, was one way the joke was not on them but on patriarchy. Indeed, the intimate pleasure of the joke relies on a deep relation to violence and passivity of the body versus the promiscuity of the tongue. These were women who were seasoned in violence and seasoned in pleasure, both gained in communal and familial formations with one another. Their capacity to cultivate the latter (pleasure) was through a manipulation of the former (violence). Theirs was a dialectic of laughter and anger. This was the in-between space of the pornographical and the pedagogical. Tarrying in the sex-negative, here was an epistemology that responded to the demands of the patriarchal familial structure and to the very survivalist and furtive possibilities of the feminine. By retelling this joke, I hope to clarify this other archive, one where women teach each other how to lie, deceive, thieve, and whore.

Taking my cue from Black feminist writers such as Gayl Jones, Toni Morrison, and Patricia Williams, I think about laughter as a latent gender affectivity that comes into the body, a mode of bodily, psychic, and social deception. In *Alchemy of Race and Rights: Diary of A Law Professor*, Patricia Williams offers a striking analytic reading of Tawana Brawley, the fourteen-year-old girl who was found unconscious in Wappinger Falls, New York, in 1987, covered in feces, urine, with racial slurs written on her body, her hair and nails pulled out, gang-raped by five white police officers.[10] As the story unfolded in the minefield of gender, sexual, and racial grammars of the late 1980s, Brawley was accused of fabricating the whole story, doing the violence to herself, and falsely accusing the white officers. As the legal trial-cum-media spectacle seesawed for and against Brawley, Williams argues that the exposure that haunted Brawley was equivalent to metarape, writing, "There is no medicine circle for her, no healing circle, no stable place to testify and be heard, in the unburdening of one's heart." Recounting a moment at the height of the controversy, Williams writes of a moment when Brawley attended a comedy show at the Apollo Theatre in Harlem. One of the comedians called attention to Brawley's presence, and in a parody of the federal antidrug campaign, he advised her, "Just say no next time." As the audience roared in laughter and the spotlight fixed on her, Brawley threw her head back and laughed with the crowd. Williams writes that this is the only image she has seen of Tawana Brawley with her mouth open, "in false witness to this cruel joke, caught in the position of compromise, of satisfying other people's pleasure, trapped in the pornography of white people's fantasy."[11]

I think of Brawley's laughter at her own violence delivered instantaneously and deceptively to her audience and my mother's laughter at the young girl's fuckedness by her uncle. Both moments are sites of knowledge, thus deception. Both moments recall Veena Das's description of the complex relation of women with violence—"women drank the pain so that life could continue."[12] The comedic dictum, in both fleshy moments, is that violence doesn't kill you; it forces you to live on. My mother's private joke and Tawana Brawley's public laughter reveal how signs, symbols, metaphors, positions, identities matter, even if they are sometimes untranslatable, transient, other times immutable, and, more often than not, dirty. Both moments reveal the semiotic and word games through which we mask the necrosexual dimensions of brown/Black femininity. Both moments of laughter move in the orbit of the libidinal and the painful; both moments put us in the room with sex-violence stories; both moments reveal the everydayness of sexual violence and the inconvenience of sexual disturbance; both moments undo the subject and evoke feminized and racialized signatures of pessimism.

But Brawley's public laughter under the spotlight at a nightclub is different than my mother's laughter among other brown women in the secret corners of their lives. Both are moments of sexual violence, one engaged as a (brown) secret, the other engaged as a (Black) spectacle, and this distinction between brownness in the domesticated but potentially agentic diaspora and blackness as always and already white colonial possession is crucial and one I do not want to downplay. But even in this uneven terrain, there lies something in both moments that allows me to think epistemologically, to address how violence against brown girls/women and violence against Black girls/women are both ongoing causalities of white patriarchal supremacies and imperialisms; how both brown and Black femininity/sexuality/promiscuity gets tied to excess and accessibility; how laughter is commanded, demanded, incited, or expected from women of color at their own expense; and how we are still at a loss for language and appropriate metaphors with which to speak about sexual violence against women of color within a patriarchal and imperial culture of consumption. My mother's stories repeatedly compel me (and her listeners/readers) to confront the troubling coincidence of flesh, language, and the feminine precisely at its most devastating of moments, moments of profound unmaking: rape, abuse, abandonment, precarity. With what utterance do we describe Black and brown emotional loss, trauma, need, wound?

Unsurprisingly then, my mother's first encounter with male sexuality occurred when her great-grandfather, after pulling his erect penis out in front of her, invited her to touch it. She was seven years old, and at the sight of his penis and his hand gesturing her closer, she ran from the room. Two days later, given the extended family formations that shaped my mother's life, she and her nine-year-old girl-cousin were asked to deliver tea to his room, and this time the invitation turned into coercion and aggressive touching. The scene my mother describes is that of a grotesque hardening phallus, a forceful hand, an aroused laugh, and threatening words. The encounter lasted twenty minutes. Eventually the two girls ran out of the room. They ran through the house and out into the courtyard, where they fell onto the floor, panting for breath. As the two girls looked at each other, their panting breath turned into piles of fearful laughter. Their response to violence was laughter. What sex tried to destroy, they reconstructed in laughter. Fear moved through their body and released itself through laughter, in that muddled middle zone between event and escape.

I think again of these different moments of laughter—laughter as a bodily genre, laughter as momentarily liberation, laughter as a mode of deception, laughter as matter of fact, laughter as the landing pad of brutality. Embedded in each moment is the phantom of violence, of being driven away from our bodies. Hélène Cixous once wrote it is laughter that allows women to function outside of the male economy and that is why it needs to be contained.[13] Ironically, when my mother recounted this story of her great-grandfather molesting her to my then seventeen-year-old daughter, she tells it laughingly, as a joke, getting full joy out of the idea of an old man trying to chase two energetic little girls for his erotic arousal. My daughter, however, doesn't laugh. She has a learned a different feminism, one that sees her grandmother's memory as moment of horror, of violence. Growing up in the United States as the daughter of a feminist professor with a certain amount of middle-class privilege, she has been acculturated into a liberal feminist genealogy that sees violence as a shock. But the disturbed look on my daughter's face doesn't perturb my mother. On and on my mother laughed, her laughter so irresistibly contagious that I also joined, and eventually, unexpectedly, so, too, did my daughter. Contagious laughter has a biosocial force. There we were: three generations of brown women merrily laughing at the idea of a perverted old man chasing two little girls for a hand job, to the point that the girls ran so fast and so hard and so far that they were panting for breath, one of those little girls being my mother.

The exterior life of laughter strangely allowed for a handling of the interior life of sex and of violation, each moment oddly fitting into the another, supporting, reinforcing, penetrating, and engendering each other. The coterminous realities of sex and violence in the lives of women of color, in both the public and private realms, illustrate the seamlessness (if not the ease) with which women of color have long come to see themselves and the violence against them as objects of laughter. So deeply entrenched were these formations of violence and sexuality, so suffused through and through with violence was intimacy, that in perpetuity I would come to see how unsafe and close to the abject sex can be.

Two

When my mother and her cousin walked back into the house, their great-grandfather, along with a group of other aunties, were all gathered in the sitting room. He was the only man sitting among the women, the women sitting on the floor while he sat in the single armchair. The women were talking about another woman's sister-in-law, who, after three sons, had given birth to a daughter. Within days of her daughter's birth, the woman's husband died of a heart attack. Speaking in hushed tones, the women said, *The daughter ate her father* (*beti baap ko kagaye*). The daughter's birth and the father's subsequent, almost immediate, death spurred everyone's superstitions. The nearness of the daughter's life to the father's death was too coincidental, too heretical: it must be mystical. This was the conclusion to which they had come. *Some girls are like that*, they said, *their hunger is a phantom in their mouth that aggresses men. Their mouth is a grave for men, of men.* My mother and her cousin listened, as these women constructed and circulated this figure of speech, a colloquialism through which meanings of *girl* were carried across, embodied, and lived out, an utterance that allowed men to enact (and justify) abuse, mockery, power, and domination over these girls. My mother's great-grandfather cocked his head back and laughed.

Twenty years later, three years after my mother married my father, her oldest brother-in-law died a week after his daughter's birth. He was a young and energetic patriarch, and his death hit my father's family hard, forcing the younger brothers to contend with familial and financial responsibilities they had otherwise left to him. His widow, a mother of four, was immediately pushed down the hierarchy of wives. The women in the family had begun to talk. The daughter, they said, *ate her father*. My mother heard the other women say these words, swallowing their haunting sounds awkwardly, uncomfortably. The phrase in play echoed retrolexically. It was an old story told and retold, a haunting speech act. A phrase that kept popping up, offering simultaneously abjection and redemption.

At the time, my mother was new to the family, somewhat naïve and intro-verted (a circumscribed self-description to which my mother is attached). By the time my mother had married, she had (almost) completely internalized the tensions between and among brown women and men. She had tried to resist, but she was keenly aware of how deeply ensconced in the fantasy, sometimes extreme, of patriarchal omnipotence these women were: an almost pathologi-cal belief in the truth of misogyny. And this they practiced from day one on my mother, beginning with the warning to my father about his new wife that "a woman with a long forehead and a short neck is very dangerous." She lis-tened to these women link the newborn girl's life to a spectral understanding of a patriarch's death—an expression made possible in the affective vernacu-lar available in upwardly mobile Pakistani communities, where the heretical offshoots and the mystical traditions still laced the available vocabularies of life and death. Part of what undergirded this utterance was a mystic under-standing of life and death, where life and death are cyclical, circuitous, and connected, and where neither necessarily have positive or negative valences. But these women's psychic insistence of a daughter *eating* her father existed in their social memory as more than just mystic and mythic Islam. It strangely and clandestinely allowed them to imagine a newborn baby girl eating her father's life with the same urgency with which she suckles her mother's breast. It strangely, and ironically, allowed them to ruminate on how girls' power was imagined by these men, how its possibilities castrated these men, even if it was subsequently annihilated also by these men.

As this utterance circulated among the women in her new family, my mother recalled her great-grandfather laughing at the ridiculousness of this exact phrase twenty years earlier, just minutes after aggressively sexually mo-lesting her and her cousin. His laughter was a pretext suggesting that these brown mothers were unfit for modernity; it gestured to his arrogance, to his ability to effectively, if only momentarily, absorb his own violent patriarchal destructiveness by laughing at the illogical conclusions of women's speech. In the echoes of her memory of his laughter, my mother began to hear a pinch of insecurity. The idea of a daughter's mouth as a grave for the father turned the patriarch into a bottom, who, at any moment by the right woman, could be eaten, fucked, castrated, buried. With so delicious an irony in her thoughts, my mother added her voice to their collective grammar: *yes*, she said, *beti baap ko kagaye*.

For my mother, and for so many women she grew up with and around, lan-guage was their object. It allowed them to mock, interpret, disassemble, and refute the attachments imposed by the world. Their speech acts were psychic acts that allowed them to adjust to and resist the material conditions of their life. This denunciatory narrative of the daughter's life as aggressive to/ward men gave rise to a melancholic morbidity that shaped all the women I grew up with, in their varying roles as wife, daughter, lover, mother, sister, whore, maid. It was strange the kind of language these women collected.

When my mother and her older widowed sister-in-law told me this story, both their tones were matter-of-fact and sarcastic, my aunts slightly inflected with a banal authority of having survived that complex and complicated treatment of her daughter and herself after the death of her husband. She tells me that the diffusion of this rumor among the men of a cannibalistic daughter tapped into the men's own visceral fear of feminine and maternal conspiracies. The notion that women could bear daughters who would consume their fathers drove home the fear of women's/girls' ability to rupture relations, to persistently be dangerous—emotionally, sexually, and politically. The phrase laid out the anxieties of consumption, hunger, heteroeroticism, and incestuous patriarchy. The rumor justified the dominant heteronormative order and fed its practice of snuffing out women and girls who were seen as having excessive appetites. These women's explanations of dangerous, *father-eating* daughters simplified a misogynistic fantasy and animated the magic projected onto women's power. Men's power was rational, justified, worldly. Women's power was magical, mythical, other-worldly.

In this traditional slippage between femininity and Black, thus, bad magic, eating signifies the scared and divine act of death, just as it signifies a sexual taboo. And to be clear, eating's carnality and sexuality is not lost on these women. Indeed, they derived some voyeuristic pleasure from this notion of a father's flesh being consumed by and for the daughter's life, literalizing eating as both a mode of life and a path to death. The women rolled their eyes, their mouths turned up in a wry smirk, their tongues in their cheek. I saw this mischief, these secret thoughts, as part of the promiscuity of that metaphorical expression, a figure of speech that, if only momentarily, successfully castrated men. The psychosexual dimension of a daughter eating her father exposed a kind of agency on the part of the women, who, on one hand, came to see that daughter as less fungible (her coming into life constituted the fungibility instead of the patriarch), just as it also circumscribed the widowed mother and her daughter's mouth to lifelong conditions of fungibility. From the moment she became a widow, both the mother's and her daughter's food intake was monitored, including counting the number of rotis they ate, hiding under lock and key ghee and milk, denying access to any sugar or sugary sweets, and so many other modes of food surveillance throughout their lives.

The epistemic power of this rumor mitigated violence (to a certain degree) against the women circulating it, just as its latent grammar exposed the complicated terrain of Global South and feminized epistemologies.

But truth be told, my mother was unsure of whose power was being sheltered, as the words cocooned around the little girl and her widowed mother. And if I am to be (even more) honest, the intelligence and the sharpness I saw in these women was not governed by logics of repair or agency. The absence of wanting to repair the young girl's life, for whom this enduring rumor literally moved from spectral to material, was deeply gripping and uncomfortable to my feminist sensibilities. But for these women, carnal misery was part of larger corporeal embodiment of womanhood, class, and sex that they understood as a given, as part of the citizenship of our family. The image they drew and circulated was not innocent or "eyes-closed"; neither was it arbitrary or uncomplicated. It could not be simply explained as a rhetorical duplication of patriarchy with no history of its own.[14]

In order for me to understand this speech act, a kind of unsettlement had to happen; another register of riven-ness and sociality had to be exposed, had to be gathered around. I had to learn how to work with—rather than dismiss, overcome, transcend, or struggle against—my mother's defeat. I had to think about how my mother and other brown mothers produced capacious and porous figures of speech to understand the everyday necropolitical, how these vernacular moments allowed them to speak promiscuously about the abject conditions of their lives and what they knew would be their daughters' lives, how this form of language became the means through which they metabolized fear and violence. This form of language—its metaphors, its force, its feminized and racialized signatures, its appeals to magic, myth, witchery, blood, flesh, and other forms of nonlife/nondeath—was as promiscuous as it was melancholic, as masochistic as it was sadistic: close to the body, close to suffering, close to the erotic, to excess, to pleasure, to pain. It was a language that never quite coalesced with modernness. The way in which these women were so intimate with God and death, always at home (but not quite at home) in their bodies, in their kitchens—but not at all in the modern world—had much to teach me about how to live in the world, had much to teach me about the power of language in shifting the terms of engagement with violence. I am at home in this archive of words, even as bits and pieces make me feel like a misfit, as if I left something behind by not paying enough attention to their immodernities, infatuated as I was with modernity.

Three

In 1972, a few days after my mother had her first daughter, she returned to her mother's house for six weeks, a custom in which the new mother is taught to mother by her mother and other mothers. For six precious weeks, my mother's body healed from thirty-six hours of labor and an emergency C-section, as all the women in the house cared for her and her newborn baby girl. When it was time for my mother to return to her husband and in-law's home, my grandmother pulled my mother to the side and whispered in her ear: *The mother of a daughter is always a thief.* My mother looked at her mother quizzically, wanting more of an explanation, but her brother-in-law had arrived to retrieve her, so she simply nodded knowingly at her mother and left. Four years later, when I was born, my mother went directly from her third, and last, emergency C-section to a house full of needy in-laws, who immediately took me from my mother's arms so she could cook for a hungry family of sixteen. Her mother and father were at the time living in Dar es Salaam, Tanzania. A few days after my birth, my mother spoke to her mother on the phone, who ended their conversation with the same maxim: *Remember, the mother of a daughter is always a thief.* My mother, wrapped up in the demands of a house full of needy in-laws, two small children and a newborn, quickly responded to her mother affirmatively and again, didn't, wouldn't or couldn't give these words another thought.

Eighteen months later, in the fall of 1977, when we were leaving Karachi for the United States, my mother had an emotional farewell at her mother's house. My grandmother, now a widow, pressed her warm wrinkled hand against my mother's arm, leaned into her face and repeated: *Don't forget, the mother of a daughter is always a thief.* Immersed in the practicalities of her upcoming migration West, my mother tightly hugged her mother, solely focused on the fact that she had no idea when they would meet again. Twenty-six years later, in 2003, when I gave birth to my daughter, my mother, who was in the delivery room with me, put my daughter in my arms, stroked my face, leaned into my ear, and said: *Remember this, the mother of a daughter is always a thief.*

I hear this language. It hangs in the air. I feel suspended by my own memories of my mother stealing for me, teaching me how to steal, training me how to lie, coaching me to keep secrets, schooling me to move through the world with furtivity. I grew up watching my mother stash money, sometimes dollar bills, sometimes coins, in the folds of socks, in the backs of drawers. Money, like sex, needs to be tucked away, in a drawer full of anxieties. Because I was the youngest, I was almost always with her. My older sister, deep in her science books, and my older brother, concerned mostly with outdoor play, paid no attention to these furtive and fugitive practices. Indeed, my mother's secrets and gossips and pithy aphorisms had something furtive and dirty about them that both my sister and brother found backward and unnecessary. But my curiosity was aroused.

Because she had no relation to the formal economy, my mother's livelihood was completely and utterly tied to my father, and prior to that, to her father. She went from her father's home to her husband's, both structural locations and trajectories that saturated her in men's will, so both gave her a particular clarity about the social forces in which she was situated. My grandmother's conviction that the mother of a daughter is always a thief handed repeatedly down to my mother and the subsequent practices it produced were one way to control some particularities in that relation. The dense grid of affective structures that my mother was yoked to produce this controversial figure of speech, crystalized its small, knotted meanings into the partial and fugitive practices that my mother developed. The dark allusiveness and the melancholy of this particular life lesson were also the perfect antidote to the men's optimistic ramblings about the life they provided for their wives and daughters. That the "safe" transfer of a woman from her father's house to her husband's house could be incomplete was something with which they couldn't, at least overtly, contend. Yes, these women had (some) stability, but along the way, they had learned acutely the lesson that stability was here today, gone tomorrow. *Chanchal*, my mother called it, meaning mercurial, moving, changing. I think of a line from Warsan Shire's poem: "Stability is like a lover with a sweet mouth upon your body one second; the next you are a tremor lying on the floor covered in rubble and old currency, waiting for its return."[15] This kind of stability, dripping in precarity and sensation, here today, gone tomorrow, was most familiar to my mother.

I think of how this utterance *ups the ante* of mothering, of mothering a daughter, of brown mothering, of diasporic mothering pathos. I think of how this utterance gives carte blanche financial subterfuge to the mother of a daughter. This way of thinking about mothering as a form of fugitivity— tied to theft, tied to a gendered stealing practice, tied to furtive maneuvers of saving money in dark corners—impels critical thinking about that which is seen as private property and that which is seen as theft, that which is disqualified as crime and that which is framed as rightful possession, that which is seen as the indigestible pieces of tradition and that which emerges as an ethical way of being. These practices of thieving explained, expressed, repaired (sometimes), negated, and rhapsodized the uncontrollable terrain of gendered-sexual-racial-classed life. The cunning of reason reveals the brutality of practice. That the mother of a daughter is always a thief gestures to modes of uncertainty, insecurity, unpredictability, and risky modes of being that neither Global North feminist theory nor postcolonial feminist theorizing has quite dealt with, both theories leaving feminized and maternal grit in the rubble and rubbish of the unseen and the illegitimate.

I think of what my mother said to me when my daughter was born, what her mother said to her when her daughters were born, and what was not said to her when her son was born. The different temporalities in which this saying transferred from woman to woman, mother to mother, mother to daughter reenacted, in each moment, the archival event through the craft and craftiness of survival. It offered a pedagogy; it commanded a lesson. It's worth recalling Simone de Beauvoir who wrote, "Woman is also taught from adolescence to lie to men, to outsmart, to side-step them. She approaches them with artificial expressions. She is prudent, hypocritical, playacting."[16] Like Beauvoir's indictment, hidden in this murky, muddy, mutated speech act were intense philosophies of gender, stability, economics, history, and flesh—a way to examine the invisible ways my mother and her mother and all these othered brown women, wives, mothers, sisters, aunts, maids, tricksters, whores found a way out of no way. Disobedience became the nucleus of my mother's epistemological and doctrinal ensemble.

As wisdom passed at a critical moment from mother to daughter, this is a thievery that is maternally endorsed. Deserved even. It's part of how women stick together against men. It's part of how my mother understood that what was secondary or even incidental for the men in our family was of primary importance for the women. I think of stealing as a feminist practice, a furtive route of and to securitization, not just in the Marxist sense but as a way to understand and situate the historical ways that women have always engaged in the informal economy of savings (i.e., jewelry collecting, jewelry exchange) and in the informal economy of earnings (i.e., hiding money, exchanging sex for money or reward, fantasies and seductions and play-acting for money and gifts, understanding that all sex is sex work). So early conditioned in male desire and bondage, my mother taught me and raised me in conditions in which there was no real separation of one from the other but instead a messy formation of epistemic possibilities that dodge, foil, or collude with instrumentalist patriarchal formations. The fragile border between mothering and furtivity comes through in this inchoate idiom, this vocabulary of symbolic action that allowed her to create some security in the midst of the perpetual affective and economic life of feminized precarity. I saw this speech act as the work my mother and her mother did (and in different ways that, as the mother of a daughter, I do) around the precariousness of our lives, to negotiate the derelictions that shaped our lives, to understand the modes through which we brought about care, stability, pleasure, and the future itself for ourselves and our daughters. Indeed, I have come to think that brown mothers are the best kind of thieves. Opaque, feminine, maternal, this advice performed a kind of intellectual history, if only perhaps because the elements of the story, of the secret, of the inheritance demanded it do so. But it was up to the listener (often, if not always, an audience of one daughter) to parse what was secret and what was given; what, like money, lay beneath the expected, the obvious, the visible, the sensible.

Four

How many women in her disrupted subjectivity does my mother carry in her stories? Every story my mother told me was cradled by sex, making plain the fact that sex and all its attenuations of gender, race, desire, flesh, melancholy, and violence would assume their station in every aspect of (my) life. Sex and the erotic underscore my mother's continued attachment to gendered meanings and the vexing, constitutive potential within which she developed these primarily furtive modes of being. As she saw it, sex was both the raw material and the grand design of women's oppression. It was both the belly of the beast and the beast itself. And though she would never say it out loud, sex was also the way out of the beast, becoming possibly the beast that takes down the beast.

My mother conflated the literalism of sex and gender with the metaphor of pain, and she confused or deliberately blurred (I still don't know which) the distinction between the literal and the metaphor beyond repair. And nowhere was this dialectic of sex and abjection more centrally articulated then when my mother uttered these matter-of-fact maxims, these random vernacular offerings, her brown colloquialisms. Each embodied a preoccupation with the most gruesome and traumatic and precarious aspects of women's lives. Each embodied multiple imaginaries that made sex benign in one moment and politically charged in another; that made the erotic a tense gender question; that elevated desire to the status of an "event"; that animated the clandestine, turning its every iteration into a relation to melancholy or promiscuity.

I had come home from college to attend a family party. As I shuffled around, making small talk, I found myself sitting next to a fortysomething, recently divorced Pakistani woman. There she was: a divorced, superbly feminine woman, dressed in a tightly fitted *shalwar kameez* with a low revealing neckline. A sultry and stared-at woman overflowing with panache and a hard, flirtatious, unapologetic edge. I was nineteen and suddenly and unexpectedly infatuated. I spent the remainder of the evening deep in what I felt was a profoundly flirtatious and feminist conversation with her. When I looked around, I sensed the whole party was watching us—the married women with distrust, the married men with desire, the older women with warning. She certainly knew how to hold an entire room, just by existing. I felt, too, my mother's eyes on me throughout the party. But her gaze was neither distrustful nor curious. It was sober with the subtlest expression of vigilance, focus—as if, for once, I was the cypher and she, the initiate. Later, when my mother and I were leaving the party, I shared that the woman and I had exchanged phone numbers and that I was excited about continuing my newfound friendship. My mother, who often spoke in absolutes, especially with regard to sex and gender, smiled and said: "*Well, you should never break your relations with a Vaidya (a "doctor") or a Visya (a "whore").*"

Appalled at my mother's antifeminist grammar, I retorted that my new "friend" was divorced, and not a whore. My mother sharply responded that the term *Visya* was a capacious figure of speech; that this was an enigmatic saying, not literal, and not legible to the newly developing, liberal arts college-educated logics in which I was being trained. She concluded that I was too young, too Americanized, too attached to literalness to understand. As with so many of my mother's other speech acts, my first reaction was corrective: I wanted to remedy or remove outright what I saw as the misogyny of the saying. My knee-jerk characteristically feminist reaction was to reduce her words carte blanche to an essentializing binary, a patriarchal, classed, colonized mode of thought and speech. But such a reading missed the emotional life world of my mother, the important emotional and cultural understandings that allowed her to survive in and against masculinist makings of the world. So, in retrospect, I've come to see things a little differently. My mother was right: the logics I had available would not cohere. The more I heard this strange dictum, the more I would search for its hidden, secret meanings.

The term *Visya* is Sanskrit and translates as "promiscuous woman," but it is varyingly used to reference whore, prostitute, courtesan, streetwalker, harlot, hooker, or slut. Its etymological root comes from the Brahminian period, "Besh," which means "one who is available to all."[17] The term *Vaidya* is Hindi and translates as "doctor," but it historically refers to a practitioner of Ayurveda, a medicine man, or a healer. It is generally used, if used at all, to name a noncertified doctor of Eastern medicine. Frankly, the term has lost circulation, save within some geospatial enclosures. The temporal import of these words, too, is significant, as *Vaidya* is a term no longer in common circulation, while *Visya* (pronounced as *Veshya*) continues to be commonly used and is always and already a dirty word. The word *rishta* is what my mother used to indicate relation—a Hindi/Urdu word varyingly meaning relation, relationship, bond, connection, alliance, and in some contexts, even friendship and marriage. The word that translates as "ruin" is *barbad* or conversely *tabah*, both of which also carry the meanings "destroy," "devastate," "wreck," or "annihilate." But no matter the voluminous field of English words, there is no clean way to translate this dictum, as each word is beset with difficulties, fraught with untranslatable ideology. When combined, each word's meaning becomes too cumbersome, too prone to error, too controlling, too rarified, too specialized. Perhaps what is most interesting about this saying is its imprecision, its ideological alliteration, its indigestibility, its incommensurability in translation. This was a speech act that retreated deep into the feminized and maternal spaces of the women I knew, ceding and kneading, making and breaking, in the space Audre Lorde might have called, "beneath language."[18]

Like so many of my mother's stories, this saying opened up the epistemological problem of sex (and the body) through the opacities of an abstract, yet literal, figure (a whore or a healer). Sex is the specter in this moment (the figure of the *Visya*) and is also sheltered in the narrative (*Visya* as capacious syntax and conjoined with *Vaidya*, a seemingly asexual, but still embodied figure). The injunctive demand to not break a relation with a *Visya* gestures to the interiority of sex, its unpredictable, promiscuous, precarious interiors (even as it is the sexual exteriority of the *Visya* that actually threatens the comportment of her relational world). Sex suffuses the space of my mother's advice. But the ruse of sex/lessness in her words, stretching *Visya* out of its sexual literalism, underscores how sex and its specter of the fleshy, feminine body (in that sex gets read through the feminine body) is disciplined and fragmented in and through vocabularies of condemnation and containment. Sex, even when invisible, is vestigial and ready to be revealed without intention or will. This figure of speech was, as Sara Ahmed writes, absent of coherence, a movement of words that would not cohere, "a queer disorientation."[19] This was a speech act with its own background, its own conditions for emergence, its own (queer) phenomenology. This was a speech act that illuminated a way of understanding that allowed women like my mother to be in patriarchy and to operate against patriarchal assignments of their bodies.

At various points throughout my life, my mother (and some of the other brown mothers) repeated this strange proverb, almost, but not always, in the context of divorced women. My mother didn't have much sympathy for divorced or divorcing women. Her sympathy was reserved for married women. Marriage was the devil she knew. For my mother, women who divorced their husbands were inviting more problems into their lives, spreading their legs for yet another man or men; and once spread, she would say, *Every man will come your way and most won't ask for permission.* The single time my mother actually tried to leave my father occurred in 1973, with just one daughter in tow. When she arrived at her father's house with an infant in one arm and a small suitcase in another, her father stood at the door and advised her that a woman can have one husband she manages or a world full of husbands (the world as a husband). The image of her father blocking the entryway, warning her of a world (full) of husbands, was all my mother needed to make her choice. She chose one husband. Divorce, she quickly understood, was as much a condemnation (by society) as it was an invitation (to men). A husband is both a necessary and an unforgivable figure, always suspect, loathsome, interruptive, and essential. No matter all the countless times she considered leaving her marriage, she never did. Divorce was beneath her: an easy escape, a cheap way out, a whore's errand.

Through these casual grammars and everyday commentaries, divorce was made so extraordinarily pathological that as a little girl I became convinced that when I would actually meet a divorced woman, she would look different, suspect, physically recognizable as *beneath us*. So when I actually met divorced women and realized that they didn't look any different than my mother, or my aunts, or my grandmothers, I was completely taken aback. These manless women were just like the women I knew, in dress, in language, in mischief, and in sociality. Yet to my mother, whose life was manned by many men, they were different, and their difference was dangerous, as she knew any minute that a wife could be condemned to live as a whore.

This pathological visual grammar was also grafted on abortion. My mother once told me that the pain of one abortion is equivalent to the pain of seven births. This she heard from her mother, who heard it from her mother, and so on. Mind you, all of these were women who had had abortions, who had helped other women get abortions, and some of whom had also performed abortions on other women. In some way, indeed, they had all played the role of the abortionist and the midwife. Yet the common idea that circulated in my family was that women who lived outside of monogamous marriage were getting abortions all the time.[19] Both divorce and abortion were ways to lose your way in the world, to displace feminine power for some abstract freedom. So my mother would repeat this adage ominously, casually, rhythmically, flirtingly, laughingly, and lovingly. There was a play involved in her statements, tongue-in-cheek, making her words both seductive and punitive. If we were in the midst of my aunts' ribaldry, all the women would knowingly and affirmingly nod and give me a firm cautionary look, as if to say: *Heed this, girl.*

At first glance, then, this *Visya/Vaidya* idiom (strange bedfellows, to say the least) expresses the typical critique of prostitutes, suggesting that sex workers' sex/work is equal to or the same as an inherently dangerous nature. Classically figured as taboo, unstable, untrustworthy, the figure of the whore is necessarily excluded from the home, the family, the domestic. But unlike the demands of the patriarchal sex-gender system, which excises the whore to exploit/condemn her, the implicit contradiction in my mother's retort is that while the figure of the whore is threatening, she, too, is one with whom one must remain *in* relation (not *out*, or severed, or broken from). There is, then, another worldview contained in this saying. Outside of the promised protection of virtue, the figure of the wife has always been intimately tied to the figure of the whore, and the figure of the whore has always been both absent and present, integrated and apart, domestic and foreign, dangerous and familiar. One might read this speech act as revealing how the figure of the whore is one who unveils the incomplete access wives have to power and their own bodies. Being a wife meant/demanded a certain amount of estrangement from one's body; being a whore signaled an immersion/synonymity with one's body. In this way, this proverb revealed how aware of their precarity, their instability, their estrangement these wives were, how clearly they understood that the unpropertied woman can undo the world of the propertied class, and how the propertied man determined the (property) value of women. Property, capital, money, stability, pleasure, when tied to a man, could also be taken away by that man (and his other woman). But just as it may center the precarity of the wife over the whore, this saying, too, pushes the mortality of the wife and the whore together, assuring that what befalls one will befall the other, where neither may have control over what has befallen.

What gradually emerges in the thicket of these words is my mother's overturning the assignation of *visya*—a denigrated term—into an exposé of hidden power, revealing that women's connections with each other have always been furtive and secret and that these modes of furtivity and femininity are simultaneously a reference to the wounds as well as balms for those wounds. I found the term *visya*, like so much of the surplus of my mother's speech, a figure expressed in multivoluminous linguistics—a social fact of deviance and power, a social figure of banishment. She, deviant in her body, in her sex; my mother deviant in her tongue, in her stories. I had to wager for meanings in these alternative epistemologies, wading through the folklore, the vernacular, the myth, the mystic, and the queer, searching for a cartography of femininity that is disruptive—as sisterhood, as whoredom, as motherhood, as a disruptive force that can fuck up White and male supremacy.[20]

The second time my mother repeated this phrase to me occurred when she was hospitalized a few years ago. A heart disease and diabetes patient, with a weak arthritic body, who eats too much spicy Indian pickle, my mother frequently ends up in the hospital. When I arrived at the hospital, my older sister, who is also a physician, was in a heated discussion with my mother's cardiologist over the chosen line of care. I arrived at the hospital at what appeared to be the end of a medical confrontation, watching curiously, as my sister and the cardiologist took their debate outside. My mother, depleted and drained, saw my raised eyebrow, shook her head, and said, *Remember, never break your relations with a Vaidya* (a doctor) *or a Visya* (a whore)."

Here again, my mother matter-of-factly seized these two opposing figures and held them together, offering not only an injunction that didn't follow the mandates of Western, modern, male logic, but again in a moment that couldn't quite hold the extremeness of her injunction. But just as this remark ripped open a (feminist) wound, it also rerouted me toward the (unthought) connection between incongruent dealers of the body—the healer and the whore—and how each conjures a sticky relation to the body and to the self. I realized then, as I looked at my mother's weak, worn-out, sick body, that the linguistic coupling of *Visya* and *Vaidya* drew together two figures who *fully* know the body, hold them in their synonymity. Indeed the Sanskrit root of the *Vaidya* is *Veda*, meaning knowledge or knower. The body is their life's work and thus indexes how intimate ways of knowing the body, from the outside-in and the inside-out, endows power in both figures. My sister's belligerence with my mother's doctor triggered that anxiety; it reinforced the specific vulnerability of the brown maternal body in relation to those who handle it, either through sexual or medicinal power. My mother mythologically conflated *Vaidya* and *Visya*, just as she conflated brown femininity and abjection to literally expose that what we do with our bodies (or what happens to our bodies) is connected to our way of being in the world and that there are entangled dis/identifications and dominations that might be in play in how we think of the body and those who handle, manipulate, fuck, and heal the body.

In both moments, my mother curiously cautious "never break" was announced with a flippancy, an almost fleeting, wry disdain that revealed both her knowingness and her helplessness. Her oldest daughter's fighting words with her male cardiologist (likely justifiable) catalyzed my mother's regulatory impulses of suspicion, just as, too, my quick public intimacy with a divorcee. Both were figures who held power over the body/sex (either others or their own)—a sense of corporeal agency my mother never quite held in her grip—thus, both were moments where her only agency (a troubling and presumptive word in any context) was, once again, a foretelling, a prophecy, a clairvoyance, a second sight. In that debilitated moment of dependency, the only thing she could do to protect herself from either of the doctors (one of whom was her daughter) in the midst of carnal abjection, in the midst of medical and medicalized precarity, was to repeat this old maxim. The irreverence with which my mother announced this injunction became a mode both for expressing her powerlessness and for resolving it. My mother's talismanic invocation expressed this anxiety, just as it, too, offered (her) a way out it. This sudden, full-tilt rhetorical switch developed out of her practices of surviving multiple material and carnal risks, and, indeed, she fundamentally saw the brown feminine body as always subject to these risks and the site through which others' power is exercised, mobilized, and hegemonized. Her words made seeable the consequences that emerge from "breaking" relations with those who handle our bodies, where the opposite of "breaking" gestured not to building or making but to a cognizance, a capaciousness, a porosity. This was no banal platitude.

My mother's mythopoetic construction of whores and healers shaped me profoundly. Ultimately (and ironically) through this erotic gesture and feminist sentiment, my mother convinced me that whores and whoring, like thieves and thieving, like lies and lying, like disobeying and disobedience, were the most powerful way to be in the world. "Trust her lies," Katherine McKittrick says, in speaking of an ex-slave's claim to freedom.[21] I think of the ways these mother-texts or mother as text, the grammars through which these brown tongues rearticulated the everyday necropolitical, just as they revealed that something happens to the necropolitical when it is exposed to the mother tongue. The connective tissue in each of these speech acts was the coterminous reality of femininity and disobedience, a mode of being that produced ways of figuring out (through furtivity), of staying in (rather than getting out), of producing power (through powerlessness), of staying alert (rather than becoming complacent), of understanding that the impulse to care for each other had to take place in the aftermath of violence (since *during* was often impossible). My mother's furtive maneuvers now become my theoretical maneuvers: the tongue as ontological opening, promiscuity as a form of speech, stealing as feminist practice, lesbianism as maternal inheritance, obsessing over lies, curses, secrets, stories that teeter on the brink of truth, shaped by speculation, anxieties, fears, rigidities—teetering but never quite taking the plunge.

Jamila

....

Tongue me, mothertongue me, mother me,
touch me, with the tongue of your, lan lan lang,
language, l/anguish, anguish
— M. NOURBESE PHILIP, *SHE TRIES HER TONGUE*

My mother's cathexis is feminine and maternal abjection, and these are her speech acts—of explanation, meditation, transformation, subjugation. She dispersed most, if not all, of her psychic and libidinal and intellectual energy on this abjection. Her opus of stories raised these sets of encounters (over and above others of equal concern), and her speech acts followed, in metaphor, hyperbole, warning, allusion, foreshadowing, irony, and juxtaposition. On the level of the symbolic, my mother (and these other brown mothers) created whole worlds of sexual signs and signifiers, an ornate matriarchal lexicon of irreverent words, followed through by furtive practices and promiscuous secrets. So when my mother tells me that my lesbianism is the result of her lesbianism with Jamila, I think about what it might mean to have first "stolen" and then "whored" in my mother's lesbian desire.

Audre Lorde once wrote that "the desire to lie with other women is a drive from the mother's blood."[22] For my mother, my "desire to lie with other women" is ineluctably fastened to the past, in that she understands and narrativizes my lesbianism as the embodied interarticulation of her childhood desire and actions. Just as she reasons that her deep erotic lineages etched their way into my flesh, she constructs desire as melancholic, spiritual, and dangerous. My mother's encounter with Jamila shaped her religiosity. She came to be uninvested in any singular cosmology. Each religion came with its ownership claims, its proprietorships, its modes of organized belonging, and thus, its constrains, its refusals, its brutalities. Instead, it was perhaps at that moment that my mother became curious about religion as a structure of beliefs that allowed people to pass judgement, that allowed others to calcify judgement, that allowed us to tell stories for which we otherwise do not have words. That Jamila deployed religious power (as she understood it) to shame my mother and that my mother then deployed sexual power (as she understood it) to save herself constitute an imprint in my mother's archive: a moment of desire, religiosity, sex, and class gone awry. My mother's desire for Jamila was tied to femininity, excess, risk, and urgency; it was outside the social, the spoken, the legible; it raised the specter of danger; it was an erotic-spiritual space in which (Jamila's) destruction and (my) future was created.

In this brown maternal frame, lesbianism is not a result of reasoning and identity but a spiritual dynamic, a rhythm of a return to an elsewhere, a residue of that which could not be felt/met/manifest historically. In so deflecting, my mother echoes a long genealogy of women of color rejecting/complicating/modifying lesbianism (as identity): Gloria Wekker on the politics (and desire) of naming Lesbianism, Astrid Roemer's refusal to call herself a lesbian, saying "There are after all, things which aren't to be given names, giving them names kills them": Audre Lorde's secret revelation that all Black women are lesbians, though they would loath to call themselves this; Amy Villarejo's position that lesbianism is an adjective not a noun, a modifier of normativity not a condition of being, an ethicoerotic practice rather than a sexual-political-identarian; and on and on, a litany of Black and brown women polemicizing lesbianism.[23]

I think of these Black and brown feminist renamings of secret sensations, these unnamed lesbianisms, these voluptuous desires, these melancholic genealogies. The lesbian as nonexistent, as traitor, as sacrilegious, as loathsome (at least in name) stood in stark contradiction to the lesbianism that suffused the space, the dynamic, the relationality between my mother and other brown mothers and between my mother and her motherhood. This suffusion brought a lesbian valence to the fore of my upbringing, that was by no means peripheral or casual or accidental. It was a lesbianism that shaped her sensitivity to patriarchy, to human life, to women's desire, to women's bodies, to the despair waiting to engulf brown mothers. It made her lucid, generous, and free. There was no doubt in my mind that the way these women spoke to each other, touched each other, cared for each other was as though they were lovers. These women's interactions were teeming with sensuality, shaped by and at the core of their intellectuality. The subtext of transgressive desire in these gestures of intimacy was hard to miss. But for my mother and these other brown mothers, desire didn't congeal into identities; it floated elsewhere in a plenitude of space that exceeds the lesbian body, that is in far excess of gender and sexuality identities. I think, for my mother, lesbianism is a vast array of interior libidinal experiences and affects (private, temporal, exciting, shameful, melancholic, masochistic), while lesbian identity was exterior, public, permanent, sadistic (in that it invited pain instead of enduring it). To take the pain dealt by life to women and to turn that pain into pleasure was the crown jewel of brown feminine maternal subjecthood. To bring about pain to yourself and other women by running away, becoming, as Monique

Wittig writes, "lesbians as figures who have run away from heteropatriarchy," was unwieldy and unethical all together.[24]

To be clear, my mother (and most of these other mothers) reject lesbianism as a legitimate mode of social life. These were women who would be lambasted for their complicity, whose oppositional knowledge is illegible to those who lionize resistance, whose modes of desire and solidarity still lack names, because they emerge from and are formed through myth and magic and not from the regularized practice of reason. The thick influence of the local vernaculars through which my mother framed heterosexual desire and behavior meant that my mother's sexual actions remained resolutely heterosexual and, in fact, perversely loyal to heterosexuality, but not, and I think this is an important distinction, cruelly optimistic toward it.[25]

I wonder what forms of desire and pleasure and mourning will die if certain metaphors do not survive, or do survive in the wrong way. I wonder also what it would mean to pause on the masochism in my mother's words and to take it seriously. What pain was my mother inflicting, on herself and on me? My mother's transforming of Jamila from her first love to an intergenerational lesbian curse (on me) straddles a number of different gender and sexual logics. It allowed her to name my desire as *lesbianism*, a word that she loathes and that causes her to cringe every time it is said, by her, by me, or by anyone else. It allowed her to situate her deep shame alongside her inability to discipline her desire for Jamila. In an oblique way, this rendering of a lesbian curse was a response to the power relations around which sexual desire and femininity and containment orbit. My mother's naming of my lesbianism as a curse was one way to work through melancholia, a working through of lesbian desire as spectrality, a refusal to let go of Jamila and the pain she caused her, giving primacy to the "fuckedness" of class and sex and femininity. I think of how, for my mother, lesbianism is not a naming of subjectification but a naming of theft, something stolen from her, something cursed upon me. Lesbianism figures in my mother's stories as desire (care), as affect (guilt), as spirituality (otherworldliness), as action (touch). Such a figuration severs sexuality from active desire and instead cleaves it into the spiritual and the flesh, the ghost, and the subject: lesbianism as that which is haunted by the patriarchies of the past.

Jamila is a figure from my mother's past who haunts her girlhood desire for girls with her present reality of a manned life, who tears the idea of time (heals), who gives circulatory life to lesbianism, femininity, maternity, and inheritance. And inheritance, lest we forget, is a relation of reciprocity. One has to be willing to receive that which one inherits. Jamila is the lingering presence who demands my mother's attention (just as she wants her attention demanded), who disrupts her practice of compulsory heterosexuality, and who reminds her of another field of desire (just as she provides her with a salve to refuse desire). Jamila fissures and queers my mother's lifeworld. She emanates a counterpoint to (her) lesbian phobia. She demands a return to injury.[26] She embodies (in her disembodiment) sexual knowledge and all its attenuations of shame, pleasure, nuance, criticality. Jamila is my mother's feminist and queer haunting. She is my mother's *lieux de memoir*. She, too, is mine. If the ghost of Jamila still haunts my mother, the reason is that my mother is still looking for an entryway to her desire.

....

I think of how the metaphors in each speech act—the mouse, the whore, the curse, the cannibalistic daughter, the maternal theft—depend on the evidence of memory, not just because of the absence of other forms of evidence but also because of the need to address traumatic experience through witnessing, retelling, communality, and metaphors. Taken together, these speech acts allowed my mother and other mothers to talk about the violence, injury, and harm this world had inflicted on them. These mythopoetic, melancholic, and masochistic interpretations of life (and death), sex (and violence), and survival (and disobedience) became my mother's primary outlet for the labor in her life. They reminded me that desire and flesh are central nodes in the practice of the brown maternal and her agency (if this remains a useful term). These words were a source of meaning, even as they so often escaped, decentered, and postponed meaning. There was always something in each utterance, in the grammar, in the textuality, in the metaphor, in the signification, in the multiplication that evaded my attempts to link it, directly and immediately, with other structures. And yet at the same time, the shadow, the imprint, the trace, the remains of those other formations, of the intertextuality of narrative with institutional sources of power, can never be erased from her speech. In each linguistic gesture was an analytic, a site of diacritic possibility, a way to think about how the semiotics of violence—flesh, femininity, maternity—continue to position mothers of color globally in certain kinds of precarity.

But just as I write this, I know also that there is so much phobia around Black and brown women's speech, because they express wariness and weariness, because they are seen as loose and lazy, because they shatter fantasies of entitlement and progress and political correctness, because they rupture the continuity of the present and demand an ethical encounter with the past, because they index a tremendous amount of violence, because they are read as a biopolitical failure. These speech acts coagulate, in their many and varied interpretations and applications, as fugitive, furtive, hypersymbolic, as *other*. Evocative, argumentative, infuriating, my mother's tongue bypassed the hermeneutical demands for recuperation, reproduction, revision, and reparation. I inhaled her lacerating, lustrous, fissured, violent, and tender brown maternal socialities. I inherited her caustic, suffocating, negative, antisocial, needlessly repetitive stories, speech acts, and utterances. I relished in her thick, hallucinatory, and promiscuous words. She touched me with this tongue, ravishing me, her words moving faster, her tongue moving stronger, spinning me around and around in the folds of her mouth. They seduce me, deflower me, embolden me.

4

the other end
of the tongue

―

I decided to return here because I was afraid to.
—JAMES BALDWIN, *NOBODY KNOWS MY NAME*

One day, shortly after I told my mother that I was writing this book, I went to visit her. She probed me about my project, curious and suspicious. Lacking the words to summarily describe my intent, I described the book as part love letter, part feminist anguish, part critical theory, part history, part myth, part archive, part seduction, part me, part her. After a few moments of silence, my mother responded by relating a popular Hindu myth. In her version, Parvati, the mother of the Hindu gods Skanda and Ganesh, ordered both her sons to go around the world in a race. Parvati promised the fruit of knowledge, a mango, to whichever son circled the world the fastest. Skanda immediately jumped on his magic Peacock and flew off around the world, returning home pleased with himself, ready to report his triumph and to receive the fruit of knowledge. But he quickly realized that his younger brother Ganesh had beaten him. Without leaving the room, Ganesh had circled around his mother and said, "You are my world." Ganesh was awarded the mango. However, when Ganesh excitedly bit into his prized fruit (of knowledge), off broke one of his tusks.[1]

When I began writing about tongues, a dear colleague suggested I research everything on tongues, including their anatomical realities. My disdain of Western science and medicine and their cold and arrogant doxas (aptly captured by Wendy Simonds's brilliant phrase, "the other s&m") kept me from delving too deep into the s&m histories of the tongue.[2] I did, however, learn (just briefly) that tongues are anchored inside our bodies by a single bone, called the hyoid bone (known also as the lingua bone). It is the only bone in the body that does not connect with any other bone; it is the only bone that relies solely on muscular, ligamentous, and cartilaginous attachments. Given this peculiarity, the hyoid bone has been described as "free floating"—a unique bone surrounded by flesh (contrary to the tongue's material reality, flesh surrounded by bone). The lingua bone is a lonely bone. I also learned that this is the bone that breaks during death by strangulation and that women are more likely to be strangled to death than men. I'm not sure why I found these medical facts interesting or even worth engaging. But there was something curious about this particular anatomy lesson that I found intriguing—the vulnerable life of the tongue, literally surrounded by hard teeth, affixed to a single, lonely bone. I wondered how this single anchoring of the tongue allows it to do its fleshy and linguistic work. There was something in the body of this medical fact that substantiated my mother's story—soft flesh moored to hard structure, flesh as simultaneously tied to the conditions of its harm and possibility, isolation, and intimacy. Interestingly enough, I also learned that the tongue in Ayurveda is a key diagnostic site. According to Ayurveda, the tongue is the mirror of the viscera (our internal organs). By looking at the tongue, its landscapes, its fleshy details, its color, a *Vaidya* (loosely, a doctor of Ayurveda) can get a good idea of a person's health. It is not without irony that a key recommendation of Ayurveda is to daily scrape one's tongue to remove the white impurities (mucus accumulation and/or bacteria) that builds up on the flesh. These two bodily facts—the fleshy tongue anchored by a lone bone and the tongue as holding the impurities of the body—came to be my mother's point of view in the world and literally and metaphorically resounded in her body. And since my entry point for the exploration of my mother's archive and the conditions in which she traversed this world is her tongue, it perhaps follows that I close with a conjectural reading of the other end of her tongue: my mother's body.

It is likely clear by now that my mother's tongues and her subsequent sociality of excessive storytelling made her a problem. The Manicheanism at the heart of my mother's misery was the division of sexes, but it was amplified by *that something rotten* in the encounter between White supremacist classed efficacy and the brown feminized maternal body. Early on, my mother developed a voluntary servitude toward these machinations of power, a servitude that many saw, variously, as meek, neurotic, foolish, and masochistic, but also unrealistic, backward, and fantastical. The telos of the good life was so apparent in our brown family that my mother's attempt to be critically melancholic was always condemned, even in the moments when she omitted the worst of it. There was a tendency to want to parse (her) bodily sickness from worldly suffering, separate and distinct from immigrant history and class struggle, or at least from the malignant, or the more unsavory aspects, of that history. So most everyone avoided her storytelling: the sting of her utterances cut into their fashioning of themselves as modern, liberal, happy, successful immigrants. They would not let her history, which they chalked up to an odd cocktail of fragmented memory and imagination, sully their fictional selves. But I let her stories reign me in, bring me closer to her, hold me in their secret embrace, connect me to the intimacy of her thoughts. Her stories were the promised fruit that I set out to archive. And in that intimate proximity, a part of me was destroyed, damaged, broken off. My prized tusk—my studied speech, my regimented syntax, my scholarly training—is now all steeped in the ugly and complicated history of my mother's life. I tried to help expunge from her tongue some of the pain, offering her, at the least, an audience of one daughter. But even my maternal enchantment couldn't save her. She had successfully been written into the nucleus of our family as irrational and servile. And as each of her illnesses arrived, they too were entered into this script.

The logic of feminine fragility masked the calculative rationale of the ubiquitous machinations of power that distributed illness on my mother's body and organs, sometimes in plain sight and sometimes in muted, benign forms. Her body and her illnesses were alternatively marked as disabled, weak, feeble, feminine, excessive, made-up, exaggerated, and hyperbolic, obfuscating the debilitating formations that shaped my mother's life. The economy of power peculiar to my mother's life was internally sustained by the interplay of liberal, good immigrant life and conservative gender roles now all grown up to a robust individualism and gendered freedom. Her failing body and her prickly tongue were anathema to these self-congratulatory deflections. So she learned to collaborate with the flow of familial discourse with amenable statements like, *I have always been sick; I am not a strong woman, I was stupid, naïve, made bad decisions.* Others would reinforce this, nodding their heads, as if to say: yes, yes, she is a weak woman, and weak women are always sick. These sentiments and their accompanying patronizing articulations were common refrains among the members of our family, naturalizing the condition of her pained embodiment as aging, performing their distinction from my mother's sickness through an expressed unique fragility that belonged solely to her. It was a compulsive negation of her intellectual understanding, and in it, she would participate. This cadence allowed for an acceptable banality to take place in both our family and the medical discourses around my mother's illness. It is this banality that I want to suspend.

Ironically, as soon as the seriality of migration, money problems, mothering, mundane racism, monotonous violence relaxed their grip and the multiple moving parts of patriarchal power lost its virulence and just when she could retire from the constant interface with power, debility stepped in. Her body, which had pushed her through life, now collapsed. It was as though sickness was waiting in the shadows, surveying until it could take over. Each sickness took its place in her body, finding its own flesh to feast on, overlapping and working in concert with the others. The act of living was not ever meant for the fragile: three heart surgeries (the doctors tell us her heart functions at less than 20 percent); severe diabetes, with blindness lurking behind her inflamed retinas; a variation of Parkinson's disease that has left her with everyday hand tremors that make even the simplest task or pleasure precarious; a horrible bout of shingles that has blurred her vision and has given her splitting migraines; severely arthritic joints that have caused her knees to give out; leg pain that has gotten worse year by year; and arthritic gout on her feet that has discolored her skin and twisted her toes over one another. Despite the eleven pills she takes daily, pain is an everyday occurrence. If she falls, which has happened several times, it takes her months to recover, and her thin blood produces football-sized bruises that last months wherever the impact of the fall is—usually her lower back. The pain that grips my mother's body is weakening, draining, encumbering, hindering, sometimes incapacitating, but almost always invisible. What holds up her bones are skin and some remaining tendons. Muscle is all but gone. Blood is thin like water. She lacks the words to explain her pain, to articulate how unfamiliar, even unrecognizable, her body has become: "a body that seems beyond the reach of language."[3]

For most of the writing of this book, my mother's arthritic body and Parkinsonian tremors punctuated our time and space together. She has become frail, something she had never been before. Her rounded, curvy, voluptuous body is now sagged and thinned. By the time I began archiving her stories, her cane—which she had resisted for many years—had become commonplace; occasionally she uses a walker now. I remember the days she went up and down stairs quickly, unthinkingly. Now stairs make her nervous, demanding too much energy and promising precarity. She walks slowly and cautiously, as though the act of walking, like so many other acts in her life, could betray her, could bruise her. She now loves handicap ramps, wheelchair grocery carts, and random strangers who stop to walk her to the door, to help her balance herself if she looks shaky, to offer their kind assistance at the sight of her physical frailty. Sickness was, for my mother, a multiple, multiplying, complex, complicated, fluid, and forever becoming. Debility sped up. Death stood by and watched. As Audre Lorde wrote of herself in the *Cancer Journals*, my mother also carried death around in her body, "like a condemnation." My mother was not a woman who repressed mortality. Death, like sex, like violence, was everyday kitchen table talk. But the border between life and death, unlike the border between sex and violence, proved to be far less retractable.

I try to think about how illness, ailment, sickness, and disease in my mother's life are (mere) extensions of the necropolitical facets of her life, how each brutally objectified her in different, separate, and conjoined ways. To think about the conditions in which my mother became sick and how each sickness amplified and transmogrified into another and another and another is to understand that the brown maternal is tethered to the patriarchal, misogynistic, capitalist, racist conflicts of our lives and that our illnesses are a container and an expression of this much more painful and complicated history. It is to understand that the debilitating effects of the structures of power don't escape our bodies. It is to understand that our illnesses are as symptomatic as they are historical, that they repeat the structures of a larger social reality. It is to understand that debilitation is germane to living through male and White and hetero and capitalist domination. It is to see illness as the normative horizon.

My mother saw this horizon clearly and expressed it. She had no illusions about the fate of women like herself, women who are embedded in a distribution of risk already factored into the calculus of debilitation. Precarity, vulnerability, frailty, and other necroproximities were familiar modalities for my mother. Each trauma, fear, and loss that contoured her life absorbed into her flesh and marked her, coagulated as slow but intense illness making—over time, accelerating its assault on my mother's body. Through metaphor and analogy, in story and in memory, through hyperbole and deadpan, she anticipated debility. *Death*, she said, *is always closer to women*. The alchemy of her persistent proximity to violence, witnessing, longing, and fear meant that her body became the repository for what the tongue couldn't work through, couldn't hold. Her tongue, in its riskiness, its abjection and its excess, had rhizomatic effects on her body. It compounded the biopolitical effects of this slow wearing down of the body, as it assembled the past and took her backward and inward. Her memories, her traumas, her stories floated through her body, materializing on her skin, on the domain of flesh, on the surface of her organs, on the flesh of her tongue. My mother was, as Jasbir Puar might say, in "debility's position."[4]

....

To bite the tongue. Swallow. Deep. Deeper.
Swallow. Again even more. Just until there would
be no more of organ. Organ no more.
—THERESA HAK KYUNG CHA, *DICTEE*

How many of her stories fell violently back down her throat, never to register in the air in front of her mouth, never oxygenated, disintegrating her organs, and turning into sepsis in her blood? In January of 2013, twenty days after my mom's third heart surgery, she developed what appeared to be a severe case of the flu. It happened too soon after the surgery, and her recovery was incomplete. Already terribly weak, she withered away even more for a few days, insisting that because it was winter, she had developed a bad cold. When my father finally rushed her to the hospital and called the three of us, I was about to board a flight back to Atlanta. At the time, I had been commuting from Atlanta to New Orleans, completing a two-year postdoc program in gender and sexuality studies at Tulane University, commuting because of an embattled custody case over my daughter. The evening I arrived back in Atlanta, I went straight to the hospital. My father and both my elder sister and brother were at the hospital. Both my older sister and my sister-in-law (my brother's wife) were pregnant at the time, my sister in her first pregnancy and my sister-in-law in her third. My mother was in critical condition. She had sepsis, a condition in which the chemicals her body produced to fight the postsurgical infection were instead inflaming and poisoning her organs. Not wanting to relate the news to my pregnant sister (although she, too, is a medical doctor), the attending ER doctor, and not her regular cardiologist, related to me that my mother would not make it through the night. We might, he continued in a clinical manner, want to say our good-byes. The doctor's eyes were serious, mechanical, focused. I looked down at his hands, not wanting him to see my face. His hands fiddled nervously, maybe because of boredom or just medical banality. My throat constricted, as I stared at his white coat, his white hands—and I thought of the "cool hands of white men" that Toni Morrison described in *Paradise*.[5] For a split second, I enjoyed turning him into a caricature. I would do the abjuring, not he. He had turned my mother into his medical property, had inducted my mother's body into a system of anatomical and medical meaning, and I was powerless in the face of his prognosis, his decisions.

Yes, my mother was sick; she had always been sick. Yes, she was dying; she had always been dying. But illness and death were always awaiting, always there-not-there. But my mother was here, flesh and fat, skin and eyes and mouth and tongue. *It wasn't that time. It wasn't her time. There was still more time. Time. Time.* The word echoed in my head, crushing all other words with its weight. I stayed with my mother in the ICU that night, watching her breathe, heavy, disoriented, poisoned, holding in her body life and death, the past and the present, poison and possibility. *Waqt* [time], she whispered, *nazook hai* [time is fragile] . . . *waqt ko sambal lo* [take care of time]. *Time is something,* she would say, *we cannot touch, hold, contain, satisfy, gather around. Time is always moving, slipping away, passing away. You can walk with it, but it will always betray you. It moves slow when you move fast; fast when you move slow. Time contains us and we endure it.* I thought of how, for my mother, if anything was weird—uncontainable, unpredictable, tense, fluid—it was time. In the temporality of sickness, time had become even more suspect, less graspable, simultaneously more and less meaningful, more open and more closed, more slow and more fast, more symbolic and more banal. The order of (colonial) time has always been suspicious of different temporalities (Black time, brown time, maternal time, women's time), and my mother knew this. She found time to be a very masculine construct and, thus, like women and sex, subject to all forms of control. *Time is untrustworthy because it made women desperate. Time is untrustworthy because it shifts proximities. Time is untrustworthy because it creates illusions of healing, delusions of recovery.* But time, my mother would say, *simply marks the endured, the quotidian.* It holds no other power. It, too, is fragile. Where others lamented the passing of time, for my mother, it was the *fragility of* time that she leaned on that night in the ICU. *Waqt ko sambal lo*, she added: "Take care of time"; time also needs care.

That happened ten years ago, and, had we all known better, we wouldn't have believed the clinical words of that White ER doctor. He didn't know. My mother still had to see her first born's *first born*, who appears to have come into this world with a lifeline for my mother. But this push-pull between death and life, almost-death, not-death, not-yet-death became and continues to be the most familiar model of my mother's life, an ongoing, persistent entanglement of the life and death drives.

The race between death and medicine had technically begun at the end of 2008, when my mother experienced, according to her doctor, an asymptomatic heart attack. She was immediately scheduled for her first open-heart surgery in January of 2009. That first postsurgical look at her body—eyes closed, mouth open, tubed up, cut open, the bandages, the gauze, the skin on her bare chest blue from bruising—was something I was not prepared for. I had always felt so connected to my mother's body. I saw it as my own. I knew her body so well that I knew the patterns of her breathing and could observe even the slightest of changes. I had developed a language, even within the patriarchal contours of our life, to encounter my mother's body with intimacy, eroticism, sensuality, respect, and care. My mother's postsurgical, sick body disrupted my vision and my history of *looking* at her. It fragmented me and exhausted me; it moved me into slowness; it extracted (and I un/willingly gave) my emotional, intellectual, and visual labor. And in that moment, I recognized that illness, as a direct by-product of patriarchal coloniality, is what would (eventually) take my mother's life instead of what I had always thought, which is that patriarchy alone would kill my mother. I had to contend with another force of power. It was something that at the time I was not ready for. It was a psychic lacuna that neither my feminist theories nor my maternal enchantment could fill.

In fact, this first surgery marked the point where my mother's body began to seriously deteriorate. She never fully recovered from this first bodily and medical invasion. It was as though when the doctors went in to fix her heart, they punctured the deep well of pain that lived there, pain that, previously manifested only on her tongue, now seeped through the rest of her body. The doctors went *in* to remedy, and in so doing, they let something even more dangerous *out*. Since that surgery, whenever she got sick, it was never mild or temporary. It felt instead like a proxy to permanence, to death. And while her illnesses, like her stories, didn't invoke crisis, they were accompanied by the temporal urgency associated with virality, infection, or sickness. My mother's everyday life came to be shaped by the debilitation of her body. Her body was now a locus of conflicting illnesses and a fleshy meeting ground of histories, traumas, power relations, and medicines. If one medicine treated one illness, then another—treating another condition—contradicted the effect of the first, yet another pharmaceutical antidote was offered to create equilibrium effects of the first two. Another condition or drug threatened to mess up the harmony of the previous pill. Each condition threatened her already very low-functioning heart. And on and on and on, my mother learned about the deterioration of her organs, and, in so doing, she yet again developed a hyperawareness of flesh.

Some time ago, long before her first heart surgery in 2009 cemented debility in her consciousness, I noticed that my mother began performing a different relation to illness, one I would describe as masochistic, self-righteous, and reparative. When she became sick, my mother quickly understood that neither her sicknesses nor her social reality undid time. Instead both relied on time; both continued to be shaped by heterosexual and masculine temporalities. Both were governed by it, scripted by it, dependent on it, stuck in it. Both animated time and foreclosed it. Both gathered around multiple registers and multiple volumes of suffering and death. So sickness, like patriarchal social reality, required an affective and epistemological response, tactic, maneuver, scheme, and trickery.

Her first bout of the American flu that persisted for weeks and that landed her in a doctor's office for hours became an oblique moment from which she would develop her habitual resort to illness. On that particular day in 1979, she sat in a little clinic in Cherry Hill, New Jersey, and wept for hours and hours, even though her doctor had given her a strong medicine with the promise that she would be feeling better within days. But my mother, finally alone with her feelings (even in the company of a stranger), kept weeping. The doctor handed her a box of tissues and left her alone, offering her the room for as long as she needed it. After several hours of crying, my mother finally wiped her tears and went home, an unusual levity in her step. She realized, then, that sickness was a peak, an intensification of the body, that, while familiar and mundane, released her from the grip, even if only temporarily, of external power. She realized in that moment that sickness, for all its wretchedness, could also be a reprieve, a silo away from the demands of men and children, a reason to be cantankerous, a reason to openly, without explanation, cry. Once she accepted this relation, this inscription of self, she was released from the illusion that she hated being sick. She had made a choice. She wasn't preparing for sickness; she was eager for it.

In this way, illnesses became part of my mother's *technologies of self*, practices by which she bound herself to her identity and consciousness and, at the same time, to and against external power. Manifesting in and through coexisting scales of loss and privilege, illness became the mode through which she expressed her powerlessness and escaped external power, a cipher for the way she contended with the intimate dimensions of social and material violence. But illness, of course, paves the way to becoming flesh but in a radically different way than the matrix of sex, gender, class, and race. Illness is something that comes from within; it emerges from the viscera and not from its exteriority. For my mother, unlike trauma, sickness wasn't melancholic or anxiogenic or even threatening. It was instead exhausting and ambivalent and weakening. Unlike trauma, sickness gave her permission to sleep. Ironically it excused her (to a certain extent, for a small period of time) from patriarchal duties. Physical pain sanctified my mother, as it provided the material ground for symbolic hurt. Illness freed her tongue, even as it actively constrained her body. It offered her an open space to dwell on her body, to dwell in her body.

And this combination of becoming pain and becoming flesh emboldened my mother. She refused the (White) androcentric style of being rational, stoic, and calm about illness and pain. There was no zone of sentient neutrality. She made it clear to anyone who would hear, could hear, that she was in pain, that *this hurt*, or *that hurt, that our bodies will always fail us, that we will always fail our bodies, that aging is a terrible thing, aging is a punishment, aging is natural, aging is a disease, aging is malignant,* and so goes just the beginning of her list of analogies. She wasn't loud or dramatic or animated. Just deadpan with excessive descriptors. And because my mother was not beholden to any class politics of containment or interested in any bourgeois attachments to privacy, her illnesses, like her stories, were available for consumption and critique. Sickness, like her stories, made her epistemologically incoherent. I suppose it was just a matter of time before her body joined her tongue, both intertwined, recursive, and unrelenting in their practice of feminine spectacle. I suppose it was just a matter of time before she became the figure of the death drive itself.

The paradox is that while subjectivity is a game my mother had internally mastered, her illnesses were conversely unavailable for mastery, simultaneously taking over the inside and the outside of her body. Pain that came from the world could be manipulated, appropriated, narrativized. But physical pain had a different formation and temporality; it was part of a different economy, marked by a different lack of agency. Her frequent hospitalizations and medicalizations were events to which she had to submit. Signification alone could not account for the appearance and manifestation of illness, which finds its home in symptomizing the body toward pain. Instead, my mother, being sick and hospitalized, reproduced her lifelong obsession with feminine abjection in a different register. The disturbance of illness profoundly slowed life, just as it too slowed death. Sickness, in its multiplicity, in its inevitability, oriented my mother toward death, but one which would not come, one which could not be beckoned, one for which mere submission was not an option. The biopolitical impulse to make life last through modern Western medicine (medicine as letting live) was in a tense relation with my mother's orientation toward death, an orientation she had developed through a lifetime of accumulated hurt and witnessing.[6] Like the death drive, both the imperative to treat her body and the impulse to let go of her body were bound to practices of repetition. The compulsion to repeat and to destroy are components of both the death drive and my mother's tongue; her death drive and speech drive are tied together in a sustaining cycle of cynicism, irony, negativity, protest, and submission.

In the early years of my mother's repeated and lengthy hospital visits, I found myself in hospital rooms watching her sleep, feeling bitter resentment at the mechanical handling of her body. Watching my mother disappear into expert medical syntax, metal instruments, and medical machines was gutting and silencing. Her self absented, my self raging. Language, both our pleasure, both our object, fell flat on our tongues, speech buried in our mouths. We communicated through our eyes, both our gaze sharpened by mutual distrust and unavoidable dependency, filled with observations, complaints, critiques, propulsions that couldn't make it to our tongues.

To pass the endless hours of sitting, waiting, watching, I began rereading (among many other things) Michel Foucault's *Birth of a Clinic*, in which Foucault takes a genealogical approach to trace the medical shift from treating the disease to a broader medical mission to sustain the patients' health toward life. Foucault's analysis exposed the omnipresence of the medical gaze on the ailing body, orienting the sick body—regardless of the subject's own desires, feelings, perceptions, beliefs—toward life. I found the hospital procedures around my mother's body and the words in Foucault's book both a drab necessity. But reading Foucault absorbed some of my rage at the hospital's mechanical handling of my mother's body, at its regimes of subjectification that rendered my mother's subjectivity irrelevant, that made her body a biomarker of the doctors' success or failure, that established her expression of pain unbelievable or communicable primarily through infantilized emojis—smiley to sad to shocked yellow-faced emojis. This dialectical intimacy between pain and witnessing, and the patronizing disavowal of both, is one I observed my entire life, with each family member and each physician, each rationale and each foil, each subjective handling of her body and each objective illness. My witnessing, like her pain, was utterly lonely and utterly unbelievable.

There is nothing exceptional about my mother's illnesses. Many of her generation with complicated migration journeys and struggles of men, money, family, and children grow old and into a litany of illnesses, cancers, heart diseases, diabetes, and so on. She also knew that old age was a privilege, *an American privilege,* she called it. But there was something particular, even peculiar, about my mother's sicknesses, the weakening of her body over and through time, the fact that others around her aged better, more gracefully, appeared stronger, and the relentless perception of her as always and already suscep- tible to illness. I think of how being sick and staying sick is, to a large extent, dependent on the economic and social relationships that sustain or exploit us. It is indissociable from that dimension of feeling that allows us to feel pro- tected and valued and alive. Having so many medical conditions that shaped my mother's everyday life recurrently demonstrated to me how fragile and necessary her interdependency was to her husband, and later to her children. This interdependency put her in a perpetual state of precarity. It still does.

I have also always been struck by the difference with which my father was able to steadfastly avoid sickness and even appeared to avoid aging. Sickness meant that my mother aged rapidly, almost overnight, while my father contin- ued to appear younger, stronger, slimmer, fitter, healthier, robust in his body and personality, making clear the distribution of health as a gendered and classed resource. Being healthy allowed my father to be also optimistic and egotistical, expressing his good health in proud statements like, "I've never even had to take an aspirin my whole life," tethering sickness and pain to my mother's shortcomings. Shortsighted, my father thought that aging for him would have a different outcome.

But when my father became a heart patient (in the spring of 2017), his characteristic and lifelong domineering posture succumbed to the fragility of his internal organs. If White men got stronger and more active after the highly treasured Western medicine's life-saving open-heart surgery (a popu- lar medical narrative offered by many a cardiologist), my father, conversely, became weak and passive and dependent. His pride in mastering his body, in being the normative (Western-ish, bourgeois) subject, debating religion and philosophy and economy and politics, all disintegrated, collapsed, shrunk. Late in life heart surgery combined with severe hearing loss and sharp painful debilitating spasms in his mouth (a mysterious illness even in the voluminous Western medical vocabulary), was enervating. His daily pharmaceutical regi- men involves seventeen different pills (to my mother's eleven), a practice that shames him and that he shares with just enough irony to reveal introspection. My father loves life and living. He loves being in control. It come so naturally to him as to never give it a second thought. But loss of mastery and loss of strength made my father physically gaunt and imbalanced, socially isolated and emotionally tender. There is a fragility about him now that is unfamiliar, both to him and to us. The abuse and masculine foulness that was scattered about in our childhood is now replaced with soft masculinity and engaged fathering. He implores my mother, longing for affirmation of his disavowals, innocently probing her for a history he doesn't have the courage to hear, fool-ishly asking questions about a past he has almost wholly denied. His weak-ness and tenderness make my mother awkward, but they also make her less secretive, less instinctually protective. She answers him favorably, balming his festering wounds with lies. Meanwhile, she turns to me, deadpan, and says, *The lion has become a frog.*

....

As far as I can remember, my mother was fat and round and loved eating and was shamed for it. When it came to eating, control and discipline were de-manded of her, not because of any hegemonic suspicion of female pleasure or a demand of feminine slenderness (although these, too, were coded man-dates) but in the name of good health. *Health is wealth*, we grew up hearing, in particular whenever my mom was eating. But my mother's love of spicy food and sweet fruit are two things she could not control. Her love of spicy food was so excessive that in her early days in the United States, she would never leave the house without a little, sealed plastic bag of Thai chilis and a lemon, a little bag she would pull out whenever she got hungry or when we ate at American fast-food chains or bland franchise restaurants. Unwilling to accept the tasteless food of various restaurants in the States, she would squeeze the fresh juice of the lemon onto her bag of chilis, sprinkle it with salt, and, instantly, everything tasted better. I saw this small act as a small way back to (some) lost objects of desire.

She now says this habit of hers is what has caused her ulcers. Worry, she explains, is what has caused her always-elevated blood pressure; even when she was young, she worried, worried, worried. Worry, she says, is in her ma-ternal blood. Her trembling hands, she declares, are a gift from her mother, whose hands also shook till the end, also mysteriously undiagnosed. Diabe-tes, which came much later, she attributes to Quetta, her favorite childhood city, a city often referred to as the fruit basket of Pakistan. Fruit evokes for my mother a melancholy eros, a longing that goes back to her childhood years. Quetta, my mother describes, is a city full of all sorts of fruit trees—peach, apple, cherry, pecan, almond, pomegranate, grapes—where she and her older sister would run from garden to garden, perch on tree after tree, eating every juicy, sticky, wet fruit they could get their hands on. The week my mother's family left Quetta when her father's two-year post ended and her youngest sister was born, my mother packed as much fruit as she could into her *dupatta* (shawl) for the train ride to Peshawar, fruit, which, of course, in the Peshwari heat, rotted right through her shawl and clothes. But even the memory of her father's wrath at the sight and smell of her stenchy and sticky clothes couldn't curb my mother's love of fruit, couldn't scar this delicious food memory.

She still has this love for fruit—sticky, messy, white-black-yellow-seeded fruits that leave unbelievable messes in the kitchen and a big, contagious smile on her face. If she breaks into a pomegranate, wet red spots cover the countertops, some even splattering to the closest white wall. When she eats mangos, she sucks on every last fiber attached to the oblong seed, her hands and face and the table and the chair sticky with the moist sugars of the fruit. Every season, she used to buy and gift cases of seasonal fruit: one for each of her three kids' homes, one for her home, and one for her older sister's home. In the summer, mangos and guavas; in the winter, pomegranate. There are few things my mother loves more, and almost melancholically, never felt she ate enough. My mother eats this fruit against her doctor's orders, against her doctor-daughter's orders. Her diabetes means that she cannot process these sugars. Sugars, even natural ones, inflame her joints, cause retinal in-flammation, which can, or will eventually, lead to blindness and which can, at any time, fatally damage her kidneys. Sugar pushes my mother's body, as my physician sister says, "into the danger zone." But I admit I love the smile that emerges when she eats fruit. It is a smile that is reserved for two things only: fruit and indicting men. It is undisciplined, uncontained, mischievous, ecstatic, excessive.

For my mother, eating is the most intimate act. Unlike sex—which while private, is accompanied by spectacle, display, taboo, and conventions—eating is intimate, unruly, pleasurable, and a time to be with sensation. Eating for her was the most private of things. More than desire. More than *language*. It was a space of intimacy, of longing, a refuge, a habit, as bodily as breath, as heartbeat, as blood. Consequently, my mother was also very peculiar about eating. She rarely ate in public—never at parties, public events, social func-tions, or even small or large family dinners at restaurants. She always ate at home, at the kitchen table, alone or with one us, before these events. As both fetish and a symbol of corporeal possession, (her) eating was not available for public consumption. Eating was a private affair.

I began to suspect early on that my mother managed the extreme ten-sion of her life conditions by means of a nearly fanatical concentration on cooking. For my mother, the kitchen was a reliable place, *kind even*. It was a space that waited for her. It was more or less an infrastructure of continuity. It was a site both of affection and instrumentality, a social sphere, and a place where she could (often, anyway) be alone. She has cooked in many a kitchen, in many a city and country, in her homes and in others; it was a space that never rejected her. She loved to—and did not hesitate to—make a mess. If she ate pinenuts, the brown shells littered the carpet. If she peeled onions, the peelings lay spread and stuck on the floors, her bare feet stepping on them to reach for the next vegetable that needed chopping. Peeling garlic, chopping chilies, cutting ginger, skinning meat, scraping lemons, making chutneys all involved elaborate, mammoth messes. And in those messes, she created some of the most delicious food we ever tasted. My mother's cooking was famous in our family. No matter how many other women in our family were present, all excellent chefs in their own right, they always, without fail, wanted my mother's cooking.

As the onset of varying diagnoses took over her and our lives, her interest in food and eating waned. Food no longer holds the same appeal—a little plate of almost nothing fills her brief, bodily need for food. For me, this is the most tragic and tangible aspect of her illness. Hunger and the pleasure of eating abandoned her. Eating and cooking as intimate feminine sociality in kitchens and on kitchen tables became increasingly rare. This is an imprecise statement. Still, I feel attached to it.

The truth is that my mother eats little (too little, according to the doctors, her weight dropping by the month, by the week) and that the pleasure and unruliness that she always associated with food has significantly dissipated. The rich interdependency between cooking, eating, sociality, vulnerability, and generosity that my mother brought forward with food no longer holds the power to cocoon her, to nourish her. Still she cooks, every day even, out of habit and history, for others, but no longer for herself. But there are rare moments of return—when her younger sister visits and over puff pastry stuffed with fresh cream, warm *rotis* fresh off the stove, homemade spicy pickle (*achar*), and her doctor-daughter's disapproving gaze, the two women fall deep into food and memory.

Her body holds this history. And part of that history comes from the room in which it was created. For my mother, the kitchen is a space of nuanced feminine pleasure, a pleasure she refuses to give up, even as it too involves endless labor and confinement and expectation. It is a space where she formulates and invents responses to the various pharmaceutical regimens imposed on her by her American doctors and insisted upon and surveilled by her doctor-daughter. It is the space where she creates another practice, in retaliation to the flat, hard, narrow hospital beds, where her body is poked, prodded, measured, jabbed, and injected. It is the space where she devises her own furtive, but reparative, practice of Ayurveda. She subscribes to these healing practices far more than she does to the multiple, little white and yellow and pink and blue pills that accompany her morning tea and toast. With varying concoctions of turmeric, nutmeg, ginger, cinnamon, fenugreek, cumin, and other spices, she privately treats her illnesses outside of and in addition to pharmaceutical mandates. She combines nutmeg, ginger, and turmeric to treat a vicious cough. She soaks fenugreek seeds overnight and drinks its water to treat her arthritic pain (*methi ka paani*). She dry-roasts carraway seeds and then wraps up the seeds in a muslin cloth to create a homemade heating pouch that clears chest congestion (*Ajwain ka sekh*). Cilantro treats high cholesterol. The insides of banana peels increase bodily strength. Cardamom for gout and appetite suppression. Turmeric to clot blood. Raw onion for bee and wasp stings.

To be clear, it was not that my mother held onto any sort of *Vedik* nostalgia; quite the contrary: she is fairly suspicious of all the ways Ayurveda had developed as a trend, the way it now circulated in its own biopharmaceutical and entrepreneurial spirit. What she does claim is that Ayurveda is a completely different epistemological foundation on how the body works, an almost private feminine language handled in kitchens and bedrooms. It was that *something feminine, something brown* about healing and care. Her kitchen concoctions were but one modality with which to create a reparative space, a space where sickness exceeds its physiology and becomes a more understandable relation.

For my mother, sickness and pain were conditions of knowing (the self). And these techniques (of self) made sickness less awkward, if not necessarily less chronic, less pained, even if still inconvenient, less fearful, even as they remained visceral. Her alternative practices countered the pharmaceutical fragmentation of her body and mind, defied the antibody impulse of medicine and medical cultures. They untroubled the troubling nature of sickness. They made sickness intimate and natural, like aging, like abjection, and thus managed by all the ingredients in her kitchen.

My mother knows that her habits, like her health, teeter unsurely on the border between her body and her grave. Her respect for death and understanding of death as something fundamentally out of her hands means that she finds the insistence on long life, particularly in America, vulgar and sadistic. This is also how she describes her pacemaker and defibrillator, warning, lamenting that *this electric current won't let me die even when it is my time*, her fingers running over the hardened metal disk under her skin, now protruding because of such extreme weight loss. *I'm ready*, she tells me. *I have many questions for Allah*. My mother's relation to Western medicine is awkward and crude, even if at times romantic and Godlike. It is the apparatus that allows her to keep living just as it controls how (long) she lives.

The kitchen, then, is one way to not relinquish control. This kitchen—full of spices, powders, pastes—prevents total governance, exceeds the interpretive grid of Western medicine, conjures an opening where there is none, unfastens the promiscuity of sensation. Sickness, like racialized misogyny, had fucked her, and her remedies, like her tongue, are one relation through which she opens and practices counterintuitive power. The various touches and textures of her tonics have come to be, like her tongue, one (more) antinormative reflex in the normal and banal everyday hegemonic handling, dealing, dismissing of her body. She sticks to these practices with such an intensity that it makes others uneasy. But with each herb, each concoction, each syrup, each alchemy, she takes back her body. Each tonic gives her control over her body and its feelings—what touches it, caresses it, goes inside of it, penetrates it, lingers on it, and how and when and how often. Her relation to these antidotes is sensual and bodily and pleasurable, unlike the mechanical control that pharmaceuticals, even if effective, have over her body. This unrestrained, uninhibited, promiscuous dialectic of illness and healing produces my mother's "elsewhere, an other-wiseness, a knowledge-beyond-knowing"—a brown maternal embodied mode of relief and care from corporeal maledictions that are seen neither as crisis nor as well-being.[7]

And indeed my mother developed a promiscuous relation to her therapies, feverishly sucking the insides of banana peels until they are as thin and translucent as film, ecstatically collecting copper cups, convinced that drinking water from them reduces inflammation, sensually massaging twice and thrice a day her joints, her scalp, her hair with mustard oil, neem oil, amla oil, and coconut oil, rapturously making jars of herbal treatments, the tips of her fingers in perpetuity stained with turmeric and tacky crystal jars meant for display are now filled with oil cocktails for knee and hand pain, and so on and so on went these amorous, elsewhere, otherwise bodily remedies, even if her diseases never yielded to her treatments. Her brown feminine kitchen alchemies demanded this feverish focus, an attentiveness to the body, a turn inward to the flesh and its workings and feelings and inclinations and proclivities— what the body repels and what it pulls in, what calms its and what excites it, what centers it and what fragments it, what comforts it and what is made uncomfortable by it. Between pain and abjection hovered an aching generosity toward these herbal potions, an aching submission to the stirrings she felt in her blood, to the pleasure she felt in possessing her own body. These brown modes of remedies and reveries moved my mother into a smoother alchemy. She became her own *Vaidya* and her own *Visya* (with whom she would *never break a relation*).

afterword

I opened this book by making a proposition about how to think about an object—the tongue—which is also how I think of theory, as a series of propositions, as a series of possibilities on how to think, how to understand, how be in life and make life. In trying to save my mother's stories from disappearing irretrievably, I approached my reading and writing tongues as an experimental theoretical practice, one hinged to other practices—of healing, living, enduring, disobeying, of maybe changing the consequences of trauma and creating better objects to which we might attach. I saw tongues as one mode to work, read, think, and create across different temporalities, spaces, knowledges, and histories in order to undo patriarchal and colonial logics that thrive on owning, possessing, excluding, and extracting the brown maternal. I offered the brown maternal as one way into thinking and theorizing to get at, as Stuart Hall wrote, "the absolute unknowingness, the opacity, the density, of reality, of the subject one is trying to understand."[1] I saw my mother's tongues as opening a way to think about thinking, a way to reach for something that is just outside one's grasp—theory in perpetuity to relation and relationality. Indeed, at a time when there is so much talk about decolonizing knowledge, I wanted to ask what this really means, what are the multiple modalities through which knowledge is produced into the world and about the world, whom do we need to take (more) seriously, what forms, imaginaries, ways of being actually move us in that direction.

I remain preoccupied with tongues, with my mother's, and with those of other brown mothers. I came to tongues through my mother, through her story on tongues. But I also came to understand that such a story on tongues is sutured to my mother's brownness, her femininity, her relation in perpetuity to the abject, and her subsequent articulations of a life lived across oceans, dictated as it was by men, money, and medicine. Every story I offered was hers, but the errors, the deviations, the interpretations, the investments are mine. She trusted me, even as she guided me, corrected me, even as she knew my reading of her story was partial, even as she knew her very stories were partial. Yet even in their partiality, I came to realize that her tongues are an embodied epistemological cypher. So I grasped at her tongue, her flesh, read it closely, folded it out as a theoretical intervention to shake loose the imperceptible of the everyday brown maternal domestic, to throw into relief the obscure relationships between sociality, trauma, femininity, and motherhood, to come close to and touch her sensuous thought form, and to do so without reproducing an essential or a single truth.

My mother's stories were a mediating force in the world I was growing up in: they structured my sense of the world, sanctioning, perpetuating, and resisting cultural myths, and sometimes creating new mythologies that allowed me to engage in a constructive rewriting and rethinking of the world. I think now of how it was so impossible for my mother to come to know herself as she did, given that the circumstances of her life were so inimical to this type of knowing, given that the bionecro politics of race and sex and class and gender attempted to discipline her so completely. I think of how her tongue—even in all its agility and perceptibility—still underscores the fact that the subject is necessarily opaque to herself, just as she understands herself perpetually within a web of social relations and responsibilities and just as she, too, may develop a relation to that opacity.

Throughout this book, I position the tongue as a brown epistemological form. I think of the brown maternal not as a singular figure but as a way of being, a method of mothering, within patrilinear, colonial, and geographic norms. I offer my mother's tongue as a fleshy path into minor subjects, like brown domestic and domesticated mothers, as a lens to notice, consider, understand how they poeticize, lyricize, develop, and disobey; tongues are the fleshy path into their survivals, relationalities, fraughtnesses, imperfections, transgressions, and pleasures. The social relations of violence, dispossession, debility, and labor that shape the brown maternal expose the impossibility of romance and sentimentality. Yet sentimentality and romance were always the risks, no matter my efforts to stay at the edge of longing, to stay at the edge of love, to keep my eyes wide open.[2]

It is also true that romance and sentimentality have their own dimensions of unexplorability—their wretchedness, their torment, their ethics. Like other affective attachments, romance and sentimentality involve a whole complex dialectic of idealization and devalorization of self and *other*. Thus, for me, identification-disidentification with my mother through introjection-projection-incorporation of the self-*other*-mother opened up the smallest space of possibility for the sublime. It allowed me to stay with the negativity of her feeling/unfeeling/overfeeling; it kept me in touch with her disobedience; it allowed for deep reciprocity. Might, then, these small trace/s of sentimentality, romance, and recuperation, as embedded in this archive (insofar as they are inevitable), excite us toward solidarity, toward an opening, toward the sublime, just as in excess they blot out the possibility of knowing and in cliché exhaust the poetic imaginary? Or is this archive yet another site of melancholic cannibalism, whereby the object of my desire is better fragmented, devoured, consumed, swallowed, rather than lost? How do I "tell" my mother's stories without fossilizing them? What did my writing metabolize—vengeance, redemption, closure, all, or none of the above? What could I gain from this kind of return and whom do I put at risk? Did I, in exposing my mother, put her in a category of risk?

These were the questions that made me pause and breathe. Several sentences I never finished. Countless stories I swallowed. Myriad details I suppressed. Many memories I silenced. Certain brutalities could not find their way into expression. I tell myself that these pauses, these partialities, are part of my mother's right to escape linguistic representation, her right to opacity. *Some things they cannot have.* I tell myself that no matter how much I follow this trail of the dispossessed brown mother, I will not be able to capture how deeply or wholly marked diasporic subjects are by the traumas of our brown mothers. *Some stories can be left out.* I tell myself that an archive of tongues runs the risk of romance (even if queerly defined), of sentimentality (even if stretched toward the sublime), of recuperation (even if my mother is an unremarkable figure), of essentialism (even if I indict my (self as) brown mother), of being obsessed with violence against women (even if such an obsession is apt and necessary). I tell myself that my mother's tongue bears what I cannot (and cannot forget). *There are some things we can keep to ourselves.* So I leave some things there, deep in the recesses of her warm, wrinkled mouth, floating in the soft folds of her pink tongue.

NOTES

Preface

1. *On the body as an archive*, see Julietta Singh, *No Archive Will Restore You* (New York: Punctum Books, 2018), 27.

2. *On the necessity of reading with "thickness,"* see Anjali Arondhekar and Geeta Patel, "Area Impossible," Notes Toward an Introduction," *GLQ: A Journal for Gay and Lesbian Studies* 22, no.2: 151–71.

3. *On bad or ugly feelings*, see Ghassan Moussawi, "Bad Feelings: Trauma, Non-Linear Time, and Accidental Encounters in 'the Field,'" *Departures in Critical Qualitative Research* 10, no. 1: 78–96; Sianne Ngai, *Ugly Feelings* (Cambridge, MA: Harvard University Press, 2007).

4. *On seizing up memory*, see Walter Benjamin, *Illuminations* (New York: Schocken Books, 1968), 255.

5. *On the insistence of memory for women of color*, see Toni Morrison, "I Wanted to Carve Out a World both Culture Specific and Race-Free': an essay by Toni Morrison," *guardian.com*, August 2019, https://www.theguardian.com/books/2019/aug/08/toni-morrison-rememory-essay.

6. *On more tongues than Kali*, see Arundhati Roy, "What Is the Morally Appropriate Language in Which to Think and Write?" *lithub.com*, July 2018, https://lithub.com/what-is-the-morally-appropriate-language-in-which-to-think-and-write/.

Introduction

1. *On our childhoods being marked by our mother's stories*, see Maxine Hong Kingston, *Women Warriors: Memoirs of A Girlhood Among Ghosts* (New York: Knopf, 1976).

2. Simone de Beauvoir, *The Second Sex* (New York: Vintage, 2011), 17.

3. *On death worlds*, see Giorgio Agamben, *Homo Sacer: Sovereign Power and Bare Life* (Stanford, CA: Stanford University Press, 1995), 40.

4. *On alternative consciousness and oppositional methods*, see Chela Sandovol, *Methodology of the Oppressed* (Minneapolis: University of Minnesota Press, 2000).

5. I want to note here the embryonic historiography predating the very possibility of my writing my mother's archive, particularly as an archive of tongues. Tongues, as feminized, racialized, and violated flesh, is a conceptual framing that I develop throughout the book through the provocation of the brown maternal. But such a provocation has roots in both hegemonic linguistic formations and women of color feminisms. For example, the widespread use of the emotionally charged phrase "mother tongue" invokes nationalized and naturalized language or the term *motherland*, gesturing to one's possession of native land. In this context, the phrase "mother tongue" designates one's attachment to a particular language/space, a natural condition of language, thus subject to acquisition through the romance of originality and authenticity. The emphasis on the maternal element of tongues inscribes language into a broader network of relations, from body to kin to nation (i.e., motherland). The latent grammar of the phrase "mother tongue" positions the linguistic and the maternal as basic human needs, like food and shelter, thus providing indispensable access to the symbolic dimension shaping both affectivity and knowledge. The phrase "speaking in tongues" also comes to mind, which refers to a private, closed, and privileged communication between a (often Christian) subject and her divine, inaccessible to others, outside the realm of public discourse and known language (although such a practice is not limited to Christianity).

While this archive of tongues loosely gestures to these framings, my use of tongues primarily draws its energies and meanings from a collective archive of feminist and queer of color thought. Black feminist writer Mae Henderson, for example, invokes the phrase "speaking in tongues" to gesture to women of colors' ability to speak in the multiple languages of public discourse, given the minefield of racism, sexism, classism, and ableism that suffuse their lives. Gloria Anzaldúa once wrote that women of color "speak in tongues like the outcast and the insane." I am also reminded of Gayl Jones (in *Corredigora*) and Toni Cade Bambara (in *Salteaters*), who offer the phrase "mad black speech," by which they refer to the ritualized speech and rhythmic words condemned by the modern world as paranoid and superstitious—the illiterate tongues of the damned. James Baldwin's short story, "Black Boy Looking at White Boy," similarly summons this metaphor in his writing about surviving as a writer, despite "all metaphorical teeth of the world's determination to destroy you"; here, being a Black, queer writer means occupying the feminized, thus destroyable, site of the tongue. The tongue, L. H. Stallings (2007) wrote, is the vernacular organ that makes speech possible. Sara Ahmed (2017) refers to feminism as a history of willful tongues. For Audre Lorde (1984), language was life in the face of existential annihilation. This long genealogy of tongues as a feminist and queer of color heuristic is one to which I am indebted in this project.

6. *On mother talk*, see Trinh Min Ha, *Elsewhere Within Here: Immigration, Refugeeism, and the Boundary Event* (New York: Routledge, 2010), 103.

7. *On unscientific methods*, see Christina Sharpe, *In the Wake: On Blackness and Being.* (Durham, NC: Duke University Press, 2018), 43.

8. *On "theory in the flesh,"* see Cherrie Moraga and Gloria Anzaldúa, *This Bridge Called My Back: Writings by Radical Women of Color* (Bath: Persephone Press, 1981).

9. *On imprecision as method*, see Keguro Macharia, "Belatedness," *GLQ: A Journal of Gay and Lesbian Studies* 26, no. 3 (2020): 566.

10. *On language as matter*, see Mel Chen, *Animacies: Biopolitics, Racial Mattering, and Queer Affect* (Durham, NC: Duke University Press, 2012).

11. *On the limits of theory as liberatory practice*, see bell hooks, *Teaching to Transgress: Education as a Practice of Freedom* (London, Routledge, 1994), 60.

12. *On the feminist usefulness of psychoanalysis*, see Avery Gordon, *Ghostly Matters: Hauntings and the Sociological Imagination.* (Minneapolis: University of Minnesota Press, 42).

13. *On psychoanalysis as a mechanism to unpack the obscure*, see Albert Memmi, *The Colonizer and the Colonized* (New York: Orion, 1965).

14. *On the postcolonial utility of psychoanalysis*, see Ranjana Khanna, *Dark Continents: Psychoanalysis and Colonialism* (Durham, NC: Duke University Press, 2003).

15. *On the mother as a collection of words*, see Gilles Deleuze, *Essays Critical and Clinical* (Minneapolis: University of Minnesota Press, 1997), 18.

16. *On Mother as Other*, see Jacques Lacan, *The Four Fundamental Concepts of Psychoanalysis*, trans. Alan Sheridan (New York: Norton, 1981).

17. *For a lovely exception*, see Roland Barthes, *Mourning Diary*, a book made up of a pastiche of meditations, constructed as a diary in which he wrote each day for the first year after his mother died in 1977. Roland Barthes, *Mourning Diary.* (New York: Hill and Wang, 2009).

18. *On White male theorists' hatred of their mothers*, see Andrew Parker, *The Theorist's Mother* (Durham, NC: Duke University Press, 2017).

19. Francois Perrier. https://www.meisterdrucke.us/fine-art-prints/Francois -Perrier/73002/Veturia,-Mother-of-Coriolanus,-c.1653.html. Accessed June 2018.

20. *On forgetting the mother tongue,* see Karl Marx, *The Eighteenth Brumaire of Louis Bonaparte,* edited by C. P. Dutt, trans. anonymous (New York: International Press, 1935), 15–16.

21. *On the good-enough mother,* see Donald J. Winnicott, "The Theory of Parent–Infant Relationships," *International Journal of Psychoanalysis* 41 (1960): 585–95.

22. *On how psychoanalyses reduce the mother to her body,* see Nancy Chodorow, *The Reproduction of Mothering and the Sociology of Gender* (Berkeley: University of California Press, 1979).

23. *On the good breast/bad breast object relations theory and the devouring infant,* see Melanie Klein, *The Writings of Melanie Klein,* vol. 3 (New York: Free Press, 1975).

24. *On the primal scene of introjection,* see Nikolas Abraham and Maria Torok, *The Shell and the Kernel: Renewals of Psychoanalysis,* ed. Nicholas T. Rand (Chicago: University of Chicago Press), 1994.

25. Abraham and Torok, *The Shell and the Kernel,* 127.

26. Julia Kristeva, "The Meaning of Parity," in *The Kristeva Reader,* edited by John Lechte and Mary Zournazi, trans. John Lechte (Edinburgh: Edinburgh University Press, 2003), 207.

27. Julia Kristeva, "Motherhood Today." Kristeva.fr.com, 2005, http://www.kristeva.fr/motherhood.html.

28. Julia Kristeva, "Motherhood Today." Kristeva.fr.com.

29. Julia Kristeva, *Power of Horror: An Essay on Abjection.* (New York: Columbia University Press. 1982).

30. Luce Irigiray, "And the One Doesn't Stir without the Other," *Signs: A Journal of Women in Culture and Society* 7, no.1 (1981): 63.

31. Luce Irigiray, "And the One Doesn't Stir without the Other," 60–67.

32. Amber Jacobs, "The Potential of Theory: Melanie Klein, Luce Irigaray, and the Mother–Daughter Relationship," *Hypatia: A Journal of Psychoanalysis* 22, no. 3 (2007): 175–93.

33. *On reproduction as key site of melancholia,* see Judith Butler, "Melancholy Gender—Refused Identification," *Psychoanalytic Dialogues* 5, no. 2 (1995): 165–80.

34. *On her own mother's life and death,* see Simone de Beauvoir, *A Very Easy Death* (London: Pantheon, 1985), 4.

35. *On the undertheorizing of motherhood,* see Adrienne Rich, *Of Woman Born: Motherhood as Experience and Institution* (New York: Norton, 1976), 11.

36. *On the Black maternal,* see Hortense Spillers, "'All the Things You Could Be by Now If Sigmund Freud's Wife Was Your Mother Psychoanalysis and Race," *Critical Inquiry* 22 (1996): 732.

37. *On mother-loss and impossible motherhood in the context of Emmitt Till,* see Fred Moten, *In the Break: The Aesthetics of the Black Radical Tradition* (Minneapolis: University of Minnesota Press, 2003).

38. *On representing the Black mother in contemporary US film,* see Rizvana

Bradley, "Vestiges of Motherhood: The Maternal Function in Recent Black Cinema," *Film Quarterly* 71, no.2 (2017): 46–52.

39. *On returning to the maternal*, see Amber Jamila Musser, *Sensual Excess: Queer Femininity and Brown Jouissance*. (New York: New York University Press, 2018); Omiseke Natasha Tinsley, *Izili's Mirrors: Imagining Black Queer Genders* (Durham, NC: Duke University Press, 2018).

40. Musser, *Sensual Excess*, 170.

41. *On the unsettled relations between feminism and psychoanalysis*, see Jacqueline Rose, *Sexuality in the Field of Vision* (New York: Verso, 2006).

42. *On archive fever*, see Jacques Derrida, *Archive Fever: A Freudian Impression* Chicago: University of Chicago Press, 1998; Andre Green, *On Private Madness* (New York: Taylor and Francis, 1996).

43. *On reading slow*, see Deborah Britzman, "On Being a Slow Reader: Psychoanalytic Reading Problems in Ishiguro's *Never Let Me Go*," *Changing English* 13, no. 3 (2006): 309; Heather Love, "Macbeth: Milk," in *Shakesqueer*, ed. Madhavi Menon (Durham, NC: Duke University Press, 2010).

44. Jacques Derrida, *Monolingualism of the Other, or the Prosthesis of Origin* (Stanford, CA: Stanford University Press, 1998).

45. *On neoliberal wet dreams and other clever ways of thinking about the (faux) fruition of desire in late capitalist global and libidinal economies*, see Yasmin Nair, "Make Art! Change the World! Starve! The Fallacy of Art as Social Justice," August 2010, https://yasminnair.com/make-art-change-the-world-starve-the-fallacy-of-art-as-social-justice-part-i/.

46. *On the feminism we get from our diasporic brown mothers*, see Sara Ahmed, *Living a Feminist Life* (Durham, NC: Duke University Press, 2016), 4.

47. *On the concept of the undercommons*, see Fred Moten and Stefano Harney, *The Undercommons: Fugitive Planning and Black Study* (New York: Autonomedia, 2013).

48. *On brownness as a flicker between minoritarian subjects*, see Jose Muñoz, *The Sense of Brown* (Durham, NC: Duke University Press, 2020).

49. Muñoz, *The Sense of Brown*, 2.

50. Muñoz, *The Sense of Brown*, 40.

51. Muñoz, *The Sense of Brown*, 101.

52. Jasbir Puar, *Right to Maim* (Durham, NC: Duke University Press, 2017), xvii.

53. Musser, *Sensual Excess*, 14.

54. Musser, *Sensual Excess*, 179.

Chapter One. Abject Tongues

1. *On the caste system as a cesspit of oppression*, see Arundhati Roy, *Capitalism: A Ghost Story* (Chicago: Haymarket Books, 2014), 41.

2. *On "rememory,"* see Toni Morrison, "I Wanted to Carve Out a World both

Culture Specific and Race-Free': an essay by Toni Morrison," *guardian.com*, August 2019, https://www.theguardian.com/books/2019/aug/08/toni-morrison -rememory-essay.

3. *On keeping stories big enough*, see James Clifford, *Returns: Becoming Indigenous in the Twenty-first Century* (Cambridge, MA: Harvard University Press, 2013).

4. *On the importance of keeping our stories moving*, see Marilyn Frye, "Oppression," in *Gender Basics: Feminist Perspectives on Women and Men*, ed. Anne Minas (New York: Wadsworth, 2020).

5. *On home as the mouth of the shark*, see Warsan Shire, *Teaching My Mother How to Give Birth* (London: Flipped Eye Publishing, 2011).

6. *On stretching out Marxism*, see Fanon, who once wrote, "This is why Marxist analysis should always be slightly stretched every time we have to do with the colonial problem." Frantz Fanon, *The Wretched of the Earth* (New York: Grove Press, 1963), 40.

7. *On the present as a prison*, see Jose Muñoz, *Cruising Utopia: The Then and There of Queer Futurity* (New York: New York University Press, 2006), 37.

8. *On the ink of our mother's milk*, see Hélène Cixous and Mirielle Calle-Gruber, *Rootprints: Memory and Life Writing* (London: Routledge, 1997).

9. *On verbs as a bleeding*, see Dionne Brand, "Ossuaries I," *Callaloo: A Journal of African Diaspora Arts and Letters* 37 no. 1 (2014): 1–6.

10. *On the signature injury*, see Andrea Abi-Karam, *Extratransmission* (New York: Kelsey Street Press, 2019).

11. *On subaltern subjects as also geographic subjects*, see Katherine McKittrick, *Demonic Grounds: Black Women and the Cartographies of Struggle* (Minneapolis: University of Minnesota Press, 2006).

12. *On renarrating violence with the hope of not reproducing it*, see Saidiya Hartman, "Venus in Two Acts," *Small Axe* 12 (2008): 2.

13. *On alternative abortion procedures in the colonial Indian subcontinent*, see Ismat Chugtai, *The Greatest Urdu Stories Ever Told: A Book of Profiles* (New Delhi: Aleph Book Company, 2017).

14. *On the "deathworlds" we live*, see Audre Lorde, *Sister Outsider: Essays and Speeches* (Berkeley, CA: Clarkson Potter/Ten Speed, 2007), 38.

Chapter Two. Forked Tongues

1. *Satyam Shivam Sundarum*, directed by Raj Kapoor (1978).

2. Lata Mageshkar, vocalist, "Yashomati Maya." Spotify, n.d. open.spotify.com /track/3QrlloyWxW6N4AUXYvGxYu.

3. I want to note that in sharing these Hindu stories, I understand *Hindu/ Hinduism*, a term that originates from the Persians, the Arabs, and the Greeks, as a dynamic composite of cultural and religious stories/practices/beliefs, both indigenous and borrowed from an endless stream of visitors. My use of Hindu stories, "Yashoda Ma," and later in the final chapter, "Parvati," is not intended to shore up

Hinduism as a deep-seated antiquity (i.e., Hindutva's claim) or even as timeless, unchanging, ahistorical stories. Instead, I offer them as stories offered to me by my mother in ways that demonstrate how religious-cultural terrains of storytelling mediate and are mediated by the South Asian and diasporic mothering in domestic spaces as subcontinental pedagogy and for the sustenance of culture, philosophy, and epistemic possibility, in ways that exceed the silos of Hinduism or Islam. Of course, it is important to note that this particular song also reveals Bollywood's own affinity to Hindutva as a set of exclusive ideas, which includes, among many others, a fetishistic fascination with being *gori*.

4. *On antiblackness*, see Frank B. Wilderson III, *AfroPessimism* (New York: Liveright, 2020).

5. *On proximate, haptic colonialities*, see Tiffany Lethabo-King, *The Black Shoals: Offshore Formations of Black and Native Studies* (Durham, NC: Duke University Press, 2019), 2.

6. *On black/brown relations in the United States*, see Vijay Prashad, *The Karma of Brown Folks* (Minneapolis: University of Minnesota Press, 2001).

7. *On the "dread" of blackness*, see Toni Morrison, *The Bluest Eye* (New York: Norton, 1970), 63.

8. I want to note how Jared Sexton's priceless notion of "junior partner" comes to full bear in this moment, where other groups of people subordinate to Whites but who fall out of the category of Blacks, such as immigrants of color and, to some extent, American Indians, are "the junior partners of civil society." In Sexton's argument, the White "senior partners" are located at the center of civil society, their "junior partners" at its inside margins, and Black people are positioned "outside of Humanity and civil society." The relation of blackness to the world is thus defined as antagonistic, while the "junior partners" have a dialectic and agonistic relation to civil society that leaves room for negotiation, no matter how small. See Jared Sexton, *Amalgamations Schemes* (Minneapolis: University of Minnesota Press, 2008).

9. *On black flesh as anagrammatical*, I want to note the rich intellectual genealogy of contemporary Black studies (which draws from and departs from certain strands of Black feminism), as offering a specification of flesh to blackness and, thus, Black genderings in unique and important ways. Hortense Spillers has demonstrated that Black flesh is the very specific artifact of the transatlantic slave trade; captive bodies were made into flesh; they were "ungendered" and stripped of human attributes like womanhood, manhood, family, and autonomous sexualities. For scholars such as Hortense Spillers, Saidiya Hartman, and C. Riley Snorton, flesh is the zero sum of blackness, meaning that blackness is ground zero, the space of nothingness. Calvin Warren and Fred Moten build on this, suggesting that blackness is "nothing," and, as opposition, whiteness defines itself as something or everything. See Calvin Warren, *Ontological Terror; Blackness, Nihilism, and Emancipation* (Durham, NC: Duke University Press, 2018); Fred Moten, *Black and Blur* (Durham, NC: Duke University Press, 2017). Christina Sharpe and

C. Riley Snorton further develop Spiller's idea that gender was undone on the plantation, in the belly of the ship, both suggesting that Black gender is anagrammatical, meaning that it is malleable and mutable. See C. Riley Snorton, *Black on Both Sides: A Racial History of Trans Identity* (Minneapolis: University of Minnesota Press, 2017); and Christina Sharpe, *In the Wake: On Blackness and Being* (Durham, NC: Duke University Press, 2018). These are critical theorizations that guide my analysis of this violent linguistic event in mine and my mother's life.

10. *On the Black penis*, see Calvin Warren, "Turned into a Black Penis: Sexistence, Nihilism, and Subtraction," March 2022, https://www.youtube.com/watch?v=rDoisrH-kek.

11. *On the everyday life of racism*, see Sharon Holland, *The Erotic Life of Racism* (Durham, NC: Duke University Press, 2012).

12. *On the weight of whiteness*, see James Baldwin, *Notes from a Native Son* (Boston, MA: Beacon Press, 1955).

13. Edouard Glissant, *Faulkner, Mississippi* (Chicago: University of Chicago Press, 2000).

14. "Forked tongues" is also an American Indian phrase, which alludes to the hypocrisy of colonizers saying one thing but meaning another: the fork in the tongue embodies simultaneously White coloniality and White benevolence. In this context, not unlike my mother's use of the phrase, the phrase "forked tongues" indicates the ways language has been central to oppression of colonized peoples. Interestingly, this visuality of tongues also gestures to the Judeo-Christian image of the serpent, a forked-tongued creature, which also reveals how betrayal, historically through speech, has been both feminized and sexualized.

15. *On the never-ending specificity of whiteness*, see Richard Dyer, who argues that whiteness is "immediately something more specific." See Richard Dyer, *White: Essays on Race and Culture* (London: Routledge, 1997), 46.

16. *On whiteness as happy object*, see Sara Ahmed, *The Promise of Happiness* (Durham, NC: Duke University Press, 2010).

17. *On history as hurt*, see Fredric Jameson. "Interview with Fredric Jameson." *Diacritics: A Review of Contemporary Criticism* 12, no. 3 (1982): 72–91.

18. *On the maternal body as border*, see Laura Doyle, *Bordering on the Body: The Racial Matrix of Modern Fiction and Culture* (New York: Oxford University Press, 1994), 27.

19. *On the cornucopia of depressing options for anticolonial resistance*, see Paul Gilroy, *Postcolonial Melancholia* (New York: Columbia University Press, 2005), 36.

Chapter Three. Promiscuous Tongues

1. *On girls who like girls as double trouble*, see Sara Ahmed, "Being in Trouble: In the Company of Judith Butler." *Lambda Nordica* 2, no. 3 (2015): 184.

2. *On "touch across time,"* see Carolyn Dinshaw, *Getting Medieval: Sexualities*

and Communities, Pre- and Postmodern (Durham, NC: Duke University Press, 1999), 3.

3. Freud's *fort da* is perhaps best understood, in this context, as "a peek-a-boo or a there! And not there! game of sex and taboo" that describes the life of my mother and the other brown mothers with whom she was daily in relation. Freud himself was referring to an anecdote involving his eighteen-month-old grandson, who would throw a cotton reel and delight in its momentary disappearance and then its reappearance when his mother would bring it back to him to throw yet again. For Freud, the repetition of *fort da* (German for "gone there") invokes simultaneously a pleasure and an anxiety around seeing/not seeing or appearing/disappearing. One might draw this out to say that repetition is itself anxiogenic and orgasmic, particularly for the mother. For more on *fort da*, see Jay Watson, "Guys and Dolls: Exploratory Repetition and Maternal Subjectivity in the Fort/Da Game," *American Imago* 52, no. 4 (1995): 463–503.

4. Kristeva, *Power of Horror*, 22.

5. *On sexuality as melancholia*, see Anjali Arondhekar, "In the Absence of Reliable Ghosts: Sexuality, Historiography and South Asia," *differences: A Journal of Feminist Cultural Studies* 25 no. 3 (2015): 98–123.

6. *On pouring vinegar on men's honey*, see Tillie Olsen, *Tell Me a Riddle* (New Brunswick, NJ: Rutgers University Press, 1995), 45.

7. *On jokes and male laughers*, see Sigmund Freud, *Jokes and Their Relation to the Unconscious*, ed. and trans. James Strachey (New York: Norton, 1960), 9.

8. *On metaphors as a key method to reading Black female sexuality*, see Evelynn Hammonds, "Black (W)Holes and the Geometry of Black Female Sexuality." *differences: A Journal of Feminist Criticism* 6, nos. 2–3, (Summer/Fall 1994), 126.

9. *On "fuckedness,"* see Darreik Scott, *Extravagant Abjection: Blackness, Power, and Sexuality in the African American Literary Imagination*, (New York: New York University Press, 2010), 9.

10. *On Tawana Brawley*, see Patricia Williams, *Alchemy of Race and Rights: Diary of a Law Professor* (Cambridge, MA: Harvard University Press, 1991).

11. Williams, *Alchemy of Race and Rights*, 81.

12. *On the phrase "woman as pain"* in the context of Indian colonial and postcoloniality, see Veena Das, *Life and Words: Violence and the Descent into the Ordinary* (Berkeley: University of California Press, 2007), 56.

13. *On a brilliant reading of women's laughter as dangerous to patriarchy*, see Hélène Cixous and Annette Kuhn, "Castration or Decapitation?" *Signs: A Journal of Women in Culture and Society* 7, no. 1 (1981): 41–55.

14. *On "eyes-closed" systems of thought*, see Lois Althusser, *On the Reproduction of Capitalism: On Ideology and Ideological Apparatuses* (London: Verso Books, 2014), 180.

15. *On the instability of stability*, see Warsan Shire, *Teaching My Mother How to Give Birth* (New York: Flipped Eye, 2011), 27.

16. Beauvoir, *The Second Sex*, 271.

17. *On Indian sex life and words*, see Durba Mitra, *Indian Sex Life: Sexuality and the Colonial Origins of Modern Social Thought* (Princeton, NJ: Princeton University Press, 2019), 49.

18. *On beneath language*, see Audre Lorde, *Sister Outsider* (New York: Crossing Press, 1984).

19. *On queer orientations to language*, see Sara Ahmed, "Orientations: Toward a Queer Phenomenology," GLQ: *A Journal of Lesbian and Gay Studies* 12, no. 4 (2006): 543–74.

20. *On how contempt for women's sexuality was foundational to colonial structures*, see Durba Mitra, *Indian Sex Life: Sexuality and the Colonial Origins of Modern Social Thought* (Princeton, NJ: Princeton University Press, 2020), 129.

21. *On femininity as disruptive to white and male supremacy*, see Omiseke Natasha Tinsley, *Ezili's Mirrors: Black Queer Genderings* (Durham, NC: Duke University Press, 2018).

22. *On trusting the lies of the colonized*, see Katherine McKittrick, "Mathematics Black Life," *The Black Scholar* 44, no. 2 (2014): 16–28.

23. *On the lesbian drive*, see Audre Lorde, *Zami: A New Spelling of My Name* (New York: Persephone Press, 1982), 265.

24. *On the f/utility of naming lesbianisms*, see Gloria Wekker, *The Politics of Passion: Women's Sexual Culture in the Afro-Surinamese Diaspora* (New York: Columbia University Press, 2006); Astrid Roemer, in Gloria Wekker, "One Finger Does Not Drink Okra Soup. Afro-Surinamese Women and Critical Agency," in *Feminist Genealogies, Colonial Legacies, Democratic Futures*, ed. J. M. Alexander and C. Talpade Mohanty (New York: Routledge, 1997), 330–352; Audre Lorde, "Age, Race, Class, and Sex: Women Redefining Difference," in Audre Lorde, *Sister Outsider* (New York: Crossing Press, 1984); and Amy Villarejo, *Lesbian Rule: Cultural Criticism and the Value of Desire* (Durham, NC: Duke University Press, 2003).

25. *On lesbians as runaways from patriarchy*, see Monique Wittig, *The Lesbian Body* (New York: William Morrow, 1975).

26. I refer here to Lauren Berlant's popular concept of "cruel optimism," in which she offers an account of our affective relations to human possibility and futurity, of what keeps ticking in us, of what attachments keep us going, let us hold on, in the face of precarity, even when it is, more often than not, too slippery to hold. Berlant provocatively queried why people "stay attached to conventional good life fantasies—say, of enduring reciprocity in couples, families, political systems, institutions, markets, and at work—when the evidence of their instability, fragility, and dear cost abound?" (2). While I am drawn to Berlant's inquiry and loosely reference it as a sublimated revelation in my mother's attachment to heterosexuality. I hold certain critiques of Berlant's popular work and find it often ill-fitting, even if sometimes useful. For one, I cannot help wondering whether cruel optimisms are undergirded by an invisible, but perhaps inevitable, White or

White-adjacent ethos. The conceptual anxiety that informs Berlant's critique of attachment to the "good life" is deeply anticapitalist, but is it, I must ask, also anti-White? Does the raison d'etre of Berlant's cruel optimisms consider the experience of the colonized, or does Berlant, like her White queer theoretical counterparts, also subtly invoke a transparent White subject, or, at the least, a white(ned)-enough subject whose imagination has space for the future? Do we, instead, see the equivalent of what Fanon has already depicted: "In the colonies . . . [the] cause is the consequence; you are rich because you are white, you are white because you are rich" (5). Perhaps, you are optimistic because you are White. You are White, because you are optimistic. My mother was a woman who had little patience with happy endings. Optimisms exhausted her. And that heterosexuality is organized around these optimisms, these promises of happiness, was even more exhausting. Happiness and the massive hope that frames oppression discourses in the Global North (a key site of Western epistemological rule) were neither viable nor interesting options for her. It became increasingly clear to me in the writing of this book that optimism (toward the good life) and the cruelty of it (that such good life may never come to pass) constitute a concept that does not travel into racialized, femininized, abject interiorities, in part because the psychic and material violence that contours the lives of brown domestic/ated mothers living in the Global North (diaspora) produces instead a subjectivity that is shaped and thus shapes a descent into (life-saving) negativities. If Berlant had looked toward mothers of color, Black and brown women who live under and through colonial and patriarchal schemata, she may have a subject who, like her, finds a broken, and not optimistic, world. See Lauren Berlant, *Cruel Optimisms* (Durham, NC: Duke University Press, 2016).

27. *On returning to injury*, see Heather Love, *Feeling Backward: Loss and the Politics of Queer History* (Cambridge, MA: Harvard University Press, 2007).

Chapter Four. The Other End of the Tongue

1. *On other versions of Parvati and the fruit of knowledge*, see Swami Achuthananda, *Many Many, Many Gods of Hinduism* (North Charleston: CreateSpace Independent Publishing, 2013). For a psychoanalytic reading of this story, see Salman Akhtar, *Freud Along the Ganges: Psychoanalytic Reflections on the People and Culture of India* (New York: Other Press, 2005).

2. *On "the other s&m,"* see Wendy Simonds, *Hospital Land USA: Sociological Adventures in Medicalization* (New York: Routledge, 2017), 11.

3. *On undone bodies*, see Christina Crosby, *A Body, Undone: Living on after Great Pain* (New York: New York University Press, 2016), 3.

4. *On debility's position*, see Jasbir Puar, *The Right to Maim* (Durham, NC: Duke University Press, 2017), vi.

5. Toni Morrison, *Paradise* (New York: Knopf, 1997), 271.

6. *On the right to opacity as a way to manage accumulated hurt*, see Edouard

Glissant, *Caribbean Discourse: Selected Essays*, trans. J. Michael Dash (Charlottes-ville: University Press of Virginia, 1989), 4.

7. *On brownness as "elsewhere,"* see Muñoz, *The Sense of Brown*, 101.

Afterword

1. *On theory*, see Stuart Hall, *Essential Essays: Identity and Diaspora*, ed. David Morley (Durham, NC: Duke University Press, 2019), 302.

2. *On the limits of sentimentality*, Lauren Berlant writes, "When sentimentality meets politics, it uses personal stories to tell of structural effects, but in so doing it risks thwarting its very attempt to perform rhetorically a scene of pain that must be soothed politically. . . . The political as a place of acts oriented toward pub-licness becomes replaced by a world of private thoughts, leanings, and gestures." Lauren Berlant, "Poor Eliza," *American Literature* 70, no. 3 (1998): 635–68.

BIBLIOGRAPHY

....

Abi-Karam, Andrea. *Extratransmission*. New York: Kelsey Street Press, 2019.

Abraham, Nikolas, and Maria Torok. *The Shell and the Kernel: Renewals of Psychoanalysis*. Edited by Nicholas T. Rand. Chicago: University of Chicago Press, 1994.

Achuthananda, Swami. *Many Many Many Gods of Hinduism*. Scotts Valley, CA: CreateSpace Independent Publishing, 2013.

Agamben, Giorgio. *Homo Sacer: Sovereign Power and Bare Life*. Stanford, CA: Stanford University Press, 1995.

Ahmed, Sara. "Being in Trouble: In the Company of Judith Butler." *Lambda Nordica* 2, no. 3 (2015): 179–89.

Ahmed, Sara. *Living A Feminist Life*. Durham, NC: Duke University Press, 2017.

Ahmed, Sara. "Orientations: Toward A Queer Phenomenology." GLQ: *A Journal of Lesbian and Gay Studies* 12, no.4 (2006): 543–74.

Ahmed, Sara. *The Promise of Happiness*. Durham, NC: Duke University Press, 2010.

Akhtar, Salman. *Freud along the Ganges: Psychoanalytic Reflections on the People and Culture of India*. New York: Other Press, 2005.

Althusser, Lois. *On the Reproduction of Capitalism: On Ideology and Ideological Apparatuses*. London: Verso Books, 2014.

Arondhekar, Anjali. "In the Absence of Reliable Ghosts: Sexuality, Historiography and South Asia." *differences: A Journal of Feminist Cultural Studies* 25, no.3 (2015): 98–123.

Arondhekar, Anjali, and Geeta Patel. "Area Impossible: Notes Toward an Introduction." GLQ: *A Journal for Gay and Lesbian Studies* 22, no. 2 (2016): 151–71.

Baldwin, James. *Nobody Knows My Name: More Notes of a Native Son.* New York: Vintage Books, 1961.

Baldwin, James. *Notes from a Native Son.* Boston: Beacon Press, 1955.

Barthes, Roland. 2009. *Mourning Diary.* New York: Hill and Wang, 2009.

Beauvoir, Simone de. *The Second Sex.* New York: Vintage, 2011.

Beauvoir, Simone de. *A Very Easy Death.* London: Pantheon Press, 1985.

Benjamin, Water. *Illuminations.* New York: Schocken Books, 1968.

Berlant, Lauren. "Poor Eliza." *American Literature* 70, no. 3 (1998): 635–68.

Berlant, Lauren. *Cruel Optimisms.* Durham, NC: Duke University Press, 2016.

Bradley, Rizvana. "Vestiges of Motherhood: The Maternal Function in Recent Black Cinema." *Film Quarterly* 71, no. 2 (2017): 46–52.

Brand, Dionne. "Ossuaries I." *Callaloo: A Journal of African Diaspora Arts and Letters* 37, no. 1 (2014): 1–6.

Brand, Dionne. *Thirsty.* Toronto: McClelland and Stewart, 2002.

Britzman, Deborah. "On Being a Slow Reader: Psychoanalytic Reading Problems in Ishiguro's *Never Let Me Go.*" *Changing English* 13, no. 3 (2006): 307–18.

Butler, Judith. "Melancholy Gender—Refused Identification." *Psychoanalytic Dialogues* 5, no. 2 (1995): 165–80.

Cha, Theresa Hak Kyung. *Dictee.* New York: Tanam Press, 1982.

Chen, Mel. *Animacies: Biopolitics, Racial Mattering, and Queer Affect.* Durham, NC: Duke University Press, 2012.

Chodorow, Nancy. *The Reproduction of Mothering and the Sociology of Gender.* Berkeley: University of California Press, 1978.

Chugtai, Ismat. *The Greatest Urdu Stories Ever Told: A Book of Profiles.* New Delhi: Aleph Book Company, 2017.

Clifford, James. *Returns: Becoming Indigenous in the Twenty-first Century.* Cambridge, MA: Harvard University Press, 2013.

Cixous, Hélène, and Annette Kuhn. "Castration or Decapitation?" *Signs: A Journal of Women in Culture and Society* 7, no. 1 (1981): 41–55.

Cixous, Hélène, and Mirielle Calle-Gruber. *Rootprints: Memory and Life Writing.* London: Routledge, 1997.

Crosby, Christina. *A Body Undone: Living on After Great Pain.* New York: New York University Press, 2016.

Das, Veena. *Life and Words: Violence and the Descent into the Ordinary.* Berkeley: University of California Press, 2007.

Deleuze, Gilles. *Essays Critical and Clinical.* Minneapolis: University of Minnesota Press, 1997.

Derrida, Jacques. *Archive Fever: A Freudian Impression.* Chicago: University of Chicago Press, 1998.

Derrida, Jacques. *Monolingualism of the Other, or the Prosthesis of Origin*. Stanford, CA: Stanford University Press, 1998.

Dinshaw, Carolyn. *Getting Medieval: Sexualities and Communities, Pre- and Postmodern*. Durham, NC: Duke University Press, 1999.

Doyle, Laura. *Bordering on the Body: The Racial Matrix of Modern Fiction and Culture*. New York: Oxford University Press, 1994.

Dyer, Richard. *White: Essays on Race and Culture*. London: Routledge, 1997.

Fanon, Frantz. *The Wretched of the Earth*. New York: Grove Press, 1963.

Foucault, Michel. *The Birth of a Clinic: An Archaeology of Medical Perception*. Translated by A. M. Sheridan Smith. New York: Vintage, 1994.

Freud, Sigmund. *Jokes and Their Relation to the Unconscious*. Edited and translated by James Strachey. New York: Norton, 1960.

Frye, Marilyn. "Oppression." In *Gender Basics: Feminist Perspectives on Women and Men*. Edited by Anne Minas. New York: Wadsworth, 2020.

Genet, Jean. *Fragments of the Artwork*. Translated by Charlotte Mandell. Stanford, CA: Stanford University Press, 2003.

Gilroy, Paul. *Postcolonial Melancholia*. New York: Columbia University Press, 2005.

Glissant, Edouard. *Caribbean Discourse: Selected Essays*. Translated by. J. Michael Dash. Charlottesville: University Press of Virginia, 1989.

Glissant, Edouard. *Faulkner, Mississippi*. Chicago: University of Chicago Press, 2000.

Gordon, Avery. *Ghostly Matters: Hauntings and the Sociological Imagination*. Minneapolis: University of Minnesota Press, 2008.

Green, Andre. 1006. *On Private Madness*. New York: Taylor and Francis, 1996.

Ha, Trinh Min. *Elsewhere Within Here: Immigration, Refugeeism, and the Boundary Event*. New York: Routledge, 2010.

Hall, Stuart. *Essential Essays: Identity and Diaspora*. Edited by David Morley. Durham, NC: Duke University Press, 2019.

Hartman, Saidiya. "Venus in Two Acts." *Small Axe* 12, no. 2 (2008): 1–12.

Head, Bessie. *The Collector of Treasures*. London: Heinemann, 1977.

Head, Bessie. *Life: Short Stories*. Edited by Ivan Vladislavić. Baltimore, MD: Viva Books, 1993.

Holland, Sharon. *The Erotic Life of Racism*. Durham, NC: Duke University Press, 2012.

hooks, bell. *Teaching to Transgress: Education as a Practice of Freedom*. London: Routledge, 1994.

Hurston, Zora Neale. *Their Eyes Were Watching God*. New York: Harper, 2006.

Irigiray, Luce. "And the One Doesn't Stir without the Other." *Signs: A Journal of Women in Culture and Society* 7, no. 1 (1981): 60–67.

Jacobs, Amber. "The Potential of Theory: Melanie Klein, Luce Irigiray, and the Mother-Daughter Relationship." *Hypatia: A Journal of Feminist Philosophy* 22, no. 3 (2007): 175–93.

Jameson, Fredric. "Interview with Fredric Jameson." *Diacritics: A Review of Contemporary Criticism* 12, no. 3 (1982): 72–91.

Jones, Gayl. *Eva's Man*. Boston: Beacon Press, 1987.

Khanna, Ranjana. *Dark Continents: Psychoanalysis and Colonialism*. Durham, NC: Duke University Press, 2003.

Khanna, Ranjanna. "Post-Palliative: Coloniality's Affective Distance." *Post Colonial Text* 2, no. 1. 2006. https://www.postcolonial.org/index.php/pct/article /view/385/815.

Kingston, Maxine Hong. *Women Warriors: Memoirs of A Girlhood among Ghosts*. New York: Knopf, 1976.

Klein, Melanie. *The Writings of Melanie Klein*. Vol. 3. New York: Free Press, 1975.

Kristeva, Julia. "The Meaning of Parity." In *The Kristeva Reader*. Edited by John Lechte and Mary Zournazi and translated by John Lechte, 90–108. Edinburgh, UK: Edinburgh University Press, 2003.

Kristeva, Julia. "Motherhood Today." Kristeva.fr.com. 2005. http://www.kristeva .fr/motherhood.html.

Kristeva, Julia. *Power of Horror: An Essay on Abjection*. New York: Columbia University Press, 1982.

Lacan, Jacques. *The Four Fundamental Concepts of Psychoanalysis*. Translated by Alan Sheridan. New York: Norton, 1981.

Lethabo-King, Tiffany. *The Black Shoals: Offshore Formations of Black and Native Studies*. Durham, NC: Duke University Press, 2019.

Lorde, Audre. "Age, Race, Class, and Sex: Women Redefining Difference." In Audre Lorde, *Sister Outsider*, 114–23. New York: Crossing Press, 1984.

Lorde, Audre. *The Cancer Journals*. San Francisco: Aunt Lute Books, 1980.

Lorde, Audre. *Sister Outsider: Essays and Speeches*. New York: Crossing Press, 1984.

Lorde, Audre. *Zami: A New Spelling of My Name*. New York: Persephone Press, 1982.

Love, Heather. *Feeling Backward: Loss and the Politics of Queer History*. Cambridge, MA: Harvard University Press, 2007.

Love, Heather. "Macbeth: Milk." In *Shakesqueer: A Queer Companion to the Complete Works of Shakespeare*. Edited by Madhavi Menon, 201–8. Durham, NC: Duke University Press, 2011.

Macharia, Keguro. "Belatedness." *GLQ: A Journal of Gay and Lesbian Studies* 26, no.3 (2020): 561–73.

Mageshkar, Lata. Vocalist. "Yashomati Maya." Spotify. n.d. open.spotify.com/track /3QrlloyWxW6N4AUXYvGxYu.

Marx, Karl. *The Eighteenth Brumaire of Louis Bonaparte*. Edited by C. P. Dutt and translated by Anonymous. New York: International Press, 1935.

McKittrick, Katherine. *Demonic Grounds: Black Women and the Cartographies of Struggle*. Minneapolis: University of Minnesota Press, 2006.

McKittrick, Katherine. "Mathematics Black Life." *Black Scholar* 44, no. 2, (2014): 16–28.

Memmi, Albert. *The Colonizer and the Colonized*. New York: Orion, 1965.

Mitra, Durba. *Indian Sex Life: Sexuality and the Colonial Origins of Modern Social Thought*. Princeton, NJ: Princeton University Press, 2020.

Moraga, Cherrie, and Gloria Anzaldúa. *This Bridge Called My Back: Writings by Radical Women of Color*. Bath, UK: Persephone Press, 1981.

Morrison, Toni. *The Bluest Eye*. New York: Norton, 1970.

Morrison, Toni. "'I Wanted to Carve Out a World both Culture Specific and Race-Free': An Essay by Toni Morrison." guardian.com. August 2019. https://www.theguardian.com/books/2019/aug/08/toni-morrison-rememory-essay.

Morrison, Toni. *Paradise*. New York: Knopf, 1997.

Moten, Fred. *B. Jenkins*. Durham, NC: Duke University Press, 2010.

Moten, Fred. *In the Break: The Aesthetics of the Black Radical Tradition*. Minneapolis: University of Minnesota Press, 2003.

Moten, Fred, and Stefano Harney. *The Undercommons: Fugitive Planning and Black Study*. New York: Autonomedia, 2013.

Moussawi, Ghassan. "Bad Feelings: Trauma, Non-Linear Time, and Accidental Encounters in 'the Field.'" *Departures in Critical Qualitative Research* 10, no. 1 (2021): 78–96.

Muñoz, Jose. *Cruising Utopia: The Then and There of Queer Futurity*. New York: New York University Press, 2006.

Muñoz, Jose. *The Sense of Brown*. Durham, NC: Duke University Press, 2020.

Musser, Amber Jamila. *Sensual Excess: Queer Femininity and Brown Jouissance*. New York: New York University Press, 2018.

Nair, Yasmin. "Make Art! Change the World! Starve! The Fallacy of Art as Social Justice." August 2010. https://yasminnair.com/make-art-change-the-world-starve-the-fallacy-of-art-as-social-justice-part-i/.

Ngai, Sianne. *Ugly Feelings*. Cambridge, MA: Harvard University Press, 2007.

Nourbese, Philip M. *She Tries Her Tongue, Her Silence Softly*. Middletown, CT: Wesleyan University Press, 1989.

Olsen, Tillie. *Tell Me a Riddle*. New Brunswick, NJ: Rutgers University Press, 1995.

Parker, Andrew. *The Theorist's Mother*. Durham, NC: Duke University Press, 2017.

Perrier, Francois. https://www.meisterdrucke.us/fine-art-prints/Francois-Perrier/73002/Veturia,-Mother-of-Coriolanus,-c.1653.html. Accessed June 2018.

Phillips, M. NourbeSe. *She Tries Her Tongue, Her Silence Softly Breaks*. Middletown, CT: Wesleyan University Press, 2015.

Prashad, Vijay. *The Karma of Brown Folks*. Minneapolis: University of Minnesota Press, 2001.

Puar, Jasbir. *The Right to Maim*. Durham, NC: Duke University Press, 2017.

Rich, Adrienne. *Of Woman Born: Motherhood as Experience and Institution*. New York: Norton, 1976.

Roemer, Astrid. "One Finger Does Not Drink Okra Soup: Afro-Surinamese Women and Critical Agency." In *Feminist Genealogies, Colonial Legacies, Democratic Futures*, edited by J. M. Alexander and C. Talpade Mohanty, 300–52. New York: Routledge, 1997.

Rose, Jacqueline. *Sexuality in the Field of Vision*. New York: Verso, 2006.

Roy, Arundhati. *Capitalism: A Ghost Story*. Chicago: Haymarket Books, 2014.

Roy, Arundhati. "What Is the Morally Appropriate Language in Which to Think and Write?" *lithub.com*. July 2018. https://lithub.com/what-is-the-morally-appropriate-language-in-which-to-think-and-write/.

Sandoval, Chela. *Methodology of the Oppressed*. Minneapolis: University of Minnesota Press, 2000.

Satyam Shivam Sundarum. Directed by Raj Kapoor. 1978.

Scott, Darreik. *Extravagant Abjection: Blackness, Power and Sexuality in the African American Literary Imagination*. New York: New York University Press, 2010.

Senza, Danny. *Caucasia: A Novel*. New York: Penguin, 1999.

Sexton, Jared. *Amalgamations Schemes: Antiblackness and the Critique of Multiracialism*. Minneapolis: University of Minnesota Press, 2008.

Sharpe, Christina. *In the Wake: On Blackness and Being*. Durham, NC: Duke University Press, 2018.

Shire, Warsan. *Teaching My Mother How to Give Birth*. London: Flipped Eye, 2011.

Simonds, Wendy. *Hospital Land USA: Sociological Adventures in Medicalization*. New York: Routledge, 2017.

Singh, Julietta. *No Archive Will Restore You*. Santa Barbara, CA: Punctum Books, 2018.

Snorton, C. Riley. *Black on Both Sides: A Racial History of Trans Identity*. Minneapolis: University of Minnesota Press, 2017.

Spillers, Hortense. "'All the Things You Could Be by Now If Sigmund Freud's Wife Was Your Mother': Psychoanalysis and Race." *Critical Inquiry* 22 (1996): 710–34.

Stallings, L. H. *Mutha Is Half a Word: Intersections of Folklore, Vernacular, Myth and Queerness in Black Female Culture*. Columbus: Ohio State University Press, 2007.

Tinsley, Omiseke Natasha. *Ezili's Mirrors: Imagining Black Queer Genderings*. Durham, NC: Duke University Press, 2018.

Villarejo, Amy. *Lesbian Rule: Cultural Criticism and the Value of Desire*. Durham, NC: Duke University Press, 2003.

Warren, Calvin. *Ontological Terror: Blackness, Nihilism, and Emancipation*. Durham, NC: Duke University Press, 2018.

Warren, Calvin. "Turned into a Black Penis: Sexistence, Nihilism, and Subtraction." March 2022. https://www.youtube.com/watch?v=rDoisrH-kek.

Watson, Jay. "Guys and Dolls: Exploratory Repetition and Maternal Subjectivity in the Fort/Da Game." *American Imago* 52, no. 4 (1995): 463–503.

Weller, Gloria. *The Politics of Passion: Women's Sexual Culture in the Afro-Surinamese Diaspora*. New York: Columbia University Press, 2006.

Wilderson III, Frank. *AfroPessimism*. New York: Liveright, 2020).

Williams, Patricia. *Alchemy of Race and Rights: Diary of a Law Professor*. Cambridge, MA: Harvard University Press, 1991.

Wilson, Harriet E. *Our Nig; or, Sketches from the Life of a Free Black*. New York: Vintage Books, 2011.

Winnicott, Donald J. "The Theory of Parent-Infant Relationships." *The International Journal of Psychoanalysis* 41 (1960): 585–95.

Wittig, Monique. *The Lesbian Body*. New York: William Morrow, 1975.

INDEX

....

caste: class and, 30–31; exploitation and, 48, 59–62
Cha, Theresa Hak Kyung, 127
Chen, Mel, 6
Cherry Hill (New Jersey), 51–55, 75–77, 130
Chitral, 47–48
Chittagong, 30, 34–37, 43
Chodorow, Nancy, 9
Chughtai, Ismat, 59–60
Cixous, Hélène, 56, 102
class: care work and, 67–68, 79–80; cash savings and, 76–77, 107; colonialism and, 35–36; gender and, 51–53, 61, domestic work (unwaged) and, 34, 47–48; domestic work (waged) and, 30, 47, 67, 90–92; Marxism and, 8, 52, 109; model minority and, 67; postcolonial capitalism and, 46; precarity and, 51–55, 76–78; privacy and, xviii, 34–36, 48; property and, 53; as spectacle, 51; stratification and, 31, 53; *See also* sex
Clifford, James, 41
colonialism: class conditions and, 36, 51–52, 88; global capitalism and, 23; race and, 25; subalternity and, xvii, 25, 58, 61; temporality and, 128; trauma and, 129–34; Western medicine and, 134–37
colony (housing community), 34–37
colony (product of colonization). *See* colonialism

Dar es Salaam, 107
Das, Veena, 101
Deleuze, Gilles, 7–8
Derrida, Jacques, 8–9, 15–16, 18
Dhaka, 30–31, 37
disability: debility and, 22–23; failure and, 125, 133–34; identity and power and, 130–31; illness and, 115–16, 124–26; pain and, 131–32; precarity and, 133; temporality and, 128
dispossession, 40, 49–50, 57, 60–61
divorce, 110–13
Doyle, Laura, 86
Du Bois, W. E. B., 25

English: as colonial construction, 20, 30; as language, 4, 70; race and, 5, 12, 68, 85

Fanon, Frantz, 25, 71, 153n25
Father: failure of, 133; patriarchy and, 45, 50–52, 61, 81, 85; in psychoanalysis, 8
feminism: ethics of care and, 6; knowledge and, 21; theft and, 109–110, 116; women of color and, 15. *See also* psychoanalysis
Foucault, Michel, 132
Freud, Sigmund, 8–10, 12, 93, 151n3
Frye, Marylyn, 41

Ganesh, 122
Green, Andre, 18
Gordon, Avery, 7

Ha, Trinh Min, 4
Hall, Stuart, 25, 139
Hartman, Saidiya, 149n9
Head, Bessie, 97
health: the brown maternal and, 23, 124–27, 138; food and, 134–38; institutions and, 78, 115–16, 127. *See also* disability
Henderson, Mae, 144–45n5
Hindi. *See* Urdu
Hong, Cathy, 11
Hurston, Zora Neale, 7, 25

immigration: citizenship and, 44–46; class and, 51–52; for education and training; 37–38, 43; global diaspora and, 19, 46–47, 72; legislation and, 44. *See also* Partition of India; migration
India: Bombay, 43, 46, 54, 59; Gujrat, 29, 54. *See also* Pakistan; Partition of India
India-Pakistan partition. *See also* Partition of India
Irigiray, Luce, 10–11, 56
Islam: Muslims, 29–30, 72; Muslimness, 42–43, 80; religious practices and, xxiii, 29, 31–32, 50, 53, 79–80, 97, 117–18; Shia-Ismaili Muslims, 46, 53
Islamabad, 19–21

Sandoval, Chela, 2
Sanskrit. *See* Urdu
Sartre, Jean Paul, 9
Scott, Darreik, 99–100
Senna, Danzy, 86
sex: abortion and, xxiii, 59–61, 113–14; concept of "fuckedness," 99–100, 119; pregnancy and birth and, xxiii, 31, 45, 50, 103–4; ubiquity of, 93; the whore and, 39–40, 111–16. *See also* sexual violence; sexuality
Sexton, Jared, 149n8
sexual violence: normalization of, 49–50, 56–58, 100–102; rape, 29–31, 56, 59–62, 100
sexuality: Black and brown feminism and, 118; compulsory heterosexuality, 51; heterosexuality and heteronormativity, 51, 91–92, 119; magic and curses and, 91–93; queerness, 3, 18–21, sexual 95–96, 112
Sharpe, Christina, 5, 150n9
Shire, Warsan, 51, 108
Simonds, Wendy, 123
Singh, Julietta, xvi
Skanda, 122
Snorton, C. Riley, 149–50n9
Spillers, Hortense, 12–13, 149–50n9
Spivak, Gayatri, xvii, 25
Suleri, Sara, 11
Stallings, L. H., 145n5

tongue: anatomy of, 123; the body and, 123–26, 140; as epistemology, 5, 140; as excess, 14–15; as flesh and language, 2–6, 18; as pedagogy, 3; precarity and passivity and, 95–96; promiscuous speech and, 93–96; theory and analysis of, 144–45n5; translation and, 19–20
Torok, Maria, 9–10

Uganda, 53
Urdu: Hindi and, 4, 49, 111; phrases in, xxiii, 4, 25, 28, 31, 49–50, 70, 73–74, 78, 91, 95, 103–4, 108, 111–15, 128, 138; Sanskrit and, 111, 115

Villarejo, Amy, 118
violence: against women, 32–33, 40–41, 62, 76–77; between women, 32–33, 48–49; flesh and, 24. *See also* sexual violence

Wekker, Gloria, 118
whiteness: adjacency to, 72, 75, 82, 87–88, 152–53n25; assimilation to, 68–69, 76, 82, 94. *See also* Blackness; brownness
Warren, Calvin, 150n9
Williams, Patricia, xxi, 100–1
Winnicott, Donald, 9–10
Wittig, Monique, 118–19
Wilson, Harriet E., 63

Yashoda Ma, 63–64, 149n3